Ransomware Protection
Playbook

Ransomware Protection Playbook

Roger A. Grimes

WILEY

This book is dedicated to my wife, Tricia. She is always the brightest light in any room, blotting out the sun with her smile, beauty, kindness, brilliance, and laughter. People like me better after meeting her.

About the Author

Roger A. Grimes is a 34-year computer security consultant, instructor, holder of dozens of computer certifications, and author of 12 previous books and more than 1,100 magazine articles on computer security. He has spoken at many of the world's biggest computer security conferences (e.g., Black Hat, RSA, etc.), been in *Newsweek*™ magazine, appeared on television, been interviewed for NPR's *All Things Considered*™ and the Wall Street Journal, and been a guest on dozens of radio shows and podcasts. He has worked at some of the world's largest computer security companies, including Foundstone, McAfee, and Microsoft. He has consulted for hundreds of companies, from the largest to the smallest, around the world. He specializes in host and network security, ransomware, multifactor authentication, quantum security, identity management, anti-malware, hackers, honeypots, public key infrastructure, cloud security, cryptography, policy, and technical writing. His certifications have included CPA, CISSP, CISA, CISM, CEH, MSCE: Security, Security+, and yada-yada others, and he has been an instructor for many of them. His writings and presentations are often known for their real-world, contrarian views. He was the weekly security columnist for *InfoWorld* and *CSO* magazines between 2005–2019.

You can contact the author at:

Email: roger@banneretcs.com

LinkedIn: https://www.linkedin.com/in/rogeragrimes/

Twitter: @rogeragrimes

CSOOnline: https://www.csoonline.com/author/Roger-A.-Grimes/

About the Technical Editor

Aaron Kraus, CCSP, CISSP, is an information security professional with more than 15 years of experience in security risk management, auditing, and teaching information security topics. He has worked in security and compliance roles across industries including US Federal Government civilian agencies, financial services, and technology startups. Aaron is a course author, instructor, and cybersecurity curriculum dean with more than 13 years of experience at Learning Tree International, and most recently taught the (ISC)² CISSP exam prep. He has served as an author and technical editor for numerous Wiley publications including *The Official (ISC)² CISSP CBK Reference*; *The Official (ISC)² CCSP CBK Reference*; *(ISC)² CCSP Certified Cloud Security Professional Official Study Guide, 2nd Edition*; *CCSP Official (ISC)² Practice Tests*; *The Official (ISC)² Guide to the CISSP CBK Reference, 5th Edition*; and *(ISC)² CISSP Certified Information Systems Security Professional Official Practice Tests, 2nd Edition*.

Acknowledgments

I want to start by thanking Jim Minatel, my Wiley acquisitions editor. We've been together for at least four books now. Jim always figures out the right book for us to write at the right moment and brings together the rest of the talented team to make it happen. I want to thank the rest of my production team, including project manager Brad Jones, managing editor Pete Gaughan, Sacha Lowenthal, Saravanan Dakshinamurthy, Kim Wimpsett, and tech editor Aaron Kraus. I didn't know Aaron before this project, but I now know he's a rock star. He's one of the best tech editors I've ever had. Brad was just perfect in tempo and responsiveness.

Special thanks to Anjali Camara, M.S., M.A., partner, and cyber practice leader for Connected Risk Solutions. She took time out from her PhD work to educate me on cybersecurity insurance issues and the big changes in the industry that ended up becoming a whole chapter. Special thanks for my multidecade friend, Gladys Rodriguez, Microsoft principal cybersecurity consultant for the information she gave me on recovering Microsoft environments and is usually the smartest person in the room on any Microsoft technology subject she's interested in.

I have to thank my KnowBe4 co-workers, starting with Erich Kron. It was his early ransomware slide decks I viewed when first learning about newer breeds of ransomware many years ago. I stand on his shoulders. My friend and co-worker, James McQuiggan, was my constant sounding board, and is great for turning my 30-minute rants into more memorable 30-second quips that people will actually listen to and read more often. Fellow author Perry Carpenter has forgotten more about social engineering than I'll ever learn. My awesome co-workers, Javvad Malik (check out his YouTube videos and his and Erich's Jerich Show podcasts), Jacqueline Jayne (she puts the Human in Human Firewall), Anna Collard (South African rock star!), and Jelle Wieringa (he knows how to read, write, and talk in 5 languages, including C-Level Boardroom). All taught me about how ransomware impacts their countries and regions.

A big thanks is owed to my CEO, Stu Sjouwerman; direct leader Kathy Wattman (I have never had a bigger supporter); SVP Michael Williams; our excellent marketing team, including Mandi Nulph, Mary Owens, and Kendra Irimie; our PR team, including Amanda Tarantino, Megan Stultz, and Reilly Mortimer, for either letting or forcing me to speak about ransomware hundreds of times over the last few years. Nothing fine-tunes your understanding of subject matter more than speaking about it hundreds of times and using the resulting comments to get it right. Thanks to co-worker Ryan Meyers for helping me to look for the right phishing clues that are or might be used by ransomware gangs.

Lastly, thanks to the hundreds of existing ransomware resources— articles, presentations, whitepapers, and surveys—that provided much of the education that I tried to consolidate into this book. Defeating ransomware is going to take everyone. I hope I've added some value to the path of defeating ransomware.

Contents

Introduction

I've been doing computer security since 1987, for more than 34 years now. I remember the first ransomware program I, or anyone else alive at the time, saw. It arrived in December 1989 on a 5-1/4″ floppy disk and quickly became known as the *AIDS PC Cyborg Trojan*.

Wess didn't call it ransomware then. You don't make up entirely new classification names until you get more than one of something, and at the time it was the first and only. It remained that way for years. Little did we know that it would be the beginning of a gigantic digital crime industry and a huge blight of digital evil across the world in the decades ahead.

It was fairly simple as compared to today's ransomware programs, but it still had enough code to thoroughly obfuscate data, and its creator had enough moxie to ask for $189 ransom in order to restore the data. The story of the first ransomware program and its creator still seems too strange and unlikely even today. If someone tried to duplicate the truth in a Hollywood hacker movie, you wouldn't believe it. Today's ransomware creators and gangs are far more believable.

Dr. Joseph L. Popp, Jr., the creator of the first ransomware program, was a Harvard-educated evolutionary biologist turned anthropologist. He had become interested in AIDS research and was actively involved in the AIDS research community at the time of his arrest. How he got interested in AIDS research isn't documented, but perhaps it was his 15 years in Africa documenting hamadryas baboons. Dr. Popp had co-authored a book on the Kenya Masai Mari Nature reserve in 1978 (https://www.amazon.com/Mara-Field-Guide-Masai-Reserve/dp/B000715Z0C) and published a scientific paper on his baboon studies in April 1983 (https://link.springer.com/article/10.1007/BF02381082). AIDS is thought to have originated from nonhuman primates in Africa, and those theories were starting to be explored more around the same timeframe as people searched for "patient zero." Dr. Popp was in the right place at the right time. His study of one could have led to the other.

Back in the late 1980s, AIDS research and understanding was fairly new and very rudimentary. There was still a widespread fear of the relatively new disease and how it was transmitted. Unlike with today's treatments and antivirals, early on, getting HIV/AIDS was a death sentence. At the time, many people were afraid of kissing or even hugging people who might have AIDS or were in high-risk groups. There was great interest for the latest information and learnings, inside and out of the medical community.

No one besides Dr. Popp knows why he decided to write the world's first ransomware program. Some have speculated he was disgruntled at not getting a much-desired job in the AIDS research industry and wanted to strike back, but it can just as easily be stated that he just wanted to make sure he got paid for his work. Still, there are definite signs of hiding and malevolent intent from a man who knew his creation would not be taken well. It's hard to say you didn't know something was illegal when you try to hide your involvement.

Dr. Popp purchased a mailing list of attendees from a recently held October 1988 AIDS conference in Stockholm put on by the World Health Organization and purportedly also used the subscriber lists of a UK computer magazine called *PC Business World* and other business magazines.

Dr. Popp created the trojan horse program using the QuickBasic 3.0 programming language. It must have taken him months of code writing and testing. When he was finished, he copied it onto more than 20,000 disks, applied labels, printed accompanying usage instructions, applied postage manually, and then mailed them to unsuspecting recipients in the United States, United Kingdom, Africa, Australia, and other countries. Dr. Popp must have had help doing all of this, because creating 20,000 software packages and manually applying postage would likely have taken weeks and weeks of work by one person. But no other person's involvement was ever declared in court documents or volunteered by Dr. Popp.

The trojan floppy disk was labeled "AIDS Information Introductory Diskette" (see Figure I.1).

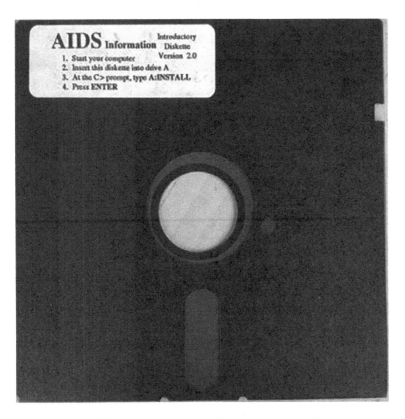

Figure I.1   Picture of disk that AIDS PC Cyborg trojan arrived on
Courtesy Eddy Willems

The floppy disk instructions introduced the disk as purporting to be a program with information about AIDS. After viewing, the user would be asked a series of personal behavior questions. The answer to those questions would be used to give the user a report on their personal risk of getting AIDS along with recommendations on how to avoid getting it.

The instructions included the warning, "If you use this diskette, you will have to pay the mandatory software licensing fee(s)." This latter warning would later be used by Dr. Popp in his defense as to why his program should not be considered illegal extortion. You can see the instructions and ominous warning in Figure I.2.

AIDS Information - Introductory Diskette

Please find enclosed a computer diskette containing health information on the disease AIDS. The information is provided in the form of an interactive computer program. It is easy to use. Here is how it works:
- The program provides you with information about AIDS and asks you questions
- You reply by choosing the most appropriate answer shown on the screen
- The program then provides you with a confidential report on your risk of exposure to AIDS
- The program provides recommendations to you, based on the life history information that you have provided, about practical steps that you can take to reduce your risk of getting AIDS
- The program gives you the opportunity to make comments and ask questions that you may have about AIDS
- This program is designed specially to help: members of the public who are concerned about AIDS and medical professionals.

Instructions

This software is designed for use with IBM● PC/XT™ microcomputers and with all other truly compatible microcomputers. Your computer must have a hard disk drive C, MS-DOS● version 2.0 or higher, and a minimum of 256K RAM. First read and assent to the limited warranty and to the license agreement on the reverse. [If you use this diskette, you will have to pay the mandatory software leasing fee(s).] Then do the following:
Step 1: Start your computer (with diskette drive A empty).
Step 2: Once the computer is running, insert the Introductory Diskette into drive A.
Step 3: At the C> prompt of your root directory type: A:INSTALL and then press ENTER. Installation proceeds automatically from that point. It takes only a few minutes.
Step 4: When the installation is completed, you will be given easy-to-follow messages by the computer. Respond accordingly.
Step 5: When you want to use the program, type the word AIDS at the C> prompt in the root directory and press ENTER.

Figure I.2 Picture of AIDS PC Cyborg Trojan disk program instructions
Courtesy Eddy Willems

Further, when the trojan program was first run, it printed a license and invoice to the screen and to the printer if the PC was connected to a local printer. The license told users they must pay the software license and even included another ominous warning that you are unlikely to see on any legitimate software program:

"If you install [this] on a microcomputer. . .

then under terms of this license you agree to pay PC Cyborg Corporation in full for the cost of leasing these programs. . .

In the case of your breach of this license agreement, PC Cyborg reserves the right to take legal action necessary to recover any outstanding debts payable to PC Cyborg Corporation and to use program mechanisms to ensure termination of your use. . .

These program mechanisms will adversely affect other program applications. . .

You are hereby advised of the most serious consequences of your failure to abide by the terms of this license agreement; your conscience may haunt you for the rest of your life. . .

and your [PC] will stop functioning normally. . .

You are strictly prohibited from sharing [this product] with others. . ."

Just like today, most people didn't read software license agreements. Normally it's not a problem, but in this case not reading the license agreement with its unusual dire warning would take on special importance. In the late 1980's, a large percentage of users also didn't pay for any commercial software they were not forced to pay for. Software was routinely illegally copied and traded. It was incredibly common for people to copy disks for their friends or even sell (even if they hadn't paid the original developer). Local computer clubs held monthly disk swaps. If you didn't have to pay for software, you didn't. In response, some developers created "copy protection" routines that prevented easy, standard disk copying.

> The author has seen other malicious programs and sites include similar "fair warnings" in their licensing information. It never hurts to read your end-user license agreements instead of simply trying your best to ignore and quickly get by them.

Dr. Popp either didn't know how to do legitimate copy protection or he counted singularly on his peculiar ransom enforcement for people who ignored his licensing instructions. Maybe he got the idea from an earlier malware program. In 1986, the first IBM PC-compatible computer virus, Pakistani Brain (https:// en.wikipedia.org/wiki/Brain_(computer_virus)), was created as a copy prevention mechanism. Its Pakistani creators were tired of people illegally copying without paying for disks they had themselves often illegally copied. You can't make this stuff up. It caused boot problems and indirectly might have caused some people to pay money to the inventors to resolve. The malware, however, did not encrypt anything nor directly ask for a ransom.

There is a chance that Dr. Popp saw his ransomware program as simply a way to legally enforce his copyright and software license. There were warnings in at least two places clearly visible to users who used his software. In comparison, today's ransomware programs never give any warning. So perhaps, in only that way, Dr. Popp's creation was a slight bit more ethical than today's ransomware programs. But being a slight bit more ethical criminal among more unethical criminals is not a particularly high standard that anyone should want to be measured against.

Either way, the first time Dr. Popp's program was run by a user, it would install itself on the local hard drive (C:) and modify the autoexec.bat file to use as a boot counter. After the involved PC was booted 90 or so times, the program would encrypt/obfuscate the user's files and folders. It would then display the message shown in Figure I.3.

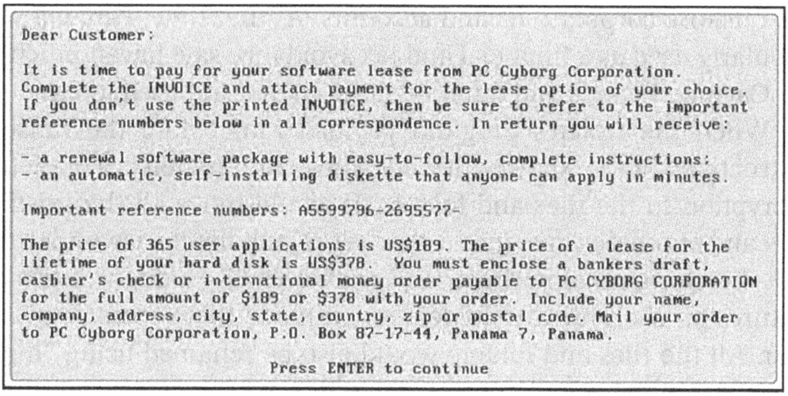

```
Dear Customer:

It is time to pay for your software lease from PC Cyborg Corporation.
Complete the INVOICE and attach payment for the lease option of your choice.
If you don't use the printed INVOICE, then be sure to refer to the important
reference numbers below in all correspondence. In return you will receive:

- a renewal software package with easy-to-follow, complete instructions;
- an automatic, self-installing diskette that anyone can apply in minutes.

Important reference numbers: A5599796-2695577-

The price of 365 user applications is US$189. The price of a lease for the
lifetime of your hard disk is US$378.  You must enclose a bankers draft,
cashier's check or international money order payable to PC CYBORG CORPORATION
for the full amount of $189 or $378 with your order. Include your name,
company, address, city, state, country, zip or postal code. Mail your order
to PC Cyborg Corporation, P.O. Box 87-17-44, Panama 7, Panama.

                        Press ENTER to continue
```

Figure I.3 Picture of AIDS PC Cyborg Trojan ransomware screen instructions
Courtesy Wikipedia

> No one knows why Dr. Popp put his trigger counter at 90. Perhaps he estimated that most people booted their PCs about once a day during the work week, and 90 workdays was more than enough time for someone to send payment for their program and for him to return a "block the lock" executable disk.

Dr. Popp had created a company with the name of PC Cyborg, which would lead to the naming of the virus. The name was shown in the original license and in the after-the-fact ransomware warning, along with asking for $189 for an annual "license" or $389 for a "lifetime license" to be sent to a Panama post-office box. It was this information that led to his quick identification and arrest. Today's ransomware purveyors use hard-to-identify-true-ownership cryptocurrencies to avoid the same easy identification and detection by authorities.

Dr. Popp had clearly tried to hide his identity and original involvement with his creation. As is still true today, it is common for unethical people trying to hide their identity and financial gains to use offshore corporations and accounts. At that time, Panama was popularly used as a financial and tax avoidance safe haven much as the Cayman Islands and other offshore islands are used today.

When the trojan's program payload ran, before the ransom instructions were shown, it did some rudimentary symmetric encryption to the files and folders. It would move all the existing files and subdirectories into a new set of subdirectories under the root directory, rename them, and enable DOS' "hidden" attribute features on each file and folder, which made them seem to disappear. All the files and folders would also be renamed using "high-order" extended ASCII control characters, which made everything appear as being invisible. Even if the DOS hidden attribute was discovered and turned off, the file and folder names looked corrupted. If the impacted user tried to do some common exploratory commands to see what happened, the malicious code brought back a fake DOS screen with fake results to confuse the user.

The main set of malicious subdirectories were created using extended ASCII character 255, which is a control code that looks like a space even though it is not. But like a space, it would not display on the screen or when printed. For all intents and purposes, all the files and folders appeared, to most users, to have disappeared or at least badly corrupted. But, importantly, none of the files were actually encrypted (unlike today's ransomware programs). The names of the files and folders were just renamed and moved.

The ransomware program created a conversion table that could be used to reverse the moving and renaming. If you found the table and understood what the trojan program did, you could convert everything back to the original file and folder names and locations. Several individuals figured this out and wrote "fix-it" programs, including early computer virus expert Jim Bates.

Bates created a free 40-page analysis report of the trojan that he would send to anyone who requested it, and he published a shorter, but still great, analysis in the premier antivirus journal Virus Bulletin (https://www.virusbulletin.com/uploads/pdf/magazine/1990/199001.pdf.) in January 1990. Bates revealed the many dubious routines of the program including the multiple steps it took to fake what the user saw when investigating. It was a great example of the antivirus and online community coming together to defeat a common foe without thinking about profit.

> The PC Cyborg ransomware encryption routine used what cryptographers called *simple character substitution* for the encryption component. This is the absolute simplest type of encryption possible, and because of that, it's probably more accurate to call Dr. Popp's encryption routine obfuscation instead. It certainly wasn't anything close to as secure as how most digital encryption had been accomplished on computers for at least a decade before Dr. Popp's program, and much less sophisticated compared to encryption in today's ransomware variants. But the point is mostly semantic. To most victims, their data was gone and their computers were unusable.

Along with his detailed analysis, Bates created a free trojan removal program called AIDSOUT and a free AIDSCLEAR program that would restore any renamed and moved files to their original locations and names. The late John McAfee, of McAfee Antivirus fame, gained some early national media attention in the United States by talking about the ransomware program and by saying he went around rescuing people's locked-up PCs.

> It was the publicity surrounding John McAfee's computer virus recoveries during that time that led this author to disassembling DOS computer viruses for John McAfee later that year and largely led to the author's lifetime career in cybersecurity.

After the antivirus industry and law enforcement determined that Dr. Popp was involved, he was arrested on a warrant while at Amsterdam's Schiphol Airport and eventually imprisoned in London. During the arrest it was immediately noted that he was having some mental health issues. Even before the arrest, he had apparently scribbled strange messages on another passenger's luggage, indicating that he, Dr. Popp, was in the luggage. He did many other unusual antics during this period of time, including wearing a condom on his nose and wearing curlers in his beard "to ward off radiation." To this day no one knows if he was really having mental health issues or just faking being insane to avoid being found guilty. Either way, he was originally arrested or detained in the Netherlands and sent back to his parents in Ohio in the United States at some point. He was then re-arrested on many crimes including blackmail and extradited back to the United Kingdom for trial.

Where the various arrests happened are swapped in some news stories, but it appears he was arrested or detained in two or three different countries at some point and faced some sort of adjudication in at least two of those countries. His final release came from a UK court.

Dr. Popp's original defense was to claim that everything he did was legal because he warned users, and they were the ones not paying for what they were legally obligated to pay. Some lawyers thought he may have a valid legal point even though it was unusual and unethical. Part of Dr. Popp's original defense fell apart because his program would also state that if users took his ransom program to another computer and allowed it to lock up that computer, that the program would then unlock the original computer so it could be used. This part of the program did not work, either intentionally or unintentionally, and both the original and additional PC would not be operational.

It's unclear if Dr. Popp ever got paid or sent a single unlock disk or if that unlock disk worked. I don't know of anyone who paid the ransom, and none of the victims in the dozens of old news stories claim to have paid the ransom or received an unlock disk from Dr. Popp. I think Dr. Popp was quickly on the run to avoid being arrested when his program started to make the news worldwide. It is doubtful that he had time to pick up his payments in Panama and send out unlock disks, and it is certainly true that he did not do this at scale. Every news story surrounding the PC Cyborg trojan starred victims whose PCs were locked up.

Dr. Popp claimed in court proceedings and to investigators that he planned to donate all the ransom money to AIDS research. That claim would be unlikely to persuade any court and would not result in the dismissal of any pending charges. Although it must be noted that Dr. Popp really did belong to several AIDS research groups that were raising money for research, and he was involved in several AIDS educational conferences and programs. In any case, one or more judges ruled that he was unfit to stand trial, and by November 1991 he was released back to his parents a free man by UK Judge Geoffrey Rivlin.

He faded back into relative obscurity and turned his interest back toward human anthropology. His infamous actions, which had both directly attacked and unfairly maligned AIDS researchers around the world, precluded his continued involvement in that field.

A decade later, in September 2001, he released a fairly controversial book called *Popular Evolution Life Lessons* (https:// www.amazon.com/Popular-Evolution-Life-Lessons-Joseph-Popp/ dp/0970125577), which contained many unconventional recommendations, including an aggressive focus on procreation, even by young females who had just obtained puberty. He strongly promoted "scientific ethics," which stand diametrically opposed to by most moral codes and ethics that the rest of us follow. Perhaps his belief in his own form of unconventional ethics played a part in his creating the first ransomware program. He was also for eugenics and euthanasia. He didn't believe in anyone having a pet. He pretty much offended almost anyone who lived a conventional life. Suffice to say, his book of recommendations was not a best seller and did nothing to diminish how strange he was seen by others even as he was pursuing other careers.

Sometimes even an eccentric man can be a gentle man and beloved by others. Just before he died in 2007, "Dr. Joe" funded The Joseph L. Popp, Jr. Butterfly Conservatory in upstate Oneonta, New York. They have their own Facebook page (https://www.facebook.com/Joseph-L-Popp-Jr-Butterfly-Conservatory-119385884741701/). The butterfly operation was still in business at least until the 2020 COVID-19 shutdowns, but the main website domain is now up for sale and there aren't any Trip Advisor reviews after early January 2020 (https://www.tripadvisor.com/Attraction_Review-g48333-d1755655-Reviews-Joseph_L_Popp_Jr_Butterfly_Conservatory-Oneonta_New_York.html). Some of the early reviews indicated things were looking a bit rundown and ragged before the COVID crunch, so maybe it has had its final opening.

In his life, Dr. Popp had a few different careers, including evolutionary biologist, author, anthropologist, and butterfly lover. But his likely biggest unwanted claim to fame, something he could not escape the rest of his life, was as the father of ransomware. There are still nearly as many stories on him today as the creator of ransomware, in 2021, as there were back in 1990 when his creation was creating digital havoc. His place in history far outlived his own life.

More information and stories on Dr. Popp and his PC Cyborg program can be found at the following resources:

- https://en.wikipedia.org/wiki/AIDS_%28Trojan_horse%29
- https://www.csoonline.com/article/3566886/a-history-of-ransomware-the-motives-and-methods-behind-these-evolving-attacks.html
- https://www.vice.com/en/article/nzpwe7/the-worlds-first-ransomware-came-on-a-floppy-disk-in-1989
- https://www.sdxcentral.com/security/definitions/case-study-aids-trojan-ransomware/

- https://www.thepitchkc.com/dr-popp-the-first-computer-virus-and-the-purpose-of-human-life-studies-in-crap-gapes-at-popular-evolution/
- https://blog.emsisoft.com/en/34742/history-of-ransomware-a-supervillain-30-years-in-the-making/
- https://www.villagevoice.com/2009/04/16/dr-popp-the-first-computer-virus-and-the-purpose-of-human-life-studies-in-crap-gapes-at-popular-evolution/
- https://www.gwinnettdailypost.com/news/business/the-bizarre-story-of-the-inventor-of-ransomware/article_bed2be94-129c-5d5a-a973-2112d99556a6.html
- https://www.knowbe4.com/aids-trojan

The PC Cyborg ransomware trojan was a startling wake-up. The lesson learned was that there are people in this world who have no ethical qualms with encrypting your hard drive and asking for a ransom to be paid to unlock it. They were willing to risk going to jail to do it.

Surprisingly, after Dr. Popp's trojan, there wasn't a lot of imitation as antivirus fighters had feared. Perhaps it was because Dr. Popp had not been successful. He didn't get rich. He ended up in jail. Lesson learned. Other criminals learned that it was hard to do digital extortion and get away with it, at least at the time. But in another decade or so, other advances in technology would give them the means to get away with the crime almost every time.

Dr. Popp's encryption wasn't very good either. But around the same time period, other types of malware, especially computer viruses, were starting to experiment with better encryption. But encryption was used only to hide and protect the malware program itself from quick antivirus detection and not to encrypt data files and ask for ransom.

Slowly a few slightly "better" ransomware programs started to appear. Most of them made up their own encryption routines, which is to say almost always resulted in very bad, easily-breakable, encryption. These early "cryptoviruses" or "cryptotrojans," as they were known then, rarely required a decryption key to unlock the data. Hobbyist cryptographers often figured how to decrypt the locked files without having to pay the ransom. Good encryption is hard to make. By 2006, a second class of crypto-malware started to show up, this time using known and proven cryptographic routines that were not so easy to break. By 2013, ransomware programs using encryption that was really hard to impossible to break were fairly common.

As the encryption issue was being fixed, the far bigger problem for criminals was how a ransomware creator could get paid without getting caught and sent to jail. Two things happened. First, Bitcoin was invented in 2009. It took a few years, but by 2014, the ransomware programs made the link to Bitcoin, and the whole ransomware industry exploded. Now, criminals could get paid without getting caught.

Second, some major countries, like Russia, became cyber safe havens for ransomware criminals. Today, many ransomware gangs are located in or around Russia and operate with near impunity. Many pay bribes to local and country law enforcement as a part of doing business, and their revenue streams are seen as a net positive in their host countries. As long as they don't encrypt computers in their host or friendly ally countries, they are free to do business with few exceptions.

With these two new developments in place, sophisticated ransomware programs started to take out entire businesses, hospitals, police stations, and even entire cities. Today, ransomware is so prolific that entire companies being taken down, and ransoms paid in the multi-million-dollar range don't even raise an eyebrow. Ransomware attacks are taking down oil pipelines, food production plants, corporate mega-conglomerates, closing schools, delaying healthcare, and pretty much exploiting everything they can with near impunity. As I write this, ransomware gangs are likely in their "golden years," causing more disruption and making more money, than ever before. At this moment, we aren't doing a very good job at stopping it.

But we can. That's what this book is about. It's about preventing ransomware from happening in the first place, as your number-one objective, and minimizing damage if your organization gets hit. Turns out there are many things any organization can do to avoid being hit by ransomware or to at least significantly minimize the odds. Fighting ransomware is more than having a good, solid backup and up-to-date antivirus program.

This book will tell you the best things you can do to prevent a ransomware attack from happening in the first place, better than any other source you can find. It will tell you the details of what you need to do before you are possibly hit by ransomware and what to do, step-by-step if you are exploited. You don't have to be a victim. You can fight back.

Anyone can be a victim of ransomware. Ransomware is difficult to defeat currently. The aim of this book is not to say that you can 100 percent defeat ransomware. You can't. No one can make that claim. Cybersecurity defense is about risk minimization, not elimination. My goal is to help you minimize the risk as much as possible. If you follow the ideas and steps in this book, you will minimize your risk of a successful ransomware exploit as best you can given the current state of what we can do until we get new defenses that work better for us all (covered in Chapter 2, "Preventing Ransomware").

Fight the good fight!

Who This Book Is For

This book is primarily aimed at anyone who is in charge of managing their organization's computer security, from the front-line defender to the top computer security executive. It is for anyone who is considering reviewing, buying, or implementing computer security defenses for the first or the tenth time.

What it will take to prevent and mitigate ransomware is what it will take to prevent and mitigate all malicious hackers and malware. The lessons taught in this book, if followed, will significantly reduce risk of all malicious hackers and malware attacks. Even if one day ransomware goes away, the lessons learned here will readily apply to the next "big" attack. Ransomware is not your real problem; it's an outcome of your real problem.

What Is Covered in This Book?

Ransomware Protection Playbook contains 12 chapters separated into 2 distinct parts.

Part I: Introduction

Part I summarizes what ransomware does, how sophisticated it is, and how to prevent it from exploiting your organization and devices. Many people don't understand how mature ransomware is and even more don't concentrate enough on stopping it before it attacks.

Chapter 1, "Introduction to Ransomware"   Chapter 1 covers ransomware starting with a little bit of history of the significant milestones and then discusses the very sophisticated and mature versions used today. The ransomware industry is run much more like a multilevel marketing firm/ecosystem than anything else. Chapter 1 will cover the common pieces and parts. As an encompassing introduction, it is also the longest chapter in the book.

Chapter 2, "Preventing Ransomware"   Preventing ransomware is something that isn't talked about enough. The most recommended "prevention" control, a good backup, is not prevention at all. Chapter 2 will talk about the things every person and organization should be doing to prevent ransomware to the best of their ability. And in the process of discussing how to defeat ransomware, it will discuss how to best defeat all malicious hackers and malware.

Chapter 3, "Cybersecurity Insurance"   The decision to purchase cyber insurance is a big dilemma for organizations facing the threat of ransomware. Cyber insurance is complex. Chapter 3 gives readers a basic understanding of cyber insurance, including the things that should be avoided when considering a policy. It ends with a frank discussion of the massive changes happening in the cybersecurity industry right now and where it's headed.

Chapter 4, "Legal Considerations" Chapter 4 covers the legal considerations involved with dealing with a successful ransomware attack, not only in the decision of whether to pay or not pay the ransom, although that is a big part of this chapter, but also how to use legal help to your benefit during an attack. Chapter 4 will contain tips and recommendations that every organization should utilize in their planning and responses to ransomware.

Part II: Detection and Recovery

Part II will help you plan for and respond to a successful ransomware attack.

Chapter 5, "Ransomware Response Plan" Every organization should have a detailed ransomware response plan created and practiced ahead of an actual ransomware event. Chapter 5 will cover what your ransomware response plan should contain.

Chapter 6, "Detecting Ransomware" If you can't stop a cybersecurity exploit from happening, the next best thing is early warning and detection. Chapter 6 covers the best ways to detect ransomware and gives you the best chance to stop it before it begins to do real damage.

Chapter 7, "Minimizing Damage" Chapter 7 assumes ransomware has been able to successfully compromise an environment and has encrypted files and exfiltrated data. How do you minimize the spread of ransomware and its damage during the first hours of the first day? Chapter 7 tells you how.

Chapter 8, "Early Responses" After the initial damage has been prevented from spreading further, now comes the initial cleanup, better assessment, and additional responses, beyond just preventing further spread. Chapter 8 is what you need to be doing after the first day or two. How well you perform this part of the response often determines how long it will take to fully recover.

Chapter 9, "Environment Recovery"   Chapter 9 covers what you need to be doing after the first few days. You've stopped the spread, minimized the damage, and started to get some initial systems back up and working. Chapter 9 is what you need to be doing after the initial worst is over. It covers the longer-term items, the ones that often take days to weeks, or even months, to recover or rebuild.

Chapter 10, "Next Steps"   So, despite your best prevention efforts, you were successfully compromised by ransomware. Chapter 10 covers what lessons you need to learn and what mitigations you need to implement to prevent it from happening again. Many ransomware victims skip this step and often get hit again, and usually the additional times are worse. Learn what you need to learn and do to become more resilient against ransomware.

Chapter 11, "What Not to Do"   Knowing what not to do is as important as what to do in an emergency. Many ransomware victims have made the situation worse by making critical mistakes early on. Chapter 11 covers the things any organization should avoid doing to not make things even worse than they already are.

Chapter 12, "Future of Ransomware"   Chapter 12 covers the likely future of ransomware, how it will evolve, and what it will ultimately take to defeat it forever.

How to Contact Wiley or the Author

Wiley strives to keep you supplied with the latest tools and information you need for your work. Please check the website at www.wiley.com/go/ransomwareprotectionplaybook, where I'll post additional content and updates that supplement this book should the need arise.

If you have any questions, suggestions, or corrections, feel free to email me at roger@banneretcs.com.

Part I

Introduction

Chapter 1
Introduction
to Ransomware

This chapter is a general introduction to ransomware starting with the basics and leading to a more mature discussion of all the features and components that make it such a mature and formidable foe today. You will learn that much of the ransomware industry is run more like a professional, corporate industry rather than like the traditional perception of a few bad guys or gangs hiding out in their basements drinking jacked-up caffeinated sodas surrounded by empty bags of chips. Instead, you're more likely to find CEOs, payroll departments, professional developers, and business partners. You will come away with a very good understanding of today's ransomware, what and how it does it, and the significant challenges to defeat it.

Note to the reader: This chapter is the longest of the book.

How Bad Is the Problem?

Many press and security experts seem to compete with each other to use the latest over-the-top superlatives surrounding ransomware. But for once in the computer security world, the statistics and scary reputation are well earned. We have had other very bad, long runs of damage-causing malware such as that from DOS boot viruses, disk-formatting computer viruses like Michelangelo (1992), worms that crashed email and pager systems like the Iloveyou worm (2000), rapidly spreading and database-crashing worms like SQL Slammer (2003), the USB-key spreading Conficker (2008), spam bots, and resource-sucking crypto-miners. We've been living with damage-causing malware for a long time. But no previous threat has produced the damage and operational interruption caused by ransomware. It's simply unparalleled in human history, and that is not hyperbole. It might be the "tipping point" event that forces the Internet to finally be made significantly safer.

As bad as ransomware has been and still is, it is still getting worse. The number of attempts against possible victims is growing. The number of successful attacks is growing. The ransoms demanded per exploitation are greater. The percentage of victims paying the ransom is increasing. The overall damage, in financial and other terms, is growing exponentially. Since the beginning of ransomware, and especially since bitcoin came around and allowed it to take off, it has been one historic year after historic year for ransomware purveyors and their programs. We are likely living in the "golden age" of malware, at least from the bad guy's perspective. Here are some of the latest stats at the time of this writing:

- The FBI says it is investigating about 100 different types of ransomware programs (https://www.reuters.com/technology/fbi-says-it-is-investigating-about-100-types-ransomware-wsj-2021-06-04/).
- Ransomware was successful in exploiting 68 percent of surveyed organizations in one year alone (https://cyber-edge.com/wp-content/uploads/2021/04/CyberEdge-2021-CDR-Report-v1.1-1.pdf). That figure alone is shocking.

- The same survey listed in the previous bullet point says the average ransom paid in 2020 was \$166,475, and 57 percent of victims paid the ransom.
- Coveware says the average ransom paid in Q1 2021 was \$220,298 (`https://www.coveware.com/blog/ransomware-attack-vectors-shift-as-new-software-vulnerability-exploits-abound`). Why is Coveware's figure higher than the previous report? It's likely because Coveware's figure is newer. When I see a low-ball ransomware figure, I usually check the date of the statistic, and it's almost always old. And when I mean old, I mean only by a year or two. Either way, ransomware is growing tremendously over time.
- The highest publicly known paid ransom the author is aware of is \$40 million, but there are many in the \$5 million to \$10 million range. There are likely many privately paid ransoms over \$40 million that we are not aware of.
- This 2019 report (`https://blog.emsisoft.com/en/34822/the-state-of-ransomware-in-the-us-report-and-statistics-2019/`) says the average ransomware incident cost \$8.1 million and took 287 days to recover from.
- This vendor states \$18 billion was paid globally in ransom and total costs are in the hundreds of billions of dollars . . . a year (`https://blog.emsisoft.com/en/38426/the-cost-of-ransomware-in-2021-a-country-by-country-analysis/`).

In summary, the problem of ransomware is pretty bad and growing over time.

Variability of Ransomware Data

Things are moving so fast in the ransomware world that trying to get up-to-date figures and statistics tends to be like trying to nail the proverbial Jell-O™ to a wall. Different vendors and surveys in different time periods often say vastly different things. For example, many cybersecurity vendors talk about multi-month average dwell times where the ransomware gang specifically figured out the exact maximum ransom they could ask for, while others will tell you that "most" ransomware attacks happen right after the break-in or within hours of the initial successful exploitation, and all the victims are asked for same fixed fee. Who is right? Likely everyone. There are at least a 100 different ransomware programs coded by all sorts of criminals of varying skill levels and experiences successfully attacking tens to hundreds of thousands of organizations and people a year. Different ransomware groups also target different industries, sectors, and regions. The figures and stats are bound to vary widely.

Even the exact same answer can have a different number from the same vendor. For example, the Coveware Q1 2021 report figure listed above states that the average ransom paid was $220,298, but in the same report it also says the median ransom payment was $78,398. The two figures don't even seem close. This seemingly statistical anomaly means that a few victims on the upper end are paying far more than the rest of the victims, which brings up the overall average for everyone. It turns out having to pay a few $5 million and $10 million ransoms will skew results.

So, if you're trying to figure out how much a ransom payment might cost your company, which figure do you use in your estimation calculation? It varies based on your perspective. The most conservative answer is if you want to be safe and set aside for the worse-case scenario, then use the highest reasonable estimate. But who knows, if your organization gets hit by ransomware, the criminals might ask for an unreasonable figure. Certainly, none of the organizations hit by multi-million dollar ransoms would agree with the reasonableness of the request.

How much you might have to pay really comes down to what type of ransomware program you got hit with, how bad things got before damage control started to happen, and how recovery goes. And no one knows those answers until they are in the thick of things. It's like going into a surgery with a bad pain in your lower left quadrant and asking the doctor what the cost of the operation will be before they've put you to sleep. No one knows.

With that said, no matter what figures you grab and whether they are using averages, medians, or last year's figures, the damage caused by ransomware is bad and getting worse. The total involved costs can easily be many millions for multimillion-dollar organizations and tens to hundreds of millions for multibillion-dollar organizations. Smaller amounts of ransom can even be devastating to smaller organizations.

True Costs of Ransomware

Many defenders when trying to argue for the need to defend against ransomware must come up with the potential damages that might occur from a ransomware event. The damages incurred by one organization vary drastically from another, according to size of the organization, revenue stream, preparation, value of the involved data, how bad the incident is, and ability to respond to a particular ransomware attack. There are a lot of variables at play. Get hit with a very simple ransomware program that was really meant to hit a consumer at home, and the cost could be less than $1,000 to clean up a single exploited computer. Get hit by another ransomware variant, and it could mean the whole network is down for weeks to months.

Still, many defenders are asked to come up with estimated costs to help with cybersecurity risk management decisions around ransomware, such as whether to buy cybersecurity insurance, upgrade that old backup system, or what to invest in next to try to prevent a ransomware attack from being successful in their organization. Unfortunately, as covered earlier, the risk from ransomware and costs abound and vary greatly.

One of the biggest disagreements you will see between vendors and reports is the "cost of ransomware" or something like that. For example, one vendor like Cybersecurity Ventures, will publish a huge figure like ransomware costing $20 billion in 2021 and to grow to $256 billion in damages by 2031 (https://cybersecurityventures

.com/global-ransomware-damage-costs-predicted-to-reach-250-
billion-usd-by-2031/). And another, you'll have someone saying the cost is only in the "low" millions of dollars. For example,
the FBI's very respected 2020 Internet Crime Report (https://www
.ic3.gov/Media/PDF/AnnualReport/2020_IC3Report.pdf)   stated,
"In 2020, the IC3 received 2,474 complaints identified as ransomware with adjusted losses of over $29.1 million." So, one vendor
is saying $20 billion in 2021, while another agency is saying just
$29.1 million in 2020. I doubt ransomware damage doubled more
than 687 times higher in one year alone.

The key to reconciling these huge discrepancies and deciding which number is more accurate is in realizing they are often
reporting drastically different things. In the FBI's instance, they
are reporting only on ransomware events reported to them. At the
most, it would only include US victims, and even then, it has to be a
very small percentage of ransomware victims. The larger figures in
the billions always include global considerations.

Still, the FBI's numbers seem low. If you divide the quoted
losses ($29.1 million) by the number of victims (2,474), you only
get an average damage loss of $11,762. I'm not sure what the FBI's
"adjust losses" figures include, but that seems very low, even if
it only included ransom. Most of the other ransomware reports
are showing numbers well over $50,000 to over $200,000 for the
ransom alone.

Perhaps a big part of the difference is that adjusted losses
likely only include "accounting" realized losses after an insurance
claim clicked in. This 2020 study (https://www.sophos.com/en-us/
medialibrary/Gated-Assets/white-papers/sophos-the-state-of-
ransomware-2020-wp.pdf) stated that 64 percent of ransomware
victims had cybersecurity insurance that covered ransomware. So,
nearly two-thirds of ransomware-hit victims likely had only a much
smaller deductible to pay (and not the whole ransom amount) unless
the ransom and damages went over the ceiling of their coverage.

Many vendors reporting ransomware statistics report on both
the ransom paid and the money spent to get the victim back up
and running. Many ransomware events can include other indirect

costs that many people don't think about that are often not listed in most reports. If you're trying to do a risk assessment calculation for either mitigating ransomware, calculating if you can afford a cyber-security insurance premium, or having to calculate all the real costs from a ransomware event, consider these related costs:

- Whether or not a ransomware event has occurred, cost of:
  ◦ Ransomware mitigations to prevent an attack in the first place
  ◦ Increase in backup costs and labor to prepare to recover from a ransomware event
  ◦ Cybersecurity insurance premiums, if any
- If a ransomware event has occurred, costs of:
  ◦ Ransom paid, if any
  ◦ Recovery expenses
  ◦ Business interruption losses, by the intended victim and downstream impacts
  ◦ Law enforcement and investigation costs
  ◦ Personnel changes, adds/deletes/changes, if any
  ◦ Productivity slowdowns due to new procedures and protections, if any
  ◦ Reputational harm
  ◦ Additional defense preparations to mitigate the next attack
  ◦ Cyber insurance deductible/retention

When you consider all the costs associated with recovering from a ransomware attack, you can see that they can be a lot over and above and beyond just paying the ransom and "recovery damages." This is to say, that preventing ransomware from occurring in the first place is almost always the cheaper option.

Types of Ransomware

There is no singular type of ransomware, although the majority of it does have common features that most of us have come to associate with the ransomware descriptor, including the following:

- It is a malicious software program (i.e., malware).
- It sneaks or is secretly placed onto a victim's computer(s) or device(s).
- It has the ability to encrypt files.
- It asks for a ransom to provide the decryption key(s).

Since the very first ransomware program, the PC Cyborg trojan from 1989, covered in this book's introduction, most traditional ransomware has followed this basic pattern for the first two decades of their existence. But ransomware has changed over time. There are many different types of ransomware, and as this book is being written, significant, evolutionary changes are continuing to happen. By understanding the different types, you can more fully appreciate that if you are involved with a ransomware attack, what the ransomware does isn't monolithic, and you can be more prepared for any differences. Here are the different types and traits of various ransomware programs:

- Fake ransomware
- Immediate action versus delayed
- Automatic or human-directed
- One device or multiple device impact
- Trojan versus worm
- File-encrypting versus boot infection
- Good versus bad encryption
- Infection versus more payloads
- Ransomware as a service

Fake Ransomware

Not all malware that claims to be ransomware is really encrypting files and taking ultimate control over someone's computer. There are many far less sophisticated malware programs and simple JavaScript applets that claim to be ransomware but are simply fake. They are not encrypting anything. They are generally known as *scareware*.

They usually take over a person's current Internet browsing session in such a way that the intended victim may believe they have lost control of their computer or phone and must pay the ransom to get back control. The fake ransomware demands are often communicated along with a claim that the victim was recorded doing something embarrassing (e.g., watching porn, etc.) or doing something illegal (e.g., watching child porn, not paying their lawful taxes, etc.). Figure 1.1 shows such a fake ransomware warning claiming to involve the US Department of Justice *and* Federal Bureau of Investigations (FBI).

Figure 1.1 Example scareware screenshot

Fake ransomware warnings are popular on mobile media devices, as well. You might wonder who could possibly believe this warning, especially with the suggested payment methods, but some percentage of people have paid the ransom demanded by fake ransomware programs for decades. There have even been multiple suicides and even at least one murder-suicide (https://hotforsecurity. bitdefender.com/blog/romanian-man-commits-suicide-and-kills-his-4-year-old-after-falling-for-police-ransomware-8168.html) by victims believing the fake ransomware notices and feeling ashamed of their purported actions. It's very sad.

In most cases of fake ransomware, all the victim has to do is figure out a way to remove the fake ransomware program from their computer. It is the easiest type to remove in that generally it simply requires restarting the involved browser program, although that can take some effort as the ransomware program "takes control" of the browser. Some fake ransomware victims can easily close their impacted browser, while others have to somehow forcibly close the program. On Microsoft Windows, that may involve hitting Ctrl-Alt-Del, starting Task Manager, and then killing the involved process(es).

If the browser cannot be closed or restarted, it may only take a reboot if the fake ransomware program has not modified any local computer files. In my anecdotal experience, most fake ransomware programs can be eradicated by closing the browser or rebooting the involved device, although if your re-started browser automatically opens your last page, it can be an additional pain to stop the automatic reloading.

If the fake ransomware program was able to modify local device files and, hence, will automatically reappear and "have control" after a reboot, then the user has to use another method to bypass the normal boot process to remove the fake ransomware files and startup instructions. On a Microsoft Windows computer, this often means booting into Safe Mode and then finding and deleting the malicious file and/or registry entries.

If you are experienced in what real ransomware programs look like, there is a certain "look" to the fake ransomware programs versus the real ransomware programs. For instance, the fake ransomware programs often try to imply that they have captured the victim's unethical or illegal actions or captured their passwords and will do even more harm if the victim does not pay up (the latter of which is something that real ransomware does but doesn't usually brag about during the initial interaction). So, if you see a ransomware notice going out of its way to claim that it has recorded you or your actions, it's more likely scareware than real ransomware.

Some damaging malware programs are closer to scareware than real ransomware, although they do a slightly better job of pretending. For example, StrRAT doesn't encrypt files, but it does rename them and add a .crimson file extension (https://latesthackingnews .com/2021/05/24/microsoft-warns-of-fake-ransomware-strrat-that-is-actually-a-potent-malware/). On Microsoft Windows systems, renaming any file to a nonlegitimate extension will result in the file's icon being represented by an invalid icon, not opening or executing normally, and in general could very easily fake many victims into believing a real ransomware event is occurring. However, in these sorts of instances, simply renaming the file to its complete original name will make the file operational again. The files themselves are not truly encrypted and do not require a decryption key to restore. If you suspect this type of malware, it can't hurt to open an "encrypted" file whose contents you understand by renaming it to its original extension and seeing if you can still read it. You can typically do this on real encrypted program files as a test, without causing further damage.

On the other side of the spectrum, you have malware programs that claim to have encrypted files that they will release if the ransom is paid, but don't have any intention of doing so. The NotPetya attack (https://en.wikipedia.org/wiki/2017_cyberattacks_on_Ukraine) in Ukraine is a great example. It impacted hundreds of thousands of computers, mostly in Ukraine. When it was executed, it claimed that it would release the encrypted files if a ransom was paid (see Figure 1.2 for a screenshot of the message). But in reality, it would never release the files even if the ransom was paid. The ransomware claim was simply a ruse to confuse the victims and cause longer-lasting damage until the victims realized a ransom-based rescue was never coming.

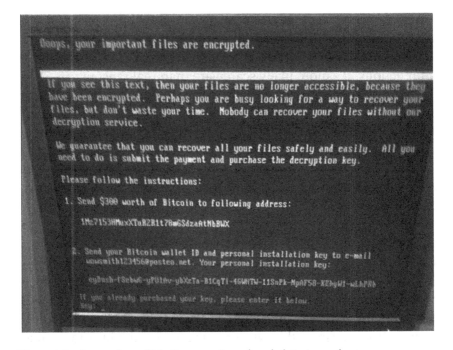

Figure 1.2   Screenshot of NotPetya activated and claiming to be ransomware
Courtesy Wikipedia

Malware that overwrites boot sectors and files with no intention of allowing an easy recovery are known as *wiper* programs. NotPetya was a wiper program, not a ransomware program, even though it is often classified and talked about like ransomware. The reason why NotPetya is talked about as ransomware is that much of the code is borrowed from another true ransomware program known as Petya. But the Petya ransomware program was modified to become a wiper program, and that's part of the reason why it is known as NotPetya. If a program asks for ransom but doesn't ever take ransom to unlock the encrypted files, then it's missing the most important part of the ransomware . . . the ransom!

Immediate Action vs. Delayed

Most early ransomware programs went off and encrypted files as soon as they were executed. Just a few years ago, perhaps 70 percent of ransomware programs did this. Immediate action ransomware programs are easier to write, less likely to be detected before executing their payload, and result in faster payments because usually they cause less damage and ask for less ransom. They are also known as *direct-action* malware.

Today, immediate action ransomware programs are in the minority. Starting at the end of 2019, immediate-action trojans started to become less common. There are still plenty of them (they are easier to write), but most ransomware programs "dwell" for days, months, and even years before executing their payloads. We will cover more about this in the "Typical Ransomware Process and Components" section below. Figure 1.3 shows an example of a common immediate action ransomware program known as Cryptic.

Figure 1.3 Screenshot of immediate action Cryptic ransomware

NOTE: A large version of this figure is available for download at www.wiley.com/go/ransomwareprotectionplaybook.

I downloaded it from a website that hosts malware programs for a webinar I was presenting. I was literally surprised that I had found a ransomware program that executed and locked up the test virtual machine environment I was running it on in under 15 seconds. Although you can't directly see the encrypted files, you can see all the newly created TXT files, which are the ransomware notices in Cyrillic and English. Some immediate action ransomware programs will quickly perform other payloads, such as collecting passwords and uploading them to the hacker gang, before encrypting files. Direct action malware is automated to do what it does when it does it, and it often does it in seconds.

Another common direct action ransomware program is called Kolz (https://heimdalsecurity.com/blog/kolz-ransomware/). It encrypts files, adds a file extension to all the encrypted files, and then asks the victim to send $490–$980 to the ransomware criminal in order for them to provide the decryption key.

However, it is clear that more and more ransomware is spending longer on victim devices and networks without being detected no matter how long they dwell. This is worrisome on at least two critical levels. First, the longer a malware program dwells, the greater the increased risk of damage. The malware program has longer to look around, if it does that sort of thing; longer to collect more passwords and longer to spread to additional computers. The longer a malware program dwells, the more increased risk to the victim.

Second, it points to a huge problem in cybersecurity defenses. Most people and organizations have up-to-date antivirus defenses, meaning some sort of program that proactively scans new incoming files and content looking for malicious markers or activity; and the vast majority of successful ransomware attacks are still succeeding despite the presence of up-to-date antivirus programs. In fact, most of the impacted victim organizations have everything they think they need to be successful against hackers and malware, and they are still being exploited. Most are doing what they think is a "good job" with computer security. They have antivirus programs, firewalls, event monitoring, secure configurations, least privilege permissions, patching, and so on, and they are still being exploited by malware and hackers.

If there was anything ransomware taught us that could be seen as a possible positive, it pointed out the glaring error that most organizations did not have good, reliable, thorough backups. For the entirety of the existence of computers, every organization has been told and/or required to have good, solid, reliable backups. Computer owners have been told this not only for ransomware, but for any disaster recovery or business interruption event. And most organizations thought they had good backups, and most have even told their compliance auditors that they had good backups. But when ransomware went off, encrypted files, and asked for a ransom to supply the decryption keys, it turns out that many victim organizations did not have good, reliable backups, at least at the scale they needed to fight an enterprise-wide ransomware attack. Additionally, many organizations actually did have good, reliable, backups but learned they were not as securely protected as they could be when ransomware gangs deleted the backups before turning on the encryption. In general, ransomware was a huge industry wakeup call that many, if not most, organizations did not have the solid, good, reliable, enterprise-wide backups they had long been claiming they had to interested stakeholders. In this one point alone, ransomware has improved the defenses of many organizations by forcing them to make sure they have good, secured, enterprise-wide backups. Having a reliable backup can be very useful in many other types of events, like disaster recovery.

Automatic or Human-Directed

Automatic or human-directed malware is one of the biggest, most significant changes in ransomware (and really all malware) maturity over the last decade. Traditional malware did what it was programmed to do. It couldn't do anything it wasn't programmed to do. Even ransomware that has delayed actions is often programmed that way. For instance, the first ransomware program, the AIDS Cyborg trojan, was programmed to obfuscate files and folders 90 or so reboots after its initial execution. It didn't have flexibility. It did what it was programmed to do.

Today, much of malware and the majority of ransomware uses some automated method, like a trojan or worm, to break in and gain initial "foothold" access to a device and/or environment, and then it allows human adversaries to ultimately come in, take control, and drive its future actions. Human-directed ransomware has "changed the game" and is much more dangerous and devious. This is because humans, unlike automated programs, can change their tactics, offensive capabilities, and defenses, on the fly, as circumstances and learnings dictate. For example, a hacker can break in, eavesdrop on email, learn some important information, and then use that information to ask for a higher extortion payment. Or a human-based attacker can drop additional malware programs, like Trickbot, a password-stealing trojan, to collect as many passwords as they can before causing the encryption issues. Human-directed, dwelling malware is a far more serious problem than simple, automated, direct action ransomware programs. More is covered on this later in this chapter.

Single Device Impacts or More

Early and simple ransomware just impacts the device it was originally executed on. Most ransomware today either directly impacts more devices or allows human adversaries to explore and compromise more assets. Consider yourself "lucky" if the ransomware program, like the Cryptic ransomware program that was shown in Figure 1.2, encrypts only the computer it is located on.

Years ago, ransomware, if it exploited more computers, did so by collecting administrative logon credentials out of a computer's memory. This usually happened on Microsoft Windows computers connected to Microsoft Active Directory networks. The ransomware program would use keyloggers or programs like Trickbot, Mimikatz, or Wince to steal passwords or password hashes for administrative logon credentials out of memory or a file, which they then used to spread across more devices using the stolen credentials.

These days, ransomware can use those same automated methods or human adversaries can come into the exploited environment, look around, and use various tools and scripts to collect the types of credentials they want and exploit additional computers (i.e., lateral movement). Today, most ransomware programs are going to exploit and encrypt multiple computers at the same time because it increases both the chance and amount of a ransom payment. I've heard of hundreds to tens of thousands of computers being locked up all at the same time. Even if it isn't most of the computers in an organization being encrypted, the organization has to assume all are compromised. The organization must clean or verify all computers are safe, before relying on them.

The ability of most ransomware gangs to exploit and encrypt multiple computers at once means any exploited victim has to assume the worst-case scenario until each possibly accessible computer is investigated and deemed clean. It is routine to hear of entire, global, conglomerate companies shut down, when only a much smaller division or location is actually impacted.

This happened with the infamous Colonial Pipeline attack (https://en.wikipedia.org/wiki/Colonial_Pipeline_cyber_ attack). According to news reports, the ransomware only directly impacted Colonial's billing system, but the much larger operational systems had to be shut down until billing resumed and Colonial verified that it could re-open the pipeline safely. Further, the pipeline shutdown impacted gasoline supply issues not at all impacted by the pipeline. For example, there was a "run on gas" in parts of Florida that were not served by the pipeline and had no interruption, simply because consumers were fearful of shortages. People in far away, untouched countries, like the Netherlands, were told to expect interruptions due to the attack. This shows that ransomware taking out even small percentages of computers of an organization can cause big problems.

Even if you think that you are only hit by direct-action, single-computer ransomware, how do you really know? An organization's risk calculation is much more complicated by the mere existence of multicomputer ransomware, both because ransomware often does impact multiple computers at the same time and simply because of the threat even if ransomware doesn't do it.

Ransomware Root Exploit

Hackers can use a variety of methods to get ransomware into an organization, including the following:

- Social engineering
- Malware
- Unpatched software
- Exploiting misconfigurations

- Password guessing
- Using known good previously compromised victim passwords
- USB key infections
- Compromised trusted third parties

The most common method for spreading ransomware is the spread and execution of a trojan horse program via a socially engineered email or website pop-up message. Social engineering is responsible for the vast majority of ransomware attacks over most time periods (although there are other leading root causes for temporary periods of time).

There are also ransomware programs, like WannaCry (https://en.wikipedia.org/wiki/WannaCry_ransomware_attack), that spread like worms. A computer worm uses its own coding, usually looking for and exploiting unpatched software or looking for misconfigurations it can abuse. WannaCry, in particular, looked for and used unpatched versions of Microsoft Windows that were susceptible to the "Eternal Blue" Server Message Block (SMB) exploit. SMB is the protocol used that underlies Windows file shares and many other mechanisms "behind the scenes" of Windows. The exploit had been discovered by the US National Security Agency (NSA), then stolen by one or more hacking groups, and eventually used in WannaCry, NetPetya, and other malware programs.

Worm-based ransomware programs are not nearly as popular as trojan-based ransomware, but they have the propensity to spread far quicker, depending on its spreading aggressiveness, ability to access exploitable devices, and number of accessible devices overall. Social engineering can potentially work with any number of different platforms and doesn't have to count on an unpatched vulnerability to be successful.

Ransomware programs acting as computer viruses, where it infects other files and then uses them to spread are rare to nonexistent. Computer viruses, in general, are less commonly used in malware, as they are more difficult to write and operate successfully over a wide range of scenarios. Because of this, most ransomware programs are social engineered-trojan horse programs or worms.

File Encrypting vs. Boot Infecting

Usually ransomware encrypts most of the files (or files with selected file extensions) that it can find on the host computer it exploits. Most ransomware programs will leave the computer's boot files and processes unimpacted so that the impacted computers run well enough to communicate what has happened, ask for the ransom payment, and possibly allow the decryption key to be entered to unlock the files. Some file-encrypting ransomware programs will encrypt everything, including the boot files, but leave enough malicious remnants for responders to find and figure out what happened.

Other ransomware programs, like Petya (`https://en.wikipedia.org/wiki/Petya_(malware)`), encrypt an operating system's boot files only, like the master boot record (MBR) or other related critical system files (like the file system table). In many instances, because all the other involved files are not truly encrypted, it can result in a greater chance of complete or partial recovery without the ransom being paid or the decryption keys being used. However, when boot files or file tables are encrypted, it erases the location of the files and all their related disk sectors. The files and folders are still there in their unencrypted state, but the impacted files and folders can be difficult to find and to reconstruct. Encrypting the boot files or file system table alone will likely be as disastrous for impacted victims as true file-encrypting ransomware, although there is a great chance (if only slightly) for the victim to get unencrypted files and their content back.

It is more difficult for a malware program to infect boot files and file system tables correctly than it is to encrypt files and folders. There have been instances where the ransomware program did not correctly encrypt the boot files or file system tables, so the ransomware did not execute correctly. It showed a ransomware warning but did not otherwise impact the system at all. In other cases, a data recovery expert was able to recover or use additional copies of the boot sector or file system tables that some operating systems make by default to restore the encrypted portions to their pre-impacted states.

This is to say, although boot file and file system table encrypting ransomware is bad, it is not quite as bad and technically disastrous to recover from as compared to true file-encrypting ransomware. If you get hit by ransomware successfully and don't have good backups, some victims might hope that the involved ransomware is just a boot sector or file system table encryptor. If there is some critical piece of information you need to get to, you may have a better chance.

There are also many ransomware programs that just look for and encrypt particular types of files, usually Microsoft Office formats (e.g., Microsoft Word .docx, Microsoft Excel .xlsx, etc.). The hacker's thinking is that they can encrypt more data quickly using a lesser number of files and still get paid. This is often true. The user's data is more valuable than the common and static operating system files.

Good vs. Bad Encryption

No matter how a ransomware program encrypts, it's important to understand what type of encryption it uses. Some early ransomware programs like the PC Cyborg trojan really do something closer to obscuration than true encryption. This is sometimes still true today. Some less sophisticated ransomware programs either use obscurity tactics instead of good encryption or use bad encryption. Good encryption is hard to make. Even the world's most trained and educated cryptographers struggle to make good, reliable, new encryption programs.

In the ransomware world, the early ransomware programs used obfuscation and homegrown (i.e., bad encryption) programs. Most of these early efforts could be reversed without much effort by a trained cryptographer or even just a regular, nontrained person (who understood what was going on and knew at least a little programming).

Today, most ransomware uses very good, well-accepted, cryptography like RSA and Advanced Encryption Standard (AES). Files encrypted by good encryption programs usually can't be decrypted without the proper decryption key. Still, if the victim is "lucky," sometimes the encryption isn't great, and the files can be recovered without the decryption key(s). There are also less sophisticated versions of ransomware out there. Sometimes the same decryption key(s) are shared by every version of the same ransomware program, and if so, once one victim learns what those keys are, others can use the same key, if publicly known, instead of paying the ransom. There are many websites dedicated to sharing ransomware keys for the types of ransomware programs that share keys (we will cover those in later chapters).

Understanding what ransomware program and version you are being attacked by can be used to quickly determine if a ransom has to be paid to recover encrypted files.

Encryption vs. More Payloads

Back in the "good old days," ransomware just encrypted files. That was the case until late 2019. Starting in October 2019, a single ransomware program called Maze started to threaten to publicly share exfiltrated data. There had been a few threats by that same ransomware gang in the months before to publish stolen data, but they had yet to follow through on threats to publish the stolen information if weren't paid. Then in November 2019 (https://www.bleepingcomputer.com/news/security/allied-universal-breached-by-maze-ransomware-stolen-data-leaked/), Maze finally followed through with the threat and released a victim's stolen data publicly in multiple locations including its personal website and Wikileaks. Pretty soon it became common. Figure 1.4 shows a real-world example of files stolen from a law office, evidence placed up on the "dark web," and an extortion demand being made.

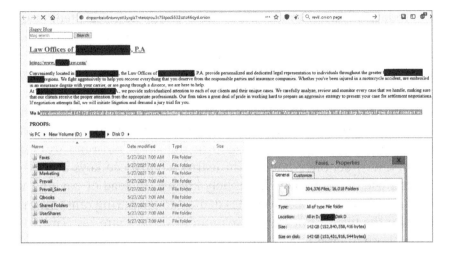

Figure 1.4   A real-world ransom data extortion demand

Courtesy Erich Kron

NOTE: A large version of this figure is available for download at www.wiley.com/go/ ransomwareprotectionplaybook.

This new tactic of data exfiltration led to Maze getting paid more money more often. Pretty soon the other ransomware groups, seeing Maze's success, followed suit. Within a few months, REvil/ Sodinokibi and Zeppelin started to use the tactic. What started out as one ransomware gang using the tactic soon turned into a majority using the tactic. By the end of 2020, more than 70 percent of all ransomware attacks were using data exfiltration as a primary tactic, by the first quarter of 2021 it was more than 77 percent, and by the middle of 2021 it is likely over 80 percent (https://www.coveware .com/blog/ransomware-attack-vectors-shift-as-new-software- vulnerability-exploits-abound). This is to say that you are far more likely to get hit by a ransomware program that exfiltrates your confidential data first before it encrypts it, than not. Many in the media started to give this a new buzzword called *double-exploitation*. But it's far worse than that.

Ransomware gangs realized that they were tired of not being paid because more victims had good backups, and also the realization that the "gold" of what the ransomware attacker had was not the ability to encrypt files but the unauthorized access to the compromised environment and everything it contains. Using their unauthorized access, the attackers could end up with complete control of a network, knowledge of passwords, and access to all critical data and systems. Operationally, they could steal and do anything the compromised systems were capable of.

Besides taking data, ransomware attackers are stealing company, employee, and customer passwords. It used to be that if they stole passwords, they only stole them to help spread laterally and exploit more machines in the same network. No more. Now, starting in about 2019–2020, their primary goal for stealing passwords is to use them to maximize their extortion pressure or in additional criminal efforts to maximize profits.

No longer just immediate action trojans, ransomware programs are dwelling on someone's device or network undetected from a few hours to more than a year. I see different figures in different time periods about how long ransomware dwells on average without being discovered, but the most common stats I see are 120- to 200-day ranges. I know of many companies where ransomware was inside the network for a year or more. I know of one where the ransomware program dwelled for more than three years without being detected.

FireEye Mandiant says 1 percent of ransomware programs dwelled for more than 700 days (https://www.bankinfosecurity.com/attackers-dwell-time-plummets-as-ransomware-hits-continue-a-16508), even as overall ransomware dwell times fell.

Today's ransomware programs not only collected network passwords to spread around the network, but collected every password used by an employee on a system or website while it was dwelling. Besides network passwords, the programs are getting passwords to the websites and services used by the systems and employees to do the work of the business, plus all the passwords employees use on their personal sites. Brian Krebs, one of the most influential computer security bloggers on the Internet, recounted a ransomware attack from the 2019–2020 period (https:// krebsonsecurity.com/2020/01/the-hidden-cost-of-ransomware-wholesale-password-theft/) that resulted in that company's loss of more than 300 different types of passwords, including passwords to their banking portals, healthcare sites, competitive bidding sites, payroll services, and even their postage accounts.

Ransomware often steals employee passwords during the ransomware's dwell time, when employees visit tons of personal websites like their banking website, stock investing website, 401K, medical websites, Amazon to order something, Instagram, Facebook, TikTok, etc. During all that time the ransomware program, or Trojan Horse program or script, is collecting all those passwords. It's the same thing with customers. If you have a website where customers log on and it's hosted on the compromised environment, ransomware gangs are collecting those too, knowing that your customers are likely to use those passwords in other places.

Once the data and passwords are exfiltrated, the hackers contact the affected employees and customers of the original victim organization and tell them what they have, and say, "If you don't pay us, we will expose your sensitive information, passwords, or personal records to the world!" They often tell the employees and customers the only reason they are extorting them is that the original victim company isn't paying. This causes reputational and trust issues, not to mention individual emotional issues, and could cause further compromise of sensitive data such as identity theft if the stolen credentials are published and used by other hackers.

In one instance (https://krebsonsecurity.com/2021/04/ransom-gangs-emailing-victim-customers-for-leverage/), customers of Race-Trac convenience stores and gas stations were ransomed. In another story (https://healthitsecurity.com/news/hackers-demand-ransom-from-patients-after-breaching-florida-linic), patients of a Florida plastic surgery center were extorted with the ransomware hackers saying that if the patients did not pay, their private medical information—including pictures—would be released to the public. One of the worst stories I've read was of a 2020 ransomware attack in Helsinki, Finland (`https://www.wired.com/story/vastaamo-psychotherapy-patients-hack-data-breach/`). The intruder stole the personal data of tens of thousands of mental health patients. Thirty thousand former patients received individual ransom demands, and hundreds of very emotional, private, stories were released publicly. At least a few former patients described themselves as nearly suicidal over the release of their personal information.

Ransomware gangs are extorting the original victim's employees and customers for money as well, causing huge reputational issues. Even if the victim's employee and customers aren't being directly extorted for money, the ransomware hacker is making sure the employees and customers are aware their information is under their control, making the threat, and making sure the customers and employees know who to blame. Figure 1.5 shows an example of the devious, emotional messages ransomware attackers are using to embarrass the original victim and to cause reputational harm.

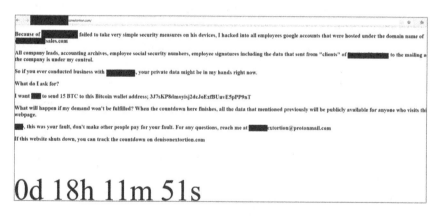

Figure 1.5 A real-world ransom extortion demand on the regular web

NOTE: A large version of this figure is available for download at www.wiley.com/go/ransomwareprotectionplaybook.

The ransomware hackers placed this warning on the main page of the victim's website so that any visiting customers could see what was happening. They then created an additional related domain, which involved the victim's original website name and added the word "extortion" to it, and opened up a new email address with the same so that employees and customers could reach out to them. They placed this warning on the victim's real website and placed it on the new website they created so that when the original website was closed or cleaned, people would still know how to check on how the countdown tracker was coming along. Whether or not a victim pays the ransom, the reputational harm is done.

While the hackers are in the victim's systems, they are also reading emails and learning about the business relationships the victim has with other vendors and trusted partners. Hackers can use this information to send spear phishing emails asking the business partners to open malicious documents or to run trojan horse programs. The new victims are getting an email from the original victim, whom they trust and have an ongoing relationship with. They don't understand why the person they trust is suddenly asking them to open some random new document or file, but many do without further hesitation. Boom! They are now new ransomware victims, too, and will likely place at least some blame on the upstream trusted partner (and of course, ransomware gang).

Ransomware hackers also publicly advertise who they have broken into (as shown in Figures 1.4 and 1.5) to get maximum pressure on the victim organization to settle quickly. If the victim was hoping the ransomware attack didn't get leaked to the media to keep it quiet, no such luck! Hackers often function as their own malicious public relations (PR) firm and send evidence of the latest compromise to the media. While I worked as the weekly security columnist for *InfoWorld* and *CSO Online* magazines (for nearly 15 years), I would routinely be contacted by ransomware gangs in late 2019 trying to see if I would publicize their latest big extortion scheme. I remember having a meeting with the editor-in-chief of the magazine's parent company as we all decided that we didn't want to be indirect PR agencies for the ransomware gangs. It looks like they met resistance from other news sources as they started to host their own websites dedicated to their latest compromise.

You can find a list of some of the most popular ransomware programs and their PR websites at `https://www.reddit.com/r/Malware/comments/ixvgoq/list_of_ransomware_groups_and_their_pr_pages/`. Unfortunately, you'll have to join the Tor network to see most of them (any with a `.onion` extension).

In the end, after all of that, if a victim is still arguing about paying the ransom, the hackers will do whatever they can to get the victim to pay. One tactic that is becoming more common is that they conduct massive distributed denial-of-service (DDoS) attacks if the victim has secondary sites not impacted by the original ransomware event. Maybe the ransomware took down only the victim's corporate network but not the victim's public-facing web servers, which are hosted somewhere else entirely. Hackers can take them down, too, to try to cause as much pain and suffering as it is takes to get paid. To summarize, this is what most ransomware does today:

- Encrypts data
- Exfiltrates emails, data, confidential information, IP addresses, and will post it publicly or give it to hackers, competitors, the dark web, or the public Internet, if you don't pay
- Steals company, employee, and customer logon credentials
- Extorts employees and customers
- Spear phishes business partners from the victim's own computers using real email addresses and subjects the partners trust
- Conducts DDoS attacks against any services the victim still has up and running
- Publicly embarrasses the victim company

That's a septuple-part problem. If you're lucky, you get only a quintuple-part problem. So, when I see double-extortion used as a term to describe today's ransomware, I think, "I wish that was all!"

I started to cover all the things ransomware did beyond just encryption for the first time in January 2020 in my webinar called Nuclear Ransomware (`https://info.knowbe4.com/nuclear-ransomware`) and an article I wrote (`https://blog.knowbe4.com/encryption-isnt-your-only-ransomware-problem-there-are-some-other-nasty-issues`).

You need to make sure the people in your organization that are in charge of cybersecurity defenses, risk management, and senior management, understand what today's ransomware does. It isn't just a data encryption problem or even only a data exfiltration problem. It's four to seven additional problems that a good backup does not solve. Your primary defense needs to be prevention, which means fighting social engineering and maintaining good patching to defeat the majority of the risk. You'll need to consider all of this in your ransomware response plan covered in Chapter 5, "Ransomware Response Plan."

Ransomware as a Service

Ransomware as a service (RaaS) is a bit of a play on the latest cloud buzzwords (e.g., SaaS, IaaS, etc.), but is definitely a real thing. Traditional ransomware was an automated program that did what it was programmed to do. Even early on, hackers and other ne'er-do-wells without any hacking skills could buy a ransomware program and use it. These ransomware programs often had to be updated to include the latest exploits, bug fixes, and new features, just like any software program. Updating software is a pain for legitimate users and ransomware criminals alike. Many ransomware programs started auto-updating themselves. They will check dozens of times a day, after infiltrating a victim computer, to see if there is a new version or other malware to download.

Ransomware creators decided that if Microsoft, Google, Salesforce, and others could offer cloud-based software, so could they. So, starting a handful of years ago, some of the ransomware gangs started to offer ransomware as sort of a cloud-based service. It wasn't truly cloud-based in the general sense, but it did start to act more like it.

Traditional ransomware could be purchased for a one-time fee or possibly a one-time fee for upgrades. This one-time, initial fee could range from the many hundreds to many tens of thousands of dollars depending on the ransomware developer and gang. RaaS does not require an expensive, initial fee. Instead, an "affiliate" subscribes to the ransomware service and can use the ransomware program, but they pay a fixed fee for each break-in or a percentage fee for the overall ransom extorted. The affiliate's percentage payment back to the ransomware program provider can range from a few percentage points to a few tens of percentage (say 30 percent). There is great competition among RaaS providers to offer lower affiliate fees, where the affiliate keeps more of their ransom. Conversely, the better ransomware programs can demand more of the affiliate's ransom haul because they offer more successful (for the attacker) ransomware programs. Even if the affiliate pays a higher percentage of what they earn, they still earn more overall than going with a lower cost provider. Here's a good article on RaaS basics: https://www.upguard.com/blog/what-is-ransomware-as-a-service.

Some RaaS providers have "rules" for their affiliates, direct some of their activities, and can punish them for misbehaving or causing unreasonable risk to the RaaS provider because of their actions. This happened when a Darkside ransomware affiliate compromised the Colonial Pipeline, which resulted in US gas supply problems. These problems ended up forcing the involvement of the US DOJ, FBI, CIA, NSA, and even President Biden. This is to say, "unwanted heat." The RaaS provider actually made several statements apologizing for their affiliate's behavior and target selection. The provider went out of their way to say they had "fired" the affiliate and changed their affiliate licensing so something like the

Colonial Pipeline attack would not happen again. It was quite the extraordinary apology and public PR campaign.

There are more differences between different types of ransomware programs, but these major types of differences give the reader a good taste of the different types of programs.

Typical Ransomware Process and Components

Because there are so many different types of ransomware programs, there is not a perfectly repeatable, standard ransomware process. As covered earlier, at the bare minimum, ransomware breaks in somehow, exploits one or more computers, perhaps accomplishes different additional payloads, encrypts files, and presents a ransom notice. Automated ransomware programs do this. Human-directed ransomware gangs do this. Ransomware as a service does this. But they can do all that far differently from the other. However, considering all the possible permutations, there are versions gaining in popularity that paint a common picture. This part of Chapter 1 will recount that most common ransomware process.

Infiltrate

Step 1 for all the ransomware programs is to somehow gain initial "foothold" access into the (first) device of the victim, however that is done. Most of the time it occurs because of social engineering, usually because the victim was sent a phishing email that asked a user to open an attached document, execute a file, or click an embedded link. Or the user was tricked when visiting a website that then presented a rogue link or pop-up. Either way a user was tricked into clicking something and launching the initial malware program.

Alternately, something in the victim's environment could have contained an unpatched software vulnerability that the hacker took advantage of. Most of the time it is unpatched client software, where a user visits a compromised website—simply visiting a malicious web page containing a rogue JavaScript ends up invisibly infecting the user's computer. This is called a *silent-drive-*

by download. Sometimes the unpatched software is found on an Internet-facing server. I've heard of every possible type of missing software, such as unpatched VPN servers (https://arstechnica .com/information-technology/2020/01/unpatched-vpn-makes-travelex-latest-victim-of-revil-ransomware/) that took down Travelex to ransomware that specifically targeted unpatched Microsoft Exchange servers (https://siliconangle.com/2021/05/31/ new-epsilon-red-ransomware-targeting-unpatched-microsoft-exchange-servers/) led by an unrelated nation-state attack. Unpatched software accounts for the second most common reason for malicious compromise for hacking attacks in general, although not always so for ransomware (although it is still a top cause).

Another common way ransomware gets into a system is by password guessing against Internet-accessible logon portals and application programming interfaces (APIs). By far the most common software for attackers or malware to guess against is Microsoft's Remote Desktop Protocol (RDP) instances. As covered in more detail in Chapter 2, "Preventing Ransomware," according to some surveys it appears half the ransomware programs in this world utilize password guessing against RDP to break into their victims, including the following ransomware programs: CrySiS, Dharma, Maze, and SamSam. To be clear, password guessing attacks are only successful against RDP logons that have very poor passwords or allow unlimited logons without ever locking the involved user account out (which is a big security failure). Oftentimes the RDP password guessing is not built into the malware program, but accomplished by hackers using another password guessing tool seeking their initial foothold onto a victim network. Then after successfully guessing the password and gaining access, the hacker uploads the ransomware program and executes it.

Coveware (https://www.coveware.com/blog/ransomware-attack-vectors-shift-as-new-software-vulnerability-exploits-abound) routinely shows RDP as the top initial access attack vector, but without the involved details, it is unknown if that includes unpatched RDP (which is a big cause of initial exploitation as well) or just RDP password guessing attacks. No other sources besides Coveware show the RDP attack percentages nearly as high. But it does point out that RDP poses a serious risk if not correctly secured.

There are other small percentage root causes such as USB key infections and insider attacks, but the three previous issues (i.e., social engineering, unpatched software, and password guessing) are the three most popular ways that ransomware gets into a victim organization with everything else trailing far behind.

After Initial Execution

It's important to remember that in most ransomware scenarios the program that will be doing the actual encrypting is not yet installed. The first malware program that is used to break into the victim is built for that purpose. We call it a *stub* malware program or *downloader*, sometimes shortened to *loader*. It usually just establishes itself on the compromised device in such a way that it will be able to automatically re-launch after a reboot or power down and provides access to the infected system so additional attacks can be carried out.

On a Microsoft Windows system this often means the loader modifying any one of the dozens of features that Microsoft created to allow the automatic execution of code after a reboot or power-up event. The most popular modified areas include the registry, as a scheduled task, or as malicious service. There are at least a dozen places ransomware can modify on a Windows system to automatically get executed after a reboot. The stub program's first task is to continue execution after the initial foothold compromise.

Dial-Home

Most of the time the stub file will collect a little information on its host environment, enough to uniquely identify it to the attacker, plus whatever the ransomware operator wants collected, and then it connects out to its controlling servers. The controlling servers/ services are known as *command-and-control* servers, or C&C or C2 servers. The C&C servers are typically just another malware program waiting for the stub files or ransomware "bots" to connect to them. They can be hosted anywhere reachable on the Internet. They are often sitting on someone's compromised computer, or multiple compromised computers to ensure resiliency of the ransomware network. All over the world there are likely hundreds of people complaining about how slow their PCs are, not knowing that their computers are hosting hundreds to thousands of "dialing home" stub and ransomware programs. The ransomware developer will typically have at least two different C&C services in different places out on the Internet for redundancy, but often have a lot more than that. They need additional C&C servers so that if one or more are taken out by antivirus programs or threat hunters, at least one will survive and remain in control.

One of the first things the stub program will ask for from the C&C is when, where, and how it should next wait until it connects to the C&C servers again. This is because the C&C service will be moving from host to host to host every few hours to days, never staying in one place long. The IP addresses of the C&C hosting service changes along with their DNS names. The DNS names are usually very short-lived, dynamic DNS domain names. They are meant to be good for only hours to days and then expire. The stub malware program will ask which new dynamic DNS domain name or names they should connect to next time. Usually there are multiple DNS names, each hooked to one or more IP addresses, changing all the time. This sort of defensive shenanigans makes it hard for defenders to find and shut down a ransomware's C&C servers. Threat hunters will often sniff the traffic from a ransomware program actively making the connection to learn where the C&C services are currently living and what the next addresses are.

To help prevent defenders from easily detecting ransomware's outbound malicious traffic, about half of malware programs tunnel their outbound connections to their C&C servers using Transport Layer Security (TLS) encryption (https://news.sophos.com/en-us/2021/04/21/nearly-half-of-malware-now-use-tls-to-conceal-communications/) over port 443, and that figure is steadily rising over time. They do this because it then makes it more difficult for their traffic to be "sniffed" (i.e., recorded and reviewed).

And port 443 is almost always allowed outbound by any inspecting firewalls. Of the malware programs that use TLS to connect to C&C servers, ransomware is more than 90 percent of the connections. So, if you find an unexpected TLS connection coming off one of your computers going to a strange place on the Internet that you can't explain, it can't hurt to investigate.

If they don't use TLS connections, they will often pretend to be some other allowed outbound, "harmless" network traffic, such as Domain Name System (DNS). DNS packets have a pretty standard look and feel. Malware and ransomware will create fake DNS packets, inserting their commands as bogus data or DNS lookups, that are supposed to look like regular DNS requests being sent to a DNS server. Anyone seeing the bogus DNS traffic and not expecting that it was created by malware would be hard pressed to quickly see anything super suspicious unless they opened up the DNS packet and took a hard look at the details. Malware and ransomware will use other common ports such as 8080 and 1433 (Microsoft SQL).

Another ransomware trick uses ordinary and well-trusted third-party products and services to communicate. For example, a ransomware program might use Google WorkSpaces, Google Docs, Amazon Workspaces, Telegram (https://www.bleepingcomputer .com/news/security/telecrypt-ransomware-uses-telegram-as-candc-server/), Discord, Pastebin, etc., to communicate or function as their C&C servers to evade easy detection.

Basically, ransomware developers often use a network port or service that is usually allowed by most firewalls and blend in as legitimate traffic. Using a third party's application or platform has a few added benefits including the information is usually encrypted by default, and the centralized portion is robust, scalable, and trusted by most reputation filters. It's hard for an anti-malware reputation service to distinguish between a legitimate user using Google Docs or Telegram and a malicious third-party program doing the same. Ransomware developers are constantly coming up with new and creative ways to communicate between bot and operator. Ransomware using this obfuscation method is especially difficult to detect and has a higher chance of exploitation success and evading detection.

Auto-Update

Usually, the next thing ransomware programs do is replace themselves with new versions and/or download one or more additional malware programs. Most ransomware is not detected by any antivirus program or maybe, at best, one or two out of the more than 100 that exist.

Anecdotally, out of all the ransomware I've tested personally for more than two years, only a single specimen was ever detected by an antivirus program as malicious, and that was only by a single antivirus program (out of the more than 70+ antivirus programs that I used to inspect every ransomware sample I test). Even in that case, I wanted to run the ransomware program to find out what it did and where it connected, so I decided to execute it. In less than 15 seconds not only did it connect back to its C&C servers but connected to another set of C&C servers on another domain, downloaded a new copy of itself that was not detected as malicious by any of the scanners I was using (i.e., Google's VirusTotal website), and downloaded and installed two other malware programs in different locations that were undetected by any antivirus program I was using. It was almost a thing of beauty to see. Seeing is believing. It explained to me why the vast majority of ransomware victims had up-to-date antivirus programs and still got exploited by ransomware. I routinely hear antivirus vendors quote stats saying they have to detect hundreds of millions of new malware programs each year, each different enough from the last that they have to use new detection signatures. And even when detecting more than a hundred million new malware programs a year, the antivirus scanners simply cannot keep up. If they could, ransomware would not be the problem it is today.

The ransomware program is not drastically changing itself. Typically, they are just re-encrypting themselves, on the fly, with a different encryption key, which makes every single copy different than the last, at least while encrypted. As different antivirus programs begin to detect the different copies better, the malware program will rename and rearrange subroutines and insert a lot of random garbage code to make inspection and disassembly far harder. Eventually, even those "polymorphic" changes get figured out by the antivirus venders, and then the ransomware developers introduce an entirely different, updated, version. It really reminds me of a criminal, digital, version of the Whack-a-Mole game.

These days the "stub file" is often just a set of scripts, such as Microsoft PowerShell scripts. See an example article at https:// www.acronis.com/en-us/blog/posts/suncrypt-adopts-attacking- techniques-netwalker-and-maze-ransomware. This is because scripts are easier to modify and far harder to detect as malware. A malicious script can do nearly anything that a regular executable can do, including compile, download, and execute other executable programs. Most scripts create other malicious executables when they are run, essentially using the script to sneak malware past any nosy firewalls or intrusion detection scanners.

At some point along the way the stub file, if used, is replaced with the main ransomware program. And it acts pretty much like the stub program did, doing frequent checks to the C&C server, doing auto-updates, and so on. But it's automated coding may include things like looking for and stealing passwords, looking for and exfiltrating particular types of data, using network passwords to move to other machines, and so on. The key difference between the stub program and a non-stub version is the more permanent program is larger in size with far more capabilities.

Check for Location

The vast majority of ransomware will check during initial execu- tion or soon after to see what written languages are installed and running on the system they have exploited. This is because most malware programs don't want to exploit or harm a system in their home country or a close ally of their home country. Doing so could more easily lead to a local arrest and/or political problems. Most major ransomware programs developers have an implicit agree- ment with their host country not to infect there. Avoiding infecting one's own citizens, along with some monied bribes, is usually more than enough to keep the ransomware cartels in business without law enforcement or governments trying to shut them down.

As an example, a lot, if not most, ransomware comes from Russia. So, when all the Russian-based ransomware starts up, it checks for the presence of any of the common languages used in Russia or its nearby allies. These languages include Russian, Azerbaijani, Kyrgyz, Kazakh, Turkmen, Ukrainian, Tatar, Uzbek, and Serbian. If Russian ransomware detects these languages, it will quit and/or remove itself. Some defenders recommend enabling Russian as a second language, if possible, on your computer to prevent many ransomware programs from causing issues. It's a crude defense, but it often works.

Cybercriminal Safe Havens

Countries that look the other way while malicious hackers and malware attack other countries are described as *cybercriminal safe havens*. Safe havens are a key reason why ransomware is so bad and why it goes unpunished so often.

Initial Automatic Payloads

If the ransomware program had any automatic payloads, such as encrypting files and displaying a ransom, they will usually happen at this point in the lifecycle. But to be clear, this can often be just seconds after the malware originally broke in. I've seen stub files break in, grant themselves continued access, steal passwords, send those passwords to the C&C servers, update themselves, download and install new programs, and then start to encrypt files all in 15 seconds. It's automated code and it doesn't take long if that is what it is programmed to do. If an auto-payload doesn't kick off, then the ransomware program simply waits, waking up every now and then to dial home to the C&C servers to get their latest updates.

Waiting

It's during this time that many ransomware programs have their longest "dwell" times. They have compromised a victim and are in "sit and wait" mode. The attacker either hasn't learned about the involved compromise, is too busy working on another attack, or simply hasn't gotten around to looking inside that victim's environment.

Hacker Checks C&C

At some point, if the ransomware program hasn't kicked off its final encryption payload event, which could be hours to years after the original exploitation event, a hacker affiliated with the ransomware program checks their C&C servers to see what the malware has reported. Sometimes they only have IP addresses, and they have to do their own research. Other times the ransomware programs are reporting the domain names of the places they are waiting in, and they have uploaded every password that they have found. At this point, a human adversary is involved and looking at the automated results. They may pivot to the latest hacked victims, re-look at the entire list, and otherwise start to prioritize and figure out which victim they will take advantage of first.

The ransomware admin consoles are often things of beauty, running as small web servers on compromised victim's computers. Among other things, the consoles usually report statistics, such as how many overall successful exploitations have occurred, what types of computer platforms have been compromised, what countries the victims are located in, domain names, what vulnerabilities were exploited, if any, to compromise the victim, and so on.

More Tools Used

It is common for automated malware and human-directed ransomware to copy additional hacking tools onto the victim's device. These tools are used to learn more about the exploited environment, to move around laterally across the network into more devices, and to search for and exfiltrate emails, passwords, and data.

Common hacking tools that are used include custom scripts, custom hacking tools, commercial attack tools (e.g., Cobalt Strike, Metasploit, etc.), Mimikatz, Empire PowerShell Toolkit, Trickbot, and Microsoft's Sysinternals' PsExec. Attackers will disable defenses, collect logon credentials, disable any backups that they find, and install other malware and scripts. Most ransomware programs are pushing away from using publicly known hacking tools to using scripts, whenever possible. Scripts are simply harder to stop and detect as malicious.

Reconnaissance

Some ransomware programs gain the initial foothold onto their victim and begin encrypting right away. Some try to see how many computers they can exploit and encrypt within a few hours. Others allow the hackers to access the environment and explore, taking time reconnoitering the new environment over days, weeks, months, and even years. They will start wandering around the environment, reading emails, looking at applications and databases, and basically trying to learn what the victim's "crown jewels" and pain points are. They want to either steal the crown jewels or determine what they need to encrypt to cause the most operational pain.

They will monitor the email of C-level executives to learn what the executives most care about, what the reporting structures are, how much money the organization makes or has, and even if the victim has a cyber insurance policy that covers ransomware. If you have cyber insurance, they want to know what's the deductible and top coverage amount? This has happened enough that ransomware defenders now tell customers to make sure their cyber insurance policies are not on the network where a ransomware attacker can find them. The attackers will often monitor email for key words such as hacker, malware, ransomware, etc., so that they can get an early warning if anyone starts to notice their activities.

If other opportunities present themselves, the hacker will take advantage of them. For example, they might come across an email between an accounts receivable clerk at the victim company and an accounts payable clerk at another. They may use that relationship and its trust to compromise the accounts payable clerk's company or to send bogus wiring instructions for the next invoice paid. When a human adversary is involved in the attack, they can and will change up their plans according to developing circumstances, attempting to maximize their potential gain.

Some of the ransomware gangs are being paid to explicitly target certain companies and/or look for certain types of data (e.g., intellectual property, plans, and even things most people would not think would be sought, such as loan terms). Sometimes the adversary is working for the victim's competitor who is trying to learn project details and costs. Other times they are stealing the top-secret engineering plans for the next stealth bomber for their government.

Readying Encryption

Toward the end of the lifecycle, ransomware programs or attackers will position and ready the encryption routines using one or more encryption keys. If ransomware has compromised multiple machines, they will attempt to encrypt as much as they can all at once. Sometimes victims get lucky and catch the first, or the first few, computers getting encrypted and are able to shut down the rest of the potential victim machines before those machines get encrypted too. Up to 25 percent of all ransomware encryption attempts are interrupted before they can launch or complete. This figure seems high because rarely do you learn of someone who interrupted a ransomware program before it started. I do hear it. I do know of success stories, but there aren't many. I figured the reason we don't hear about it as much is that if the ransomware encryption process is prevented or interrupted, it usually doesn't become a huge event, requiring paying the ransom and reporting it as a data breach.

If multiple compromised computers are involved, usually multiple encryption keys, different for each computer or file, will be used by the attacker. This is primarily because the attacker wants to be able to unlock at least one computer or file to show they have control of the ransomware and have a decryption key. By getting the decryption key, the victim can confirm it really does unlock the data. This is known as *proof of control* or *proof of decryption*. The ransomware gang will usually ask for a small ransom to be paid, "as a mutual demonstration of trust" to release the sample decryption key. If you're going to pay the ransom to get the decryption keys, this kind of arrangement works to the advantage of both parties. The victim makes sure they aren't paying for something that doesn't work, and the ransomware gang can try to charge more for a solution once they prove that the decryption actually works. Never pay the whole ransom without testing that the proof of decryption key and process works.

Data Exfiltration

The vast majority of ransomware programs exfiltrate data (e.g., database files, passwords, emails, etc.) before kicking off the encryption. The hacker will often shut down database and email services late at night, to do the copying. Watching for signs of unexpected service shutdowns late at night is a good way to detect something suspicious going on.

Attackers exfiltrating that data will usually copy it to other servers within the environment to use as local staging servers, collecting large volumes (i.e., multi-GB) of archived (e.g., TAR, ZIP, GZIP, ARC, etc.) files. Finding unexpected, unexplained, stacks of large, encrypted files around your network is not a good sign. Attackers will then usually copy them to some sort of free, shared, storage cloud service or to other organization's compromised computers, meaning that big stack of zipped-up files you find may not be your own data.

There are also reports of ransomware hackers using the victim's cloud backup services as a way to steal the files (https://www.bleepingcomputer.com/news/security/ransomware-attackers-use-your-cloud-backups-against-you/). Once they find out the victim has cloud-based backup, many times they will use the victim's own cloud-based backup instance and credentials to copy the data to another location under the attacker's control. Then they delete the victim's backups.

No matter how the data exfiltration is done, it is important to realize that if you get hit by ransomware, encryption is not your only problem usually. Most ransomware programs exfiltrate data as well.

Encryption

With a few exceptions, at some point the encryption process begins. Some ransomware encrypts all files and folders that it finds. Others, like Cerber and Locky, search for and encrypt only certain types of document files. And others, like Petya, only encrypt boot files and file system tables. Some ransomware programs look for and encrypt files stored in the cloud; others only encrypt local files. You never know which one you could get.

Most ransomware encryption uses both public, asymmetric key encryption and symmetric key encryption. The asymmetric key encryption is used to lock up the symmetric keys that do all the file encryption (very much like any good, distributed, encryption program would). The encryption process goes something like this:

1. The ransomware program generates one or more asymmetric public/private key pair and one or more symmetric keys. There could be a different symmetric key per file or computer.
2. The symmetric keys are used to encrypt the data, permanently deleting the plaintext data versions after the encrypted version is finished. Most ransomware programs add a recognizable file extension to the encrypted data file copies.
3. The symmetric keys will be encrypted with the asymmetric public key and then the plaintext version deleted.
4. The asymmetric private key will be sent to the ransomware's key storage server, awaiting further instructions.

Different ransomware programs use different types of encryption, although usually it is very good, very standard encryption. For example, the Maze ransomware gang uses RSA with 2048-bit keys or ChaCha20. If you've not heard of ChaCha20 (https://www.cryptopp .com/wiki/), it's a good symmetric cipher created by famed computer security professor Daniel J. Bernstein. He knows his stuff and is one of the best cryptographers in the world. He didn't create ChaCha20 for ransomware, but ransomware gangs know a good thing when they see it. You're not going to break it. Many ransomware programs like to use the far more popular AES encryption cipher, but ChaCha20 is strong and many times faster.

Having the fastest encryption speed is important. Once one of the ransomware-exploited computers starts to encrypt files, it's only a matter of time before someone sees the result and starts to try to stop any other computers from being encrypted. The faster the ransomware program can encrypt the data on all the machines the better . . . for the ransomware gang. Hence, ransomware gangs like to use ChaCha20 because it's fast and strong. Petya ransomware uses elliptic curve cryptography (ECDH) and SALSA20, another earlier symmetric cipher created by D.J. Bernstein.

If someone notices one of the early encryptions and recognizes what is going on, they can shut down the network and any other computers that might possibly be involved in order to minimize damage and spread.

Extortion Demand

All ransomware programs will leave either little text files all around, display an on-screen message, or send an email. It can be one text file on the screen displaying the ransomware notice and extortion demand or a bunch of text files, one in each folder and directory, displaying essentially the same message. Here are some ransomware-involved filename examples:

- Locky ransomware displays HELP_instructions.bmp and _HELP_ instructions.html.
- Torrent ransomware puts a .encryption file extension on all encrypted files with a PLEASE_READ.txt notice file.
- Dharma ransomware adds a .onion extension to all encrypted files and displays FILES_ENCRYPTED.txt.

This link displays dozens of common file extensions used by various ransomware programs that get added to encrypted files: https:// techviral.net/ransomware-encrypted-file-extensions/.

Negotiations

The victim is told how to contact the ransomware criminal via email, Skype, or some other online communication methods. Often the ransomware criminal, through their ransom notice, has listed an identifying number that must be included in the initial communications. This is so the ransomware criminal knows who is contacting them and how to identify which encrypted public key belongs to the victim contacting them. Some ransomware notices will display a fixed amount that has to be paid. Usually this will be listed in either US dollars or bitcoin (BTC). The direct-acton variants tend to be fixed amounts. Many other ransomware programs will leave off the ransom amount that will be requested and just ask for the victim to contact them. Only when contacted does the ransomware gang come back with a figure, and that's because they do some research on how much money they can get from the victim. Often, the ransomware notice will include a deadline measured in days to give the victim a sense of urgency.

In many cases the ransomware gang will come back with their high estimate of what they hope to get as an extortion payment. Of the people who plan to pay, some pay the first amount requested. Most people try to negotiate a lower amount. A few offer far lesser amounts as counteroffers. Some do so because they really don't have that much money to pay a ransom with. Others are bluffing. And others simply, because of egos or something else, aren't going to pay as much as requested. Most ransomware gangs will consider a reasonable counteroffer and agree to take less than the original requested amount.

I've also seen ransomware gangs insulted by the victim's original counteroffer amount that then increased the ransom for far more than was originally requested. I've seen ransomware gangs just tell the victim they won't give them the decryption key and cut off all communications. I've seen ransomware gangs go on to further attack the victim with additional damage (e.g., data exfiltration, DDoS, threats of embarrassment, threats to release the data to competitors, and so on). If the victim doesn't intend to pay or offers a ridiculously low counteroffer, the most common ransomware negotiation retort is that the ransomware gang has the victim's data, and they plan to release it to other hackers, the dark web, their competitors, or the public Internet if not paid a reasonable ransom. After announcing the data exfiltration threat, they will ask for the same amount as the original request or even go higher. I've seen ransomware groups ask for double the original amount after announcing the data exfiltration threat. Usually there is some negotiating for additional time to pay as well. Most ransomware groups will give a few additional days. Initial negotiations set the whole tone of how the ransom and ransomware payoff might go.

Provide Decryption Keys

If a ransom is paid, the ransomware group will provide one or more decryption keys that can be used, along with instructions on how to use them; or they will provide a custom program or script along with the decryption keys. Either way, the decryption process, even when as automated as it can be made, is not an easy process. Even with the best of intentions on both sides, it often does not work or does not work well. I routinely see statistics that say something like only 10 percent to 25 percent of ransomware victims who pay the data actually get *all* their data back. The figures usually range between

60 percent to 80 percent of paying victims that get at least some data back. Either way, data recovery is always a mess. The ransomware gangs aren't super-professional developers who spend a lot of time and energy debugging and troubleshooting their programs. Recovery, even with the decryption keys, is always a lot of work, and that's with everything working as best as it can. Again, the decryption keys are normally provided in a few batches—first a "test batch" to prove that the ransomware attackers have the decryption keys and that the decryption keys work and then the rest after the larger portion of the ransom is paid.

The attacker might also be updating their PR web pages to let the whole world know about the new victim, what was stolen, and whether or not the ransom was paid. If the ransom was paid, the ransomware criminals pick up their bitcoins, move them to a new address, or start to cash them out. There are a lot of other processes that are going on in parallel on the victim's side including the recovery efforts. We will cover those in more detail in Chapters 7 to 10.

Ransomware Goes Conglomerate

Starting off with my frequent disclaimer that ransomware purveyors range across the spectrum of different types of players, in this section I specifically wanted to cover the upper tier of ransomware attackers. Ransomware started being developed and pushed around by individuals. And for a long time, it stayed that way. Eventually small groups of like-minded malware friends and associates started to make and distribute ransomware in small, unofficial, gangs. Up until about 2013, cryptocurrency didn't make a lot of money. It was hard for the perpetrators to get paid their ransoms without being traced and arrested.

Then bitcoin showed up. Bitcoin, the leader in cryptocurrency, was launched in January 2009. Few people understood the value back then. Not even the ransomware gangs. But in December 2013, a fairly widespread early ransomware program called CryptoLocker (https://en.wikipedia.org/wiki/CryptoLocker) asked for the $300 ransom payment in bitcoin and got it. Pretty soon its creators

were making tens of millions of dollars (https://www.zdnet.com/
article/cryptolockers-crimewave-a-trail-of-millions-in-
laundered-bitcoin/). Success breeds competitors and within a few
years hundreds of millions of dollars were being paid in bitcoin to
dozens of different ransomware vendors.

A great pictorial recount of the significant ransomware
names over time can be found at https://www.watchguard
.com/wgrd-resource-center/infographic/ransomware-
timeline.

With great financial success came professionals. People who
had worked as top-level players in high-end gangs and even as
"made" men in Mafioso started to run ransomware and malware
organizations. The rise in ill-gotten loot allowed these ransomware
gangs to start hiring real talent. Ethically compromised computer
programmers, designers, engineers, and managers who might have
ordinarily gone to work for legitimate companies were lured away
by the promise of high salaries. Ransomware gangs turned into ransomware corporations, with C-level executives, managers, HR, and
payroll. This was happening with all malware creators, although
ransomware was earning the most money. The malware that stole
passwords and credit card information, Trickbot was also making
a killing. And all that money really started bringing in even more
professionals.

I remember this point being driven home clearly when a cybersecurity firm, Cyberwise, analyze one of the most popular trojan
malware programs, Cerberus. They were able to determine by looking at different trojan examples what the network infrastructure
looked like that Cerberus trojan's creator had deployed to support
it. Figure 1.6 shows a recreation of the Cerberus network infrastructure taken from Cyberwise's excellent analysis (https://www
.biznet.com.tr/wp-content/uploads/2020/08/Cerberus.pdf).

Cerberus Trojan Network Infrastructure

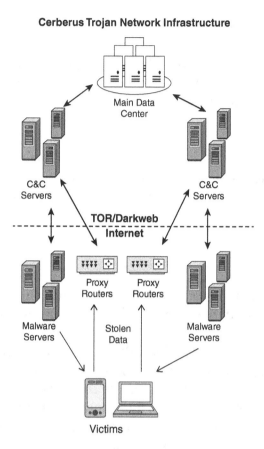

Figure 1.6   Cerberus trojan network logical diagram

I was astounded the first time I saw this diagram. This was no part-time kid running malware out of his basement. This was a professional with a lot of resources who designed a fully redundant, resilient, well-thought-out network. He had proxy servers, campaign servers, admin portals, customer service, data centers, and even license key validation. This was a guy with technical training in designing and delivering large-scale redundant networks. He could walk into any major company and apply for the head IT job and be qualified. He had likely worked for a large, legitimate, company somewhere in the world and done well. When I saw this diagram, I realized that the foe computer security defenders are up against is way more sophisticated than we had been picturing in the previous decades.

This came home again in May 2021, when the leader for the ransomware group called Darkside was in the news for attacking US gas pipeline vendor Colonial Pipeline. As covered previously, Darkside's spokesperson made statement after statement on the group's website (https://www.abc.net.au/news/2021-05-11/darkside-says-aim-as-cash-no-chaos-colonial-pipeline/100130020) in response to the unintended impact to US energy and the resulting political and intelligence agency response. The ransomware developer apologized and said they were taking steps to cull the affiliate hackers that used their ransomware-as-a-service platform. Although the written English statements were riddled with English-as-a-second-language typos, the spokesperson said the carefully measured things you would normally hear a corporate CEO say about legitimate crisis events. That's when I realized that it made sense, because the big ransomware conglomerates are closer to corporate structures than anything else.

I heard another ransomware CEO being interviewed on a radio show. He talked about his ransomware company the same way someone running Microsoft might. He was obviously proud of his product. He bragged about its feature set, its strong affiliate compensation, ease of use, and satisfied customers. When the reporter asked if it was true that another popular ransomware group split off from his group, he ignored the question as good as any politician ever did and then talked about how he welcomed competition. "Competition was good for everyone!," he said. And "just you wait till our next version is out!" He continued, "We are satisfied that we can out compete our competitors and keep and grow our customer base."

I could hardly believe what I was hearing. I might as well have been listening to a Microsoft executive fend off a question about Apple computers and its growing market share. Again, it wasn't lost on me that the leaders of the biggest ransomware groups are running professional, corporate-like organizations. And many of the people in that organization could have been well-paid executives in any organization. They just chose a life of crime to make even more money or lacked access to legitimate job opportunities that paid as well. To be clear, this is not good. We don't want our criminals acting like corporate professionals. It's easier to fight them when it is a guy in a basement drinking sodas.

Ransomware Industry Components

When I say corporate-like, what do I mean? Well, besides the fact that they have professionally run organizations, different departments, developers, executives, payroll, and so on, I'm really talking about a sort of modern-day supply chain structure. Today's ransomware corporation is just one part of the overall infrastructure. You have the main ransomware corporation, which controls the particular ransomware development and licensing. The developers may be in-house, outside hired consultants, or both. There are network people, licensing people, crypto people, web developers, and technical support people. Overall, the main ransomware corporation creates the program, funds its development, and releases the program for use to its affiliated customers. Affiliates are the people who are allowed, after vetting, to rent the ransomware program and use it to exploit victims. These people pay a certain percentage of their ill-gotten gains back to the main ransomware company.

There are also groups of people who gain the initial foothold access into various organizations and then sell that access in dark web forums. The people who have compromised these victim companies can do anything to them. They could spread malware themselves if they wanted to. Instead, they decided that their role is to get access into a company, and then turn around and sell that access to the highest bidder. You want access to such and such a company, and they will sell it to you. Larger companies with more data and resources to plunder, but also with harder to break defenses, will cost you more. For the access provider it's low risk and moderate reward. They aren't getting nearly as rich as the affiliates on a per job basis, but they try to make up for it in volume.

That's also why many of the ransomware programs have extended dwell times. The people who break in and grab the initial foothold are not the same people who then take ultimate advantage of the compromised victim organization. There are literally at least tens of thousands of companies and organizations around the world currently compromised, their illicitly-gained access waiting to be sold to the highest bidder, and they don't know it.

These types of attackers gain initial access by sending out billions of social engineering emails, compromising websites to place web exploit kits, looking for unpatched software, combing through password dumps on the dark web, and performing credential stuffing attacks against APIs to gain access. There are groups of hackers that do nothing but sell password access to the world's biggest companies to ransomware affiliates. In the professional world we might call these "lead gen" (i.e., lead generators).

There are also ransomware gangs that will pay trusted insiders to place malware inside of their companies. Tesla was the potential victim of one such failed plot (https://www.msn.com/en-us/money/companies/fbi-arrests-russian-in-tesla-malware-extortion-scheme/ar-BB18trjz). For every failure, you can bet there are other disgruntled employees who took the $1 million bribe and shut up. Their trusting parent company got infected, ransomed, and they have no idea that a traitorous employee just made a payday off their misery.

And all these groups of malware supply-side conglomerates compete against each other, trying to maximize their profit. The main ransomware companies are constantly innovating their product and adding features. They offer 24/7 tech support and even backend bitcoin exchange services to help convert the cryptocurrency into hard currency (for a fee, of course).

If you're an attacker and worried about your illegal bitcoin transactions somehow being tracked back to you, well, they have a service for that, too . . . for a price. It turns out that bitcoin blockchain, which tracks every transaction to the billionth of a cent to who sent and received it, can be gamed. Attackers have service providers whose only job is to make their bitcoin transactions more opaque and harder to follow. Just get your ransomware programs to send your bitcoins to this one central bitcoin clearinghouse wallet address. There, the leader will co-mingle your collected bitcoin with lots of other people's collected bitcoin, slice and dice, and send back your now laundered bitcoins to your other bitcoin addresses on the other side. Unless law enforcement can get inside the bitcoin launderers digital wallet, they will not be able to see where the money goes. These types of bitcoin services are known as *laundries* or *mixers*.

Sometimes law enforcement does have access to bitcoin wallets, using methods they will not disclose, and with access to the wallet, the feds can often better follow the proceeds. Sometimes, like in the case of the Colonial Pipeline attack, law enforcement can actually get some of the paid ransom back (https://www.wsj.com/articles/how-the-fbi-got-colonial-pipelines-ransom-money-back-11623403981).

There are even online marketplaces with blogs and reviews of the different ransomware groups, affiliates, and service providers, somewhat akin to what you might see on Amazon with star-ranking customer reviews. If a ransomware purveyor gets a bad, one-star, review, they will offer additional licenses, temporarily lower affiliate fees, or offer more tech support hand holding—anything to keep their customers and grow their sales base.

There are a whole cast of other ancillary characters, roles, and organizations now involved in spreading ransomware and collecting the money. There are people who help to pay bribes. People who help avoid taxes. There are fixers. And there's also payroll, time off requests, and human resource departments. There are people who go through online resumes and interview potential developers. It's big business. It looks more like a multilevel marketing company than anything else. We are not talking about huge conglomerate companies with thousands and thousands of employees. No, the largest ransomware groups are measured in dozens of people. But it's a hundred different ransomware groups and an entire competitive ecosystem driven to steal money from a large part of the world. One person told me that the ransomware industry was the second biggest industry in Russia behind only oil. That means it's important to the country's economy, revenue growth, and tax base. And there is so much money and important people involved, each taking a cut, that it's not going anywhere until it is forced to. In the days of spam worms and bots, I used to say that cybercrime had gone professional. Then as it grew, I said it went corporate. These days I don't think there's any way to describe it other than that it's gone conglomerate.

I don't want to end this chapter on doom and gloom, but things are pretty bad right now. Ransomware is making billions to tens of billions of dollars a year, and if nothing happens, many people are predicting ransomware will cause multi-hundreds of billions of dollars in damage in another ten years.

But there is hope. Ransomware will eventually be defeated. All the rest of the chapters of this book are dedicated to that goal, starting with Chapter 2, "Preventing Ransomware." Chapter 2 will tell you what you and your organization can personally do to significantly reduce your risk of a successful ransomware attack.

Summary

This chapter covered the ransomware industry, how it works, how bad the problem is, and the different types of ransomware and life-cycle processes. Chapter 2 discusses how to prevent ransomware from being successful in the first place.

Chapter 2
Preventing Ransomware

P revention should be the primary mitigation strategy for all defenders. This chapter focuses on how you as a defender can prevent ransomware from gaining access in the first place. It is the most important chapter in the book.

Nineteen Minutes to Takeover

Once any hacker or malware has gained initial "foothold" access to a device or environment, it is significantly harder to minimize further damage than it was beforehand. Prevention is easier and cheaper, even when prevention is difficult to accomplish and expensive.

The hardest part of any cyberattack is the first, initial access. After that, most attackers can more easily leverage one compromised program or device into many more. Using a single compromised device as a "base of operations" to take over an entire environment usually takes less effort than the compromise of the original device (which may, unfortunately, not be that hard either). Many studies, including `https://www.wired.com/story/russian-hackers-speed-intrusion-breach/`, show that the sophisticated attackers can move from one compromised device to many others starting in as little as under 19 minutes.

Preventing hackers and malware from gaining initial foothold access should be the primary focus of any cybersecurity defender. Unfortunately, "Have a good backup!" is often the first and sometimes only "prevention" recommendation concerning ransomware. Backups are not prevention. Backups are damage minimization. If you are using a backup to save you, your preventive controls have already failed, and ransomware has access to your environment.

Ransomware has proven itself adept at bypassing detection once executed in an environment. One survey (https://www.datto.com/resource-downloads/Datto2018_StateOfTheChannel_RansomwareReport.pdf) revealed that 86 percent of compromised victims had up-to-date antivirus detection installed. Some other studies have antivirus and other endpoint detection solutions stopping ransomware up to 50 percent of the time, but it's clear that if ransomware detection by antivirus products was better, ransomware would not be the huge problem it is today.

Once ransomware has been executed, most of it begins to do all the steps described in Chapter 1 (e.g., "dialing home," allowing the hacker in, data exfiltration, logon credential theft, encryption, extortion, etc.). It's clear that a good backup is not going to save most victims and definitely is not prevention. Prevention means stopping ransomware from executing successfully in the first place. The rest of this chapter will cover how to prevent ransomware from being successful. Not enough defenders spend adequate time and resources on preventative controls. This book will.

Eighty Percent of Ransomware Victims Suffer a Second Attack

80 percent of ransomware victims will suffer a second attack: https://blog.knowbe4.com/80-of-ransomware-victim-organizations-experience-a-second-attack. This is primarily because they did not do enough to prevent a second attack, even after the first attack.

Good General Computer Defense Strategy

Any defense is comprised of at least three major types of controls focused on three different objectives. I call them the 3×3 Security Control Pillars (as graphically displayed in Figure 2.1), but they are often described with more phases and control types by other computer defense frameworks. I like to minimize the control types and objectives to keep things simple.

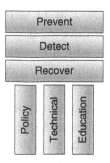

Figure 2.1   3×3 Security Control Pillars

Controls come in three main phases: preventative, detective, and recovery. Preventative controls are all the things a system does to prevent something from happening—in our specific case, ransomware. Detective controls are everything the system does to detect that a threat has successfully made it past all the preventative controls and has gained unauthorized access to an environment (or is preventing others from obtaining legitimate access). It's here that you try to accomplish early warning. If you can't prevent something bad from happening, the next best thing is early warning, so you get quick response to ideally minimize damage. The last set of controls are everything you can do to quickly recover from a malicious event to minimize downtime and expenses.

Part of your recovery may be that you cycle back around and update your preventative controls to prevent that same bad thing from being successful again. Sometimes the bad thing circumvented your preventative controls because you didn't have all the right controls—at least in the right places against the right things in the right amounts. And sometimes, it's because someone or something wasn't following the preventative controls as prescribed. Updating your preventative controls in response to lessons learned from a compromise is especially important in today's cybersecurity world. Victims that fail to properly assess their failures and update their preventative controls are at higher risk of additional failures.

Chapter 6, "Detecting Ransomware," will cover recommended detective controls. Chapters 7 to 11 will cover recovery planning and processes. One chapter devoted to prevention and five devoted to recovery should tell you which is easier to do. When people tell me that ransomware prevention is difficult to do, I respond, "You ought to see how difficult recovery is!"

To repeat, there are three major types of controls: preventative, detective, and recovery. There are three components that make up each type of control: policy, technical defenses, and education. Policies are any rules, regulations, or recommendations that are implemented and communicated to minimize risk. For example, never give out your password to an email requesting it, nor execute a program or open a document arriving in an unexpected email. Never use the same password for different sites or services. Policies can be similar to education but can have a different focus and approach.

Policies also include procedures ("a way to do things") and standards ("what must be done or what must be used"). A policy can be something like "All files must be encrypted using industry-accepted cryptography and key sizes during transmission." A procedure includes the steps that must be followed in order to do something, such as "How to encrypt files before sending across a network." A standard can be guidance for achieving something like "TLS using SHA-256 hashes, RSA asymmetric cryptography with 2048-bit keys or longer, and AES symmetric encryption with 256-bit keys or longer must be used encrypting files sent over a network."

Technical defenses are any tools that help to prevent, detect, mitigate, or respond to threats and risks. Technical defenses in the cybersecurity world include things such as antivirus software, endpoint detection and response (EDR) software, firewalls, secure configurations, content filtering, anti-phishing filters, etc.

No matter how good your policies and technical defenses are, it is likely that some amount of badness is going to make it to the end user where they will be confronted with observing and handling it. Education (also known as *security awareness training*) strives to teach end users how to recognize something malicious when it reaches them and how to handle it to minimize damage. Ideally, end users are taught to report malicious attempts and to delete or ignore them. But, as history has shown, end users being socially engineered into incorrect handling of malicious events is the number-one reason for successful malicious breaches.

When you hear the often described "defense-in-depth" metaphorical dogma, what it is saying is that every system should strive to create the best possible, layered set of preventative, detective, and recovery controls using multiple, overlapping policies, technical defenses, and education possible. You normally want overlapping controls and constituents because they decrease risk from a single control failure. One might catch what the others miss. You want to create your best, defense-in-depth, layered set of controls to prevent ransomware from being successful.

Understanding How Ransomware Attacks

To best prevent ransomware from getting a foothold on a device or in an environment, you need to focus on how those initial footholds are gained, which is called *root-cause exploits* or *initial root cause exploits* in the computer security world. To prevent ransomware, you must prevent all malicious hackers and malware, but ransomware does have some peculiarities that it helps to know. This section will discuss both.

To reiterate, because it's needed, to prevent ransomware you need to focus on how ransomware most likely gains the initial foothold access. Ransomware is not your problem. Your problem is in how ransomware gained access to a device or environment in the first place. Ransomware is an outcome of your real problem. To put this in perspective, imagine that you can make all ransomware magically disappear. In one second, it's gone and will never be again forevermore. But, if the initial root causes of how that ransomware got on a system or into an environment were allowed to continue, hackers and malware would continue successfully exploiting victims. Maybe they couldn't use ransomware, but they could use trojan horse programs, computer viruses, backdoor trojans, keyloggers, and so on, to accomplish every bad thing they want to accomplish. Ransomware is a symptom of a larger issue, that of a security vulnerability that gets exploited. And to stop all malware, hackers, and ransomware, you have to figure out the ways that they break into devices and environments and close those holes.

The Nine Exploit Methods All Hackers and Malware Use

There are essentially only nine root exploit methods that any hacker or malware program can use to exploit a vulnerable device or environment. They are listed here:

- Programming bug (patch available or not available)
- Social engineering
- Authentication attack
- Human error/misconfiguration
- Eavesdropping/man-in-the-middle (MitM) Attacks
- Data/network traffic malformation
- Insider attack
- Third-part reliance issue (supply chain/vendor/partner/watering hole attack, etc.)
- Physical attack

There is also a chance of some new attack vector that is not represented here and for which no mitigations currently exist. But for now, these nine root-cause methods have described the root-cause exploit method used by every known hacker and malware attack. To fight malicious hackers and malware, cybersecurity defenders need to mitigate all of these root-cause exploit methods, starting by focusing on the most likely to be used root exploit methods, first and best.

Top Root-Cause Exploit Methods of All Hackers and Malware

Since the beginning of computers, just two root-cause methods have accounted for the vast majority of malicious breaches to most devices and most organizations: social engineering and unpatched software. There are various other malware and hacking methods that become popular for a few years (such as boot viruses, USB key infections, etc.), but social engineering and unpatched software have been either the number-one or number-two most popular exploit methods for most years over three decades.

The fact that social engineering and unpatched software are the top causes of malicious hacker and malware exploitation has been covered in hundreds of previous articles and whitepapers, including these examples:

- 70% to 90% of All Malicious Breaches are Due to Social Engineering and Phishing Attacks (https://blog.knowbe4.com/70-to-90-of-all-malicious-breaches-are-due-to-social-engineering-and-phishing-attacks)
- CyberheistNews Vol 11 #14 [Heads Up] Phishing Remains the Most Common Form of Attack (https://blog.knowbe4.com/cyberheistnews-vol-11-14-heads-up-phishing-remains-the-most-common-form-of-attack)
- Using Threat Intelligence to Build Your Data-Driven Defense (https://info.knowbe4.com/threat-intelligence-to-build-your-data-driven-defense)
- 2021 Data Breach Investigations Report (DBIR) (https://enterprise.verizon.com/resources/reports/2021/2021-data-breach-investigations-report.pdf)

Every organization, unless they have experience and expectations to show otherwise, could benefit by better concentrating on squashing social engineering and phishing and better patching their environment. Doing so would most efficiently decrease the overall cybersecurity risk.

Top Root-Cause Exploit Methods of Ransomware

The top root-cause exploit methods of ransomware are similar to the other methods that all hackers and malware use to exploit with one substantial deviation. To determine the most common root causes of ransomware attacks, I reviewed as many public vendor ransomware reports, news articles, and blog postings, as was possible and looked to see which detailed the exact percentages of each possible type of root-cause exploit used by ransomware in a successful attack. I reviewed more than three dozen reports, nearly a hundred news articles, and dozens of blog postings. Unfortunately, only a handful of sources, listed here, showed exact percentages or even rankings of ransomware root causes:

- Coveware Blog Report (https://www.coveware.com/blog/ransomware-attack-vectors-shift-as-new-software-vulnerability-exploits-abound)
- Statista (https://www.statista.com/statistics/700965/leading-cause-of-ransomware-infection/)
- *Forbes* magazine article (https://www.forbes.com/sites/forbestechcouncil/2021/04/22/six-best-practices-for-ransomware-recovery-and-risk-mitigation/)
- Datto's Global State of the Channel Ransomware Report (https://www.datto.com/resources/dattos-2020-global-state-of-the-channel-ransomware-report)
- Hiscox Cyber Readiness Report 2021 (https://www.hiscoxgroup.com/sites/group/files/documents/2021-04/Hiscox%20Cyber%20Readiness%20Report%202021.pdf)

Most other sources simply stated the top root causes of ransomware exploitation collectively, but didn't cover exact percentages or didn't discuss percentages at all. Almost all reports listed social engineering, unpatched software, and password issues as the top causes for ransomware exploitation but did not rank or list them against each other. Luckily, some did. Table 2.1 shows the specific figures pulled from the five reports that did list ransomware root cause percentages or specific rankings.

Table 2.1 Ransomware Root Causes by Report

Report Name	Social Engineering	RDP	Unpatched Software	Password Guessing	Credential Theft	Remote Server Attack	Third Party	USB	Other
Coveware Report	30%	45%	18%	–	–	–	–	–	5%
Statisca	54%	20%	–	–	10%	–	–	–	–
Forbes magazine article	1st	3rd	2nd	–	–	–	–	–	–
Datto's Report	54%	20%	–	21%	10%	–	–	–	–
Hiscox Cyber Readiness	65%	–	28%	19%	39%	–	34%	–	–
Sophos Report	45%	9%	–	–	–	21%	9%	7%	9%
Averages	50%	24%	23%	20%	20%	21%	22%	7%	7%

Root-cause analysis is hampered by the lack of standardization among different vendors when surveying customers or victims. Different vendors call things by different names and include different categories, which could appear in a different category from another vendor.

A great example of this dilemma is RDP. RDP refers to Microsoft's Remote Desktop Protocol, which is the primary, built-in, method for users and administrators to remotely connect to a Microsoft Windows computer. It is common for some strains of ransomware to connect to remote logon portals, such as RDP, to do password guessing. Ransomware also frequently checks for and exploits vulnerable, unpatched RDP servers and clients. One vendor could classify the latter type of RDP exploit as unpatched software, and another may call it RDP. In the same vein, one vendor may call password guessing against RDP portals, "RDP", as Coveware and Statista appear to be doing, and others may place it under "password guessing" only, as Hiscox is doing. And then, other vendors, such as Datto, appear to be appropriately separating them out into separate "RDP" and "password guessing" classifications.

The data analysis gets far messier if you decide to look "upstream" about how something originally happened. For example, most credential theft happens because of social engineering, and vice versa (https://blog.knowbe4.com/new-verizon-dbir-credentials-stolen-in-85-of-social-engineering-breaches). Three of the five reports specifically call out "credential theft" as a method ransomware used to compromise a victim, but did not say how that credential theft originally happened. Credential theft, itself, is a possible outcome of a root-cause exploit, not a root-cause exploit. It is highly likely that if credential theft was broken down by the root-cause method used to obtain the credentials that social engineering percentages listed above would be even greater.

Additionally, some vendors discussed miscellaneous root-cause methods, such as USB key. One vendor reported USB key infections as possibly being involved in up to 8 percent of all ransomware attacks. No other vendor even mentions USB key attacks as a potential method used by ransomware. This seems to be a temporary outlier method at best (although we don't mean to dismiss one vendor's experience outright without further analysis).

Another vendor listed insider threats as another cause for ransomware, where a trusted insider either was bribed to install ransomware or was a direct member of a ransomware gang who planted the ransomware program. This category could be related to the USB key root causes mentioned earlier by one of the vendors. There have been court confirmed reports of trusted insiders being bribed, oftentimes up to $1 million, to install ransomware. One example story involving Tesla, Inc., can be found at https://www.wired.com/story/tesla-ransomware-insider-hack-attempt/.

But in general, three root causes: social engineering, unpatched software, and either RDP or password guessing, are involved in the majority of ransomware exploits.

Preventing Ransomware

There are three types of defenses that work far better at preventing all malicious hackers, malware, and ransomware, than all the others. We will start discussing those first, followed by everything else.

Primary Defenses

Looking at all reports, whether they reported specific percentages or not, it is safe to say that social engineering is the most consistent root cause. Social engineering was picked as the number-one reason for successful exploitation by ransomware by every report studied, except for one, the Coveware report. But even that report shows social engineering often being the top cause during some time periods. Because of the way that outcomes and root causes are comingled by most reports, it is likely that the percentages of social engineering are even higher than directly reported. This would be consistent with all malicious hackers and malware attacks, more broadly. So, anything a user or organization can do (e.g., policies, technical defenses, and education) to mitigate social engineering should be the top priority.

The best mitigation to prevent successful social engineering is to teach potential victims how to spot the different types of scams and what to do with them. A big part of spotting scams is teaching people how to recognize the rogue URLs tricks used by scammers to trick people into clicking onto malicious links. Teaching everyone to "hover" over a URL link to make sure it is legitimate before clicking it can go a long way to defeating social engineering. Users should also be suspicious of any unexpected email, especially if it contains an unexpected file attachment or link. There are dozens of other things any organization can do to mitigate the risk of social engineering, but teaching a user how to read a URL is one of the best. In general, a strong security awareness training program is one of the best defenses any organization could implement to defeat hackers and malware.

Comprehensive Anti-phishing Ebook

I prepared a comprehensive ebook for my employer, KnowBe4, which covers everything I could think of to mitigate social engineering. The book is KnowBe4's *Comprehensive Anti-Phishing Guide* found at https://info.knowbe4 .com/comprehensive-anti-phishing-guide.

However, unpatched software, which is the number-two most common root-cause exploit for all malicious hackers and malware, drops to a distant number-three (or even lower) reported ransomware root cause. This is likely due to the higher than normal involvement by several ransomware families targeting Microsoft's RDP.

All organizations should strive to make RDP and all logon portals (including any Internet-accessible application programing interfaces [APIs] allowing logons) secure. This means requiring and using multifactor authentication (MFA) whenever possible. It means where passwords are used, passwords are long and complex (at least eight-characters long with some nonalphabetic characters). Account lockout policies should be enabled on all logon portals and APIs. After too many failed logons, the user account being used to log on should automatically inactivate until an administrator has investigated and cleared it or the user has proven ownership and unlocked it.

Many guides recommend not allowing access to RDP and other remote-access tools from the Internet. They recommend requiring VPN use to access the logon portal, and this is not bad advice. However, requiring strong passwords and having an acceptable account lockout policy is just as acceptable. This advice is applicable to any logon portal or API. Additionally, Microsoft allows RDP to be protected by digital certificates. An attacker, without an installed, allowed, trusted, digital certificate, would not be allowed to even attempt an RDP logon. It's a good preventative control for RDP connections and has been around for decades. I wrote about this in the past at `https://www.idginsiderpro.com/article/3318123/experience-an-rdp-attack-it-s-your-fault-not-microsoft-s.html`.

All devices and organizations should always apply all critical security patches in a timely manner. How timely? Most guides say at least within 30 days. I'm more aggressive. I think that all critical security patches should be applied within one week of release by the vendor, of course, after appropriate testing before full-scale deployment in a production environment.

All organizations should try to be 100 percent compliant in applying patches in a timely manner on the software most likely to be attacked by hackers, malware, and ransomware. This includes operating systems, browsers, browser add-ins, Microsoft RDP, web servers, admin portals, database programs, and server-side VPN software. The latter is particularly concentrated on by ransomware gangs.

Clearly, all organizations want to best reduce cybersecurity risk should mitigate social engineering and unpatched software. Organizations that want to mitigate ransomware specifically should concentrate on those two mitigations and add in mitigations against RDP and password guessing attacks, perhaps even ahead of patching, if there has to be a prioritized order between the three recommendations.

Summarized, the top three ransomware preventions are as follows:

- Mitigate social engineering, first and best
- Protect logon portals and APIs, using MFA or strong password policies, and enabling account lockout
- Timely patching of critical security patches

Everything Else

After these three preventative controls, there are many other things defenders can do to defeat malicious hackers, malware, and ransomware. I've listed them in an order which I think decreases cybersecurity risk the most (after the top three preventative controls listed earlier).

- Use application control
- Antivirus prevention/EDR
- Secure configurations
- Privileged account management
- Security boundary segmentation
- Block USB keys
- Implement a foreign Russian language

Other controls, which are more useful for detection and damage control, will be covered in future chapters.

Use Application Control

Using an application control program in enforcement mode is the single biggest defensive mitigation any individual or organization can do to stop all malicious hackers, malware, and ransomware. I would list it in the primary defenses except for the fact that most individuals and organizations cannot implement it. Still, its singular ability to significantly reduce malicious attacks and lateral spread, if implemented, deserves coverage for organizations that can consider it. Additionally, application control, in monitoring/audit-only mode, can be implemented by any organization as a strong detective control, but is covered in Chapter 6, "Detecting Ransomware."

Application control programs have been around for decades and are also traditionally known as *blacklisting* and *whitelisting* programs. A better way to describe those modes are as block/deny mode (i.e., blacklisting) and allow mode (i.e., whitelisting). Application control programs in allow listing-mode allow only predefined, pre-approved applications and scripts to execute. By denying anything not pre-approved, this rejects all ransomware execution by default (unless it is able to bypass the allow listing controls).

Deny/block listing is when an application control program prevents only specific programs or scripts from running. The original idea of block listing was to give users as much freedom as possible, while making sure to defeat the known, malicious programs. This was a great idea when the cyber world had only dozens or hundreds of malicious programs. But now, with hundreds of millions of new malware programs being created and detected each year, deny listing has mostly become a thing of the past or used only in emergency modes when a specific bad program needs to be immediately mitigated during an outbreak.

Flu-Shot!

The first application control program I can remember was something called Flu-Shot! by Ross Greenberg in the late 1980s. His program, and his book of the same name, are largely responsible for igniting the interest I have in fighting malicious hackers and malware today. A product called Tripwire (https://en.wikipedia.org/wiki/Tripwire_(company)), released in 1992, became the first widespread application control program.

Today, there are dozens of application control programs. Microsoft has two built into enterprise versions of Microsoft Windows: AppLocker and Windows Defender Application Control. Figure 2.2 shows an example AppLocker configuration.

Local Computer Policy		Action	Name
Computer Configuration		Allow	Baseline Rules: MICROSOFT® WINDO...
> Software Settings		Allow	Baseline Rules: MICROSOFT APPLICATI...
∨ Windows Settings		Allow	Baseline Rules: WATSON SUBSCRIBER F...
> Name Resolution Policy		Allow	Baseline Rules: HttpHelper.exe
Scripts (Startup/Shutdown)		Allow	Baseline Rules: WINDOWS 10 UPDATE A...
> Deployed Printers		Allow	Baseline Rules: HTML HELP signed by O...
∨ Security Settings		Allow	Baseline Rules: SMConfigInstaller.exe
> Account Policies		Allow	Baseline Rules: MICROSOFT® .NET FRA...
> Local Policies		Allow	Baseline Rules: aspnet_wp.exe
> Windows Defender Firewall with		Allow	Baseline Rules: sxstrace.exe
Network List Manager Policies		Allow	Baseline Rules: sxstrace.exe
> Public Key Policies		Allow	Baseline Rules: ldifde.exe
> Software Restriction Policies		Allow	Baseline Rules: isoburn.exe
∨ Application Control Policies		Allow	Baseline Rules: isoburn.exe
∨ AppLocker		Allow	Baseline Rules: INTERNET EXPLORER sig...
> Executable Rules		Allow	Baseline Rules: IEChooser.exe
> Windows Installer Rules		Allow	Baseline Rules: IEChooser.exe
> Script Rules		Allow	Baseline Rules: repadmin.exe
> Packaged app Rules			

Figure 2.2   Example Microsoft AppLocker configuration

Many computer security vendors have an application control program or feature set, including McAfee, TrendMicro, Symantec, Beyond Trust, Carbon Black, Tripwire, Cisco, and Ivanti.

All individuals and organizations should implement an application control program in allow listing enforcement mode. Doing so would prevent most malicious hacking, malware, and ransomware, no matter what its root-cause exploit method was. Not all, but most.

Unfortunately, most users and organizations very much don't want to lock down their computers and devices to only pre-approved software. Users see it as an affront to their personal freedom, creativity, and productivity. Organizations are worried that implementing allow listing in enforcement mode would decrease productivity and creativity, and probably rightly so. Preventing someone from running every program and script they want (or even don't want) slows them down. It probably does stymie creativity. But stronger computer security requires that sort of control and trade-off. However, many organizations lack the technical expertise or time to implement correctly.

If allow listing enforcement mode is enabled, the organization involved should strive to be very proactive and respond to reported problems and requests for new software approvals. This is where most application control allow listing projects fail. In real-world implementations, approvals for new legitimate software can take weeks to months. This approval delay essentially kills acceptance of an allow listing program by most users and then eventually by the organization. But still, if allow listing enforcement mode could be accomplished, it would significantly defeat most malicious hackers and malware, ransomware included. And it is because most individuals and organizations can't deploy or enforce widespread allow listing, that we have to do all the other defenses. And everything else will likely not work as well. This is one of the major security conundrums of the last three decades.

Even application control in enforcement mode cannot prevent all malicious attacks, but it can *significantly* reduce the risk of successful attack and lateral movement.

Antivirus Prevention

Even though 50 percent to 85 percent of ransomware victims had up-to-date antivirus or EDR solutions (and other related types of defenses), these types of defenses are successful at stopping or mitigating some ransomware attacks and for that alone must be included in anyone's defense. There are millions of instances where antivirus protection (or any of the other related types of computer security defenses) did stop ransomware from initially executing or caught it fairly soon after the initial execution. No security control is perfect. But up-to-date antivirus or EDR defenses should be running on every device susceptible to ransomware. Just don't overly rely on it to be 100% accurate and perfect. Doing so is probably why most ransomware victims become victims.

Secure Configurations

Every device, service, and application should be securely config-ured. Most operating systems, services, and applications are fairly secure by default from the vendor that created it. However, it is common for administrators and users to use those products in an insecure way or to set insecure configurations. For example, it is not uncommon for administrators to accidentally grant overly per-missive permissions to confidential files and folders. Many ransom-ware attacks have occurred because a ransomware purveyor found an overly permissive site or storage area and then used that flaw to plant and execute ransomware. All file, folder, service, and site permissions should be "least permissive." This means always only configuring permissions to the least potentially dangerous setting for each user, computer, and service—the bare minimum necessary to perform the task or role.

It is also fairly common for users, services, and applications to be running using overly permissive security contexts and group memberships, such as administrator and root. Malware exploiting programs or services running in these overly permissive security contexts are able to obtain those same overly permissive permis-sions and privileges, which allows for easier and faster exploitation and spread. All users should use the least permissive security con-text needed to perform their job and role. All services and applica-tions should run in least permissive security contexts.

Privileged Account Management

In the same vein, privileged groups and users should be minimized to reduce the risk of an attacker gaining control of those highly priv-ileged accounts. All hackers and most malware are always looking to use the security privileges and permissions of the highest privileged groups and accounts on a compromised system.

All highly privileged groups should be minimized to the bare minimum number of permanent members at all times. Additional members should be added, as needed, on a task-specific basis, for a limited period of time. Microsoft, which I used to work for, calls this *just enough, just-in-time* privileged account management.

There are many programs and features of larger programs that allow Privileged Account Management (PAM). PAM programs allow privileged groups and users to be securely and effectively managed to decrease security risk. Some PAM programs allow privileged group membership (or members or privileges) to be "checked out" as needed. Any unexpected uses of privileged groups or members should be investigated until resolved.

Security Boundary Segmentation

The "least privilege permission" recommendation applies to all security and network boundaries. Any "blocks" between two security boundaries decreases the risk of an attack and compromise on one side from more easily being leveraged as an attack on the other. Security boundaries can be enforced physically and logically. Security boundary segmentation is often provided by software and devices, including firewalls, routers, switches, VLANs, and software-defined networks.

Different security boundaries should also *not* use the same logon credentials. Credential reuse increases the chances that the compromise of one security boundary will be able to more easily be leveraged to attack the other security boundary. In general, security boundary segmentation is losing some (or all) of its appeal over time in favor of "zero trust" defenses, but there is no doubt that separate security boundaries can provide significant benefits when managed correctly.

Zero Trust

Zero Trust is a cybersecurity defense that essentially says security boundaries have never worked particularly well. Instead, they say to treat each user and request as untrusted, and to look at the totality of what the user (or computer, service, connection) is doing to determine intent. To read more Zero Trust see this great introductory document: `https://www.nist.gov/publications/zero-trust-architecture` .

Data Protection

There are many ways to protect and encapsulate data so that it cannot be easily exfiltrated by attackers. Most organizations don't do enough to prevent large chunks of data from being copy and stolen by unauthorized intruders. Attackers, once they have gained access to an environment, simply copy whatever they want to wherever they want. They may need to temporarily stop databases or an email engine to do so but copying gigabytes and gigabytes of information to another location is, unfortunately, all too easy to do, and usually does not set off alerts.

One of the most protective things a defender can do is make it difficult to impossible (for anyone) to copy large chunks of data, at least in an unauthorized way. One method is to encrypt the data so that it cannot be copied in its unencrypted state outside the system it resides. Another is to keep the data in a highly secured enclave where all the other systems can request only limited views of the data at any one time. In general, look into data protection or data leak prevention systems. You may not be able to stop malware from getting into your environment, but you can make it harder for them to access and steal your confidential data.

Block USB Keys

A small minority of ransomware was uploaded into an environment from USB keys. Blocking USB access can reduce risk of malicious compromise. Ideally, using allow listing enforcement would be preferred over complete blocking, if allowed.

Implement a Foreign Russian Language

This is almost a "joke" recommendation, except that it works. The majority of ransomware comes from Russia or its allies. Accordingly, most ransomware programs will attempt to see if it is running on a computer with a common language spoken in Russia or one of its close allies. If so, the ransomware program will quickly terminate. Here are some of the languages that Russian-based ransomware checks for on computers and attempts to avoid exploiting.

- Russian
- Ukrainian
- Armenian
- Azerbaijani
- Belarusian
- Cyrillic
- Georgian
- Kazakh
- Kyrgyz
- Tatar
- Romanian
- Serbian
- Turkmen
- Uzbek

Some experts recommend enabling one of those commonly avoided languages in your operating system (usually Microsoft Windows) because doing so will significantly reduce the risk that the ransomware program will continue to execute. Cybersecurity journalist and best-selling author Brian Krebs covers this recommended defense at https://krebsonsecurity.com/2021/05/try-this-one-weird-trick-russian-hackers-hate/.

From a security "expert" point of view, this sort of defense is not a strong one. First, non-Russian ransomware may not even check, and even some Russian-based ransomware programs may not check. Second, you cannot be guaranteed how the Russian-ransomware might check to confirm its presence on a Russian-based device or computer. Third, whatever defense method is used, the Russian-based ransomware can attempt to program around.

Still, there is much evidence to show that enabling one of the commonly checked for Russian languages can stop many, if not most, Russian-based ransomware programs. So, if it can be done easily and quickly, it might be worth the effort it takes to enable it, at least until it stops working as a defense.

All individuals and organizations should implement these recommended preventative controls, starting with fighting social engineering and phishing, preventing password attacks, and better patching. The other recommended prevention controls should also be considered.

CISA Ransomware Readiness Tool

The US Cybersecurity Infrastructure Security Agency (CISA) has a great, free ransomware readiness assessment tool (`https://github.com/cisagov/cset/releases/tag/v10.3.0.0`) anyone can use. It's essentially a self-assessment checklist of protective controls that any defender can use to protect themselves against ransomware.

Beyond Self-Defense

There is only so much individual users and organizations can do to prevent malicious hackers, malware, and ransomware. The previous advice should not be surprising to anyone in the cybersecurity industry for very long. They are the security controls that we have all had recommended to us for decades (if you've been in the cybersecurity industry long enough). Every computer security regulatory guide (e.g., HIPAA, SOX, NERC, PCI-DSS, etc.) has been recommending the same things for as long as they have been in existence. Perhaps the only new thing I bring to the recommendations is an intense focus on preventative controls, root-cause exploits, and the right prioritization.

We don't need any new controls or new control documents or frameworks to prevent ransomware. But individual and organizational efforts to defeat ransomware alone are not enough. The underlying geopolitical environment and insecurity of the Internet allows malicious hackers and malware to go unpunished. We need more than just individual and organizational controls; we need the following: geopolitical solutions and a more secure Internet.

Geopolitical Solutions

There are several geopolitical solutions that could significantly minimize the threat of ransomware.

International Cooperation and Law Enforcement

Most ransomware either originates from intentional cybercriminal safe havens, like Russia, or benefits by the lack of legal jurisdictional cooperation between many countries. Malicious hackers and their malware creations thrive because the criminal perpetrators cannot be identified, and even if identified, are almost never successfully prosecuted. It is all gain and nearly zero risk for cyber criminals. What criminals would not take advantage of those conditions? Rob a real bank and face a very real chance of being caught and going to jail. Rob an online bank, get far more money, and have almost chance of going to jail. We need to eliminate cybersecurity safe havens and establish minimum levels of international cross-jurisdictional cooperation when investigating cybercrimes and charging and arresting cybercriminals.

There are some pockets of international cooperation already between close allies, but certainly not with countries with traditional adversarial tension such as the United States with Russia and China. Russia and China have rarely enforced warrants or subpoenas that originated from the United States for their citizens within their borders, and vice versa. Because of this, we have a lot of cybercrime originating out of one country into another. Some countries, like North Korea and Russia, appear to not only tolerate ransomware but are thought to encourage it and use it to their own advantage. As long as cybercrime is allowed, and even encouraged, between adversaries, we will have a far harder time stopping it.

It will require politicians agreeing to work on a global cybersecurity framework and countries agreeing to accept those new rules.

It is hard to get any group of people to agree on anything. Your close family likely does not agree on everything, much less the entire world and stakeholders on all sides of an issue. But some organizations and people are trying.

For example, the United Nations (UN) has been working on a global, agreed upon set of cybersecurity and cyberwarfare standards for at least six years, and there were other global agreement attempts made for decades before that. The UN got something passed. On March 10, 2021, they issued their first report on global cybersecurity recommendations (https://front.un-arm.org/wp-content/uploads/2021/03/Final-report-A-AC.290-2021-CRP.2.pdf), a sort of digital Geneva Conventions. It elevates and affirms the authority of international law in cyberspace and the set of norms for responsible behavior, sets expectations for responsible nation-state cyber behavior, and discusses the need for all nations to become more cyber-resilient. Of course, major nations are pushing back on it, but the French and other countries are also proposing a way forward (https://front.un-arm.org/wp-content/uploads/2020/10/joint-contribution-poa-future-of-cyber-discussions-at-un-10-08-2020.pdf). All in all, we are closer to global agreement on what should and should not be tolerated cyber wise.

It is also going to take global agreement on digital crime rules of evidence and on how different countries will accept and enforce subpoenas and calls for arrests of suspects made by other countries. It will likely also take widespread, global condemnation of the major nations who are safe havens for cyber criminals. We have got to make it more painful than not for nations to avoid doing what is needed to make our cyber activities safer.

Coordinated Technical Defense

The newly formed US Ransomware Task Force's report entitled "Combating Ransomware: A Comprehensive Framework for Action: Key Recommendations from the Ransomware Task Force" (https://securityandtechnology.org/ransomwaretaskforce/

`report/`) lists 48 separate actions it recommends the US government take to mitigate ransomware.

Many of its recommendations call for a centralized, coordinated, government/private-sponsored organization to directly fight ransomware. It recommends many actions, including the following:

- Establish an inter-intelligence agency working group and team to fight ransomware
- Designate ransomware as a national security threat (this was done after the report was issued)
- Establish an international coalition to fight ransomware criminals
- Create a global network of ransomware investigation hubs

Disrupt Money Supply

The Ransomware Task Force's report also recommends disrupting the money supply via cryptocurrencies that ransomware gangs enjoy today. The report clearly ties the rise in cybersecurity insurance coverage for ransomware payments and the use of cryptocurrency to the increase in ransomware incidents and cost per incident. The task force recommends significantly disabling the ability for victims to pay ransom and for ransomware gangs to collect ransom payments. The report says that just 199 bitcoin addresses accounted for 80 percent of all ransomware payments sent in 2020. By disrupting those payments, it would likely decrease ransomware gang incentives.

Fix the Internet

But if you want to decrease cybersecurity risk significantly, truly from all cybercriminal sources, including ransomware, we must "fix" the Internet. That is, make the Internet a significantly safer place for devices and people to be. That is no small task. It is considered by most observers to be an impossible task, especially in an acceptable time period, say 10 years or less.

You might ask why the Internet hasn't been made significantly more secure already. It comes with a few main problems, including the fact discussed earlier about how most hackers cannot be successfully prosecuted. Other challenges include the following:

- The Internet was not built with security in mind when it was created and bolting on more security later is never optimal.
- The Internet is so huge that changing it would be a massive, multiyear undertaking even if 100 percent of everyone was on board on how to do it and wanted to do it.
- There are many large groups who are opposed to making the Internet more secure in the ways it would likely require, ranging from privacy advocates to governments to law enforcement (for diametrically opposed reasons).
- Many people believe the "pain" so far is acceptable, equating it to the crime we all live with in the real-world, and don't want changes.
- Getting global consensus, like better securing the Internet would require, is unlikely without a cataclysmic collapse, "tipping point" event to bring everyone together to fix it.

I discuss the reasons the Internet is not more secure in more detail at `https://www.linkedin.com/pulse/why-isnt-internet-more-secure-roger-grimes`.

Surprising to many people is the fact that the Internet can be made more secure. Most people think it can't be done because we don't have the technology or know-how. It isn't a technical issue, but rather it's a sociological issue of getting people to come together to agree that it needs to be done and then agreeing on how to do it.

I've written about how I think we could do it many times over my career, including several whitepapers, dozens of articles (mostly in *InfoWorld* and *CSO Online*, where I was a weekly security columnist for nearly 15 years), and even scholarly defenses of those ideas in top university forums. There are many ways to better secure the Internet. Mine isn't the only way, but here's a quick summary of my proposal:

- Build a second, opt-in, more secure version of the Internet (the original Internet continues unimpeded for those who want to use it) using the same, existing Internet connections and nodes. On the new, more secure, version of the Internet:
  ○ Default, pervasive, strong authentication of users, devices, and network traffic replaces the current Internet's pervasive default anonymity.
  ○ All users, devices, networks, and services can establish a minimum level of assured authentication they are willing to accept to and from willing parties.
  ○ A centralized, DNS-like service, but for dynamically collecting and reporting pockets of originating maliciousness.
  ○ All based on open standards and protocols.

This new, more secure Internet described in my proposal would not prevent anyone who wants to remain completely anonymous from staying anonymous. In fact, my design allows anyone to choose their desired level of authentication, ranging from total anonymity to strong authentication of their true, real-world identity for every different service and connection. Hence, you might want to stay anonymous when talking to your cancer support group, but your bank may only allow you to make withdrawals when you use strong authentication. Some services could cater to people who desire absolute anonymity and others for people who desire the opposite end of the spectrum. And if someone's device gets compromised and is sending out malware, the entire world would know and be able to react accordingly, with their own desired actions. And when that device was cleaned and safe to use again, the world would also know that as well.

A more secure Internet could be implemented by the various groups that control it (e.g., IETF, ICANN, W3C, etc.) coming together on what to implement. All the planning could be done in a few months. And it would not interrupt a single current operation or require the buying of anything new. Most of it could be implemented through software updates. It could even jumpstart a ton of new startups and services that wanted to take advantage of the new feature sets.

If you are interested in more details on how my solution could fix the Internet, please see `https://www.linkedin.com/pulse/wanna-fix-internet-roger-grimes`. My proposal is just one possible solution, but there are other ways to make the Internet more secure. We just need to decide on one solution and implement it. Will that ever happen, in a substantial way, without a tipping point event? Most people don't think so. Me, I think the gravity of ransomware is its own tipping point event. Perhaps not a cataclysmic collapse of the Internet, but ransomware is pretty bad. It's about as bad as it can get without it being a true collapse of the Internet. And enough people may feel the same way to start an evolution.

Summary

In closing out this chapter, the key point to remember is that prevention is the key to minimizing the damage and impact from ransomware. A backup is not a preventative control. Most individuals and organizations would benefit the most by mitigating social engineering, preventing password attacks, and patching more regularly. There are many other things defenders can do to help mitigate ransomware. All organizations need to focus more on preventing ransomware from being successful in the first place. In the end, preventing ransomware is always cheaper than trying to deal with it after it has successfully exploited your environment. We all need to do our best until the geopolitical and Internet solutions come around to better help.

Chapter 3
Cybersecurity Insurance

In this chapter, we will discuss cybersecurity insurance, the industry, and how it is adjusting to the mega-ransoms paid out over the last few years. The most important part will cover how to pick cybersecurity insurance and what to watch out for, so you don't end up with inadequate coverage.

Cybersecurity Insurance Shakeout

Cybersecurity insurance helps to provide financial protection from cybersecurity incidents. These days cybersecurity insurance firms are even stepping up to the plate as a primary cybersecurity risk accessor, giving you additional ways to gauge your cybersecurity readiness, along with recommended/required controls and education. For many smaller organizations, their cybersecurity insurance broker may be their first exposure to a mature cybersecurity risk assessment and stronger cybersecurity controls and tools. Ironically, ransomware is often the reason many companies had to implement better and stronger computer security.

Cybersecurity insurance has been around in various forms for decades, albeit not in the distinct, focused, "we'll pay the ransom" way it is now. It first started as a "rider" on other business insurance policies, and mostly covered *third-party* claims, or damages that occurred to downstream (i.e., not to the insured party) people and organizations that ended up with loss or injury due to the upstream hacked, insured victim. *First-party* coverage, directly covering the insured party because of hacking, didn't start to appear until the early 2000s.

To be fair, before then, malicious cyber hacking was still a rare event. There were some hackers stealing small amounts of data and getting free services, but most hacking was fairly benevolent. It was more about teenagers and young adults proving they could hack something than hurting something or making money. Sure, there were always malicious hackers and malware from the start, like the 1992 Michelangelo virus that attacked hard drives, but they were few and far between. Most hackers broke into places just because they could, looked around, and got out. Malware was more likely to play tunes like Yankee Doodle Dandy and print messages asking for the legalization of marijuana than to cause real harm.

In the mid-2000s, spam bots, bot nets, identity thieves, and credit card stealing programs began showing up and turned yesterday's hacks and malware programs into profit-driven projects. But even then, most of it was unauthorized use of resources and not directly malicious and damaging to the compromised host. The "business" of hacking caused more hacking and hackers to come on the scene, not all of it so harmless. A plethora of corporate and industry regulations were developed (e.g., PCI-DSS, SOX, NERC, HIPAA, etc.) to fight back. Cybersecurity insurance offerings started as a way to compensate businesses for losses related more to data theft than business interruption and recovery.

The real driver of change in cybersecurity insurance, as covered in Chapter 1, was the result of the intersection of ransomware with bitcoin in 2013. Now cybersecurity criminals could directly make large sums of money from their victims. They didn't have to steal information and resell it or buy something to make a profit. They could demand a ransom and get paid with far shorter payoff dates. Within a few years, the biggest cybercrime problem, based on risk and damage alone, was ransomware by a longshot (although nearly one-half of cybersecurity insurance claims are related to other issues by sheer numbers).

For a handful of years, the number of insurance firms offering cybersecurity insurance climbed year after year. At its peak, nearly 200 different insurance firms offered cybersecurity insurance that covered ransomware attacks. Cybersecurity insurance would (and usually does) cover paying the ransom, restoration costs, and business interruption costs—up to the limit of the coverage.

Insured entities could pick from a bunch of offers, nearly any maximum desired coverage amount, with a small deductible, and affordable premium. For example, in 2019, it was fairly common for an organization to be able to get a $1,000,000 policy with a $10,000 deductible for an annual premium of $1,500. It was a very profitable and competitive field for the insurance company. They didn't dare raise rates. If anything, they considered lowering rates to keep a current customer's business as other insurance companies vied for their business.

For the insured, cybersecurity insurance allows a (large) part of the financial risk to be "transferred" to another entity (the insurance company). This is known as *risk transference*. For many years, cybersecurity insurance was relatively low cost, as compared to other types of insurance covering the same amount of financial risk. There were a lot of different types of offerings, with a wide range of deductibles and coverages, for organizations to pick from.

As recently as a few years ago, the insurance carriers that offered cybersecurity insurance were making a lot of profit. It was "easy money." Insurance carriers would routinely make 60 percent or more of every dollar they charged for cybersecurity insurance. Ransomware and their ransoms were increasing, but they were still comparatively uncommon events. The average ransoms paid were only in the tens of thousands of dollars.

A year or two later, as the number of ransomware events grew and average ransoms paid grew even more, insurance carriers were still making 40 percent of every dollar in premiums paid. It was still good profit for the insurance companies that provided cybersecurity insurance. It was good for the insured. Insured organizations could get millions of dollars in coverage for a reasonably low cost. It was win-win for both sides, and many cybersecurity insurance firms didn't work that hard to assess actual client cybersecurity risk. The profit they were making didn't require lengthy cybersecurity risk assessments. As one insurance broker told me, "I remember the days when the cybersecurity risk survey required by insurance companies had only five questions on them, and three of those were name, address, and phone number."

It has all changed. The incredible profitability the cybersecurity insurance industry enjoyed has vanished in recent years—mostly due to ransomware. The number of ransomware attacks and amounts of ransoms paid have shaken the cybersecurity insurance market. Figure 3.1 shows the percentage change in cybersecurity insurance premiums over time based on data from the Council of Insurance Agents and Brokers (https://www.gao.gov/assets/gao-21-477.pdf).

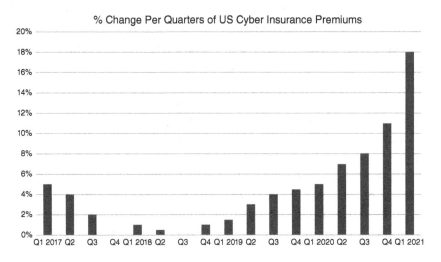

Figure 3.1   Percentage increases in cybersecurity insurance premiums over time

Many insurance firms, suffering losses or tired of the ever climbing risk, got out. Those that are still offering cybersecurity insurance policies require far more confidence in the insured's cybersecurity defenses, offer less coverage, have higher premiums, and have more "outs" (i.e., policy coverage exclusions).

Ransomware Wasn't the Only Problem

Ransomware was the primary driver of the drastic changes to the cyber insurance industry, but other threats were also a big part of the change in risk, including traditional phishing threats and business email compromise scams. Many organizations have lost millions of dollars because they were tricked into sending money to a rogue bank account, but data-destructing ransomware was the primary reason for the big changes in insurance coverage.

Today, most organizations seeking cybersecurity insurance coverage face far fewer choices and will have to prove they have fairly strong cyber defenses to get any policy. Cybersecurity insurance risk surveys often have 30 to 40 questions that have to be answered, and most organizations seeking cybersecurity insurance will have to undergo vulnerability scans and audits. Insurance firms are looking for clients who take cybersecurity defense seriously. Most cybersecurity insurance firms will require that the clients use multifactor authentication (MFA) and undergo routine, continuous patching checkups, vulnerability scans, and ongoing assessments. It used to be that an organization that was found to have a cybersecurity deficiency could still get coverage along with a 30- to 90-day "grace period" called a *contingency* or *subjectivity* to get the issue resolved, after getting the coverage. Today, that grace period is likely to be nonexistent. Organizations seeking insurance today, will likely have to be fully protected from day one. And if the insurance agency finds that the insured organization has a newly found security vulnerability during the coverage period, the insured will have to fix it very quickly or risk losing their coverage prior to the policy's original, intended termination date.

Many firms that offer cybersecurity insurance don't cover ransomware events or, more often, offer significantly diminished coverage or what is known as *co-insurance* for an additional fee. For example, a $1 million general cyber insurance policy covers only up to $100,000 to $250,000, if ransomware is involved. That's a pretty huge exclusion. An organization may have to pay an additional, much larger sum of money to have ransomware covered under a completely different policy. Times have changed.

What happened? Ransomware gangs started attacking far more targets, getting far more ransom paid per incident, and causing far more damage and recovery cost per incident. Ransoms paid under a million dollars often do not even make the headlines anymore. Five- and ten-million dollar ransoms are fairly common. Ransoms paid in the many tens of millions of dollars are not unheard of. Recovery costs for single firms are often more than a hundred million dollars. A few ransomware attacks have been closer to a billion dollars for some of the bigger, nation-wide, attacks. Most ransomware victims will be completely down for weeks, with full recovery often taking over a year. Most victims don't get all their data back, even if they pay the ransom. Victims refusing to pay the ransom have their confidential data leaked and, in general, take far longer to get back up and operating as compared to the victims that do pay the ransom. This has led to a vicious cycle where no one wants to pay the ransom because it only encourages the cybercriminals and creates more victims. But each individual victim, assessing their own chances and cost of recovery, often do pay. Rinse. Repeat.

Did Cybersecurity Insurance Make Ransomware Worse?

One of the big questions is whether the growing cybersecurity insurance industry caused ransomware to get worse than if cybersecurity insurance didn't exist. There is much debate on this issue, but it is likely that the availability of cybersecurity insurance is increasing ransomware attacks and the number of ransoms paid, at least in some cases.

An individual victim organization may have an ethical dilemma on its hands on whether to pay the ransom or not, but not cybersecurity insurance companies. When a covered victim is hit, it is common for the cybersecurity insurance firm to pressure the victim to pay the ransom. This is because victims that pay usually get back up and operating quicker, and the resulting involved expenses are far less. It's only a business decision for the insurance companies. And companies covered by cybersecurity insurance are more likely to pay the ransom because all the money isn't coming out of their pocket.

This fact is not lost on cybercriminals. Many ransomware gangs specifically target insured organizations or look for evidence of cybersecurity insurance policies within the organization they have just compromised. During negotiations, many ransomware gangs have immediately asked for the maximum amount of ransom allowed to be paid by a particular policy, letting the victims know they have read the details of their policies.

It is recommended that if an organization has cybersecurity insurance that they do not keep the policy document online, or at least protect it in a way that if the hackers get complete control of the environment, they cannot read the policy (i.e., separate encryption or isolation). Also, don't publish the fact that you have cybersecurity insurance in public documents if it can be avoided.

There have been several news stories claiming that ransomware gangs have broken into cybersecurity insurance firms, stolen their customer lists (or simply read their names off the marketing web pages of those firms), and then used the customer names as a preferred shopping list of new victims. At least one ransomware gang, Maze, has publicly confirmed this is the case, although no one knows if this claim was true or simply false braggadocio.

Several of the largest cybersecurity insurance firms themselves have been hit by ransomware attacks. At least one cybersecurity insurance underwriter was specifically attacked and their data encrypted (and not decrypted) because the underwriter publicly said they would no longer be paying any ransom. A ransomware gang punished them to send a warning to other underwriters.

While many people are asking if the cybersecurity insurance industry has done more harm than good, as far as ransomware goes, it does not change the fact that cybersecurity insurance is a good business risk decision for many companies, which want to limit the maximum amount of money they might pay out of pocket due to a cybersecurity incident. And regardless of whether it is a self-inflating, self-defeating, cycle, most organizations will have to at least consider whether they will buy cybersecurity insurance. There is even a growing chance the increasing cybersecurity insurance requirements will make us more cyber resilient overall.

Cybersecurity Insurance Policies

In this section we will dig into the basics of cybersecurity insurance. There really is no "standard" way of offering cybersecurity insurance, and it's changing as I write, but it is worth looking at the broad outlines.

Although there are dozens to more than 100 insurance firms still offering cybersecurity insurance, a handful of firms (e.g., American International Group (AIG), AXA, Beazley, Chubb, CNA, Travelers, etc.) offer more than half the policies. It's important to realize that cybersecurity insurance covers more than just ransomware attacks. Most also cover (regular) data theft, identity theft, insider threats, fraud, and other types of cybercrime, even if this chapter focuses on ransomware. It's also common for cybersecurity insurance to not cover ransomware. For example, the Sophos

"State of Ransomware 2020" report (https://www.sophos.com/en-us/medialibrary/Gated-Assets/white-papers/sophos-the-state-of-ransomware-2020-wp.pdf) said that while 84 percent of surveyed organizations had cybersecurity insurance, only 64 percent had cybersecurity insurance that covered ransomware. Many of the policies that didn't cover ransomware were add-ons to other types of policies the insured already had. Either way, it's important to make sure your cybersecurity insurance policy covers ransomware since it is one of the most frequently occurring and damaging attacks.

What's Covered by Most Cybersecurity Policies

Not all costs related to a ransomware attack event are covered by insurance. The following are some of the common covered costs:

- Recovery costs
- Ransom
- Root-cause analysis
- Business interruption costs
- Customer/stakeholder notifications and protection
- Fines and legal investigations

Recovery Costs

Most cybersecurity insurance policies that deal with the aftermath of ransomware cover the costs needed to recover/rebuild the involved systems and data to put them back to their original, operational state and level of service. This is regardless of whether the victim pays the ransom. Recovery is usually the most expensive part of a ransomware event, doubling, quadrupling, or even more, as compared to the ransom extortion payment.

The cybersecurity insurance firm may have their own in-house incident responders and recovery specialists or outsource recovery to other firms that specialize in ransomware recovery. Some insurance firms brag about their ability to provide faster and better service with in-house staff, but this claim isn't backed up by the data.

Both in-house and outsourced incident responders are usually quick to respond and good at what they do. Find out if you must use the insurance firm's in-house or outsourced incident response and recovery specialists or if they are just recommendations.

It is important that whoever you use is not new at dealing with ransomware recovery. A ransomware event is not the time to let someone see what they can do tackling it for the first time. You want a specialist with lots of experience. Someone "who has been there, done that!" Whoever the insurance company is recommending is likely to be good at ransomware recovery, both in terms of lower cost and returning the victim back to operations. It is in the insurance firm's interest to keep costs, which they will pay some portion of, if not most of, low. That means quick, lower-cost recovery.

Ransom

Most cybersecurity insurance policies pay the cost of paying the ransom and pay the ransom in a ransomware event (one survey said that when the ransom was paid, 94 percent of the time it was by cybersecurity insurance firms). Insurance firms will often pay for skilled ransomware negotiators who often get the ransom requested cut in half or more (although there is no word on whether ransomware gangs just start out by artificially doubling their initial ask to compensate).

There are dozens if not hundreds of regular people around the globe who make a living negotiating ransom payments between the victim (or their representatives) and the ransomware purveyors. I'm not sure how one gets the experience for that type of job, but they do exist, and they are used a lot. Most ransomware negotiators work with one, or maybe a few, ransomware gangs. They know how the ransomware gang works, who to email, how to do it, and what the usual terms are. The ransomware gang in turn usually trusts them, well, as much as a criminal can trust. When a ransomware gang knows, trusts, and has an ongoing relationship with a ransomware negotiator, they relax a bit. They aren't as tough and impatient with the victim.

If you get cybersecurity insurance, make sure to get confirmation on who ultimately gets to decide if the ransom is paid. Most of the time the customer is the ultimate decider, but it's better to clarify before you pay for your policy if you're going to have a problem with a ransom being paid.

Root-Cause Analysis

As Chapter 2 covered, it is important to figure out how ransomware was executed in a victim's environment. Did it happen because of social engineering, unpatched software, password guessing, or some other type of root cause exploit method? A victim needs to determine this, so the existing exploited vulnerability can be closed. This prevents not only the current or future ransomware attackers from getting in or back in, but mitigates future malware and hackers using the same exploit method. Not enough victims do root-cause analysis of how ransomware successfully got in, and that is a mistake.

Many ransomware victims also want to know if there was a "data breach" as well. Traditional ransomware, which simply exploits and encrypts, may not be considered a data breach. Today, most ransomware exfiltrates data, and so it's more likely that a classical data breach event will have also occurred. In some states, countries, or regulated industries, a data breach requires a bunch of additional legally mandated steps, such as customer notification and protection. If a data breach decision is important to your organization, then inquire if an investigation to determine if a data breach has happened is included in the recovery steps. Not every insurance policy pays for forensics root-cause analysis, but if your cybersecurity insurance firm does, take advantage of it.

Business Interruption Costs

Cybersecurity insurance may or may not cover the lost revenue caused by the interruption to the business. Most organizations hit by ransomware are completely down for days to weeks.

Most organizations are not back to 100 percent operational capacity similar to what they were doing before the attack for many months to well over a year. Most cybersecurity insurance policies will cover those lost revenues. If they do, the first-party coverage will cover the insured party's lost revenue. Third-party coverage, if there is any, will cover loss revenue that downstream customers end up having because of the upstream victim's ransomware event. However, some policies, especially the "add-on" coverages, may not. So, check your policy and be sure.

Customer/Stakeholder Notifications and Protection

Depending on the victim and ransomware involved, the victim's customers and employees could also be impacted. If their confidential information was viewed or stolen, they need to be notified. They may need to have other protections services bought and enabled, like credit monitoring and identity theft alert. Some insurance companies brag about hiring "image consultants" to fix any reputation harm that was caused by a ransomware event. Either way, you just want to find out what your insurance policy covers as far as customer and stakeholder notification and protection is concerned.

Fines and Legal Investigations

Some cybersecurity incidents may invite legal or regulatory fines and/or investigations. Many, but not all, insurance firms will cover fines that need to be paid if the customer didn't commit intentionally illegal actions. Fines can be huge in some cases, so having them included in your insurance coverage is a big benefit. However, if the insured intentionally did something illegal or against regulations (or potentially just willingly neglectful), most insurance firms will not cover the cost of any resulting fines or investigations.

Example Cyber Insurance Policy Structure

The following is how a comprehensive cyber insurance policy is typically broken out. This list shows the sections that could be in a policy, although the terminology might vary depending on the insurance carrier:

- Cyber incident response (first party)
  - Incident response costs
  - Legal and regulatory costs
  - IT security and forensic costs
  - Crisis communication costs
  - Privacy breach management costs
  - Third-party privacy breach management costs
  - Post-breach remediation costs
- Cybercrime (first party)
  - Funds transfer fraud
  - Theft of funds held in escrow
  - Theft of personal funds (for senior officers)
  - Extortion
  - Corporate identity theft
  - Push payment fraud (loss of insured's customer's money)
  - Telephone hacking
  - Unauthorized use of computer resources
- System damage and business interruption (first party)
  - System damage and rectification costs
  - Income loss and extra expense
  - Additional extra expense (sometimes)
  - Dependent business interruption
  - Consequential reputational harm
  - Claim preparation costs
  - Hardware replacement costs
- Network security and privacy liability (third party)
  - Network security liability
  - Privacy liability

- Management liability
- Regulatory fines
- PCI fines, penalties, and assessments
- Media liability (third party and optional)
  - Defamation
  - Intellectual property rights infringement
- Technology E&O (third party and optional)
- Court attendance costs (third party)

It can help to review those different sections ahead of an insurance policy consideration to make sure all the different components are being covered.

Costs Covered and Not Covered by Insurance

It's also good to be aware of the costs that cybersecurity insurance doesn't pay. To be clear, if your organization gets hit by a ransomware event, any involved cybersecurity insurance firm is likely going to be paying plenty already. They will not graciously go looking to pay for things not covered by the policy, but they aren't, like in other types of insurance, intentionally looking for ways not to cover you. Still, there are costs that most cybersecurity insurance policies don't cover. Here are some common and uncommon costs that may not be covered by ransomware cybersecurity insurance. Many costs occur whether or not your organization has been successfully attacked by ransomware.

These are the costs whether or not a ransomware event has occurred, usually not covered:

- Costs of any mitigations to prevent a ransomware attack in the first place
- Resources involved in obtaining cybersecurity insurance
- Cost of cybersecurity insurance premiums, if any

If a ransomware event has occurred, these costs are usually not covered:

- Personnel changes, adds/deletes/changes, if any
- Productivity slowdowns due to new procedures and protections, if any (although they may be covered under revenue losses)

- Reputational harm (although they may be covered under revenue losses)
- Additional new defense preparations to mitigate the next attack (that did not exist prior to the attack)
- Interruptions to uninsured third parties

Note that many insurance policies cover many of the previous costs, such as business interruption, increased labor costs, revenue loss, etc. The key is to determine whether the policy you have or are considering does or doesn't cover a particular cost. And if a policy does cover it, how much coverage applies? A victim organization would be responsible for only the portion not covered by insurance.

The last two costs in the previous bulleted list deserve additional discussion. First, let's talk about additional defense preparations to mitigate the next attack. Most victims hit by ransomware want to improve their defenses, so they are never a victim again. At best, your cybersecurity insurance policy will cover getting you back to 100 percent of your original operating capacity and defenses. They will not be paying for all the new security mitigations you are likely to be buying. Most ransomware victims end up buying new endpoint detection and response client software, network and host intrusion detection software and appliances, security awareness training services, security event monitoring products and services, multifactor authentication solutions, software upgrades, and all the other things they should have been doing already that had they already been doing would have been less likely to have been compromised by ransomware in the first place. Yeah, cybersecurity insurance is not paying for any of the new stuff. They are focused on paying what it takes to get you "back to even," which in many ransomware cases, is still plenty.

Real life is complicated. Many times, the new stuff is bought to replace the stuff that was bypassed or corrupted, and you may have no other choice. For example, suppose a bunch of Microsoft Windows 7 clients and Microsoft Windows 2012 servers crashed. Most victims will end up buying Microsoft Windows 10 and Microsoft Windows Server 2019 or 2022 to replace them. The new software usually costs more than the old software. Many times, new hardware is needed to support the greater resource requirements of the new software. Somewhere along the way one of the security consultants mentions that your current Active Directory design might have caused some of the problem. So, they recommend designing it the "right way" from the ground up, and that project will require a team of other consultants for weeks if not months.

Someone else mentions how a better incident response process would have softened the damage, lowered downtime, and lowered costs. They create an official incident response (IR) team, get team members training, conduct tabletop exercises, and buy IR software for the new team. Someone else recommends buying an enterprise-level vulnerability scanning and management program. And you'll need a new employee to run and manage all of that. And so on.

So, in the process of recovering from a ransomware event, many organizations end up with new software, new hardware, new network designs, new security appliances, new services, new employees, etc. And none of that is paid for by insurance. Don't expect a good recovery to simply be getting back to where you were. Usually, you don't want to be where you were. That's what caused your big problems in the first place.

Lastly, the big ransomware events are causing operational interruption far beyond what any cybersecurity insurance company could ever cover . . . or the insured firm could never afford the premiums if they did. For some ransomware events, the real interruption costs are huge and even global.

For example, as covered in Chapter 1, regarding the Colonial Pipeline ransomware attack, it ended up disrupting gas supplies all around the southeastern United States even though its actual, direct impacts were in a far smaller area. My hometown, near Tampa, Florida, had widespread gas shortages. It wasn't because our gas supplies were decreased in any way. Regardless, everyone was panicked that gas supplies might get low, and so they rushed out to get gas immediately, which caused most gas stations in my area not to have gas within a few hours. When I went out looking to gas up my truck, there was no gas to be found within 10 miles of my home—only plastic bags on handles and darkened gas stations. I wasted two hours and a few gallons of already scarce gas to not find gas. I called work to tell them I wasn't coming into work the next day or three because I wasn't sure I had the gas to make it there and back. My co-worker in the Netherlands said they were warned about gas issues due to what was happening in the United States. That's crazy! But that's what a single ransomware event did. None of those interruptions would be covered by insurance.

Two weeks later, international meat plant JBS paid $11 million in ransom, and its meat supplies were still delayed, which impacted restaurants and stores waiting on their meat. It's clear that the operational disruption caused by ransomware can be huge and even global. It can impact millions of people's lives and make them less productive. That cost will never be reimbursed.

If you're interested in the financial protection afforded by cybersecurity insurance, make sure to find out what is covered and is not covered by the policy. You should be working with a good, smart, trusted insurance agent who knows the policy involved and can answer your questions. Reviewing a new cybersecurity insurance policy is no time to be taking guesses.

The Insurance Process

It is key to understand the normal process of getting insurance. Once you have insurance, it is important also to know what happens if you have a ransomware event. Let's look closer at getting insurance, determining cybersecurity risk, and the underwriting, approval, and incident claim processes.

Getting Insurance

Most organizations simply contact their current business insurance broker to find out about cybersecurity insurance. Some organizations connect to cybersecurity insurance specialists, and a few new customers find their new cybersecurity insurance brokers by clicking an ad on the Internet. Either way, all organizations looking to get cybersecurity insurance will go through a few different rounds of questions.

The first will be something to classify, locate, and size the organization requesting the insurance. Some types of organizations cannot get cybersecurity insurance (they are simply attacked too often or the resulting damages are too high) or the coverages will be low and/or the premiums will be high. Different industries get different pricing.

Where is the organization located, and where does it operate? Are all locations to be covered in the same area, covered in the same country, or spread out globally? If globally spread out, where? Some countries are not insurable or additionally, other insurers will have to be brought in to cover the gaps.

What equipment do you want covered? Just computers, or also mobile devices, industrial equipment, environmental equipment, and more? What types of computers do you have (e.g., Windows, Linux, etc.)? How many computers do you have? How many servers do you have? How many client computers do you have?

How much is your organization valued at? How much are the annual revenues? How many customers do you have? How many confidential records do you have? How many credit card transactions do you have, and what is the total value? Sizing your organization is important not only for the insurer to size your policy appropriately, but specifically with ransomware in mind, it ends up determining what a possible ransomware extortion payment might look like.

Cybersecurity Risk Determination

Ultimately, the insurance company wants to know if you are a good or bad cybersecurity risk. To that end, they will normally ask you dozens to more than 100 questions about specific policies, such as whether you use MFA, implement account lockout for failed logons, what your backup process is composed of, if backups are stored offline, and so on. Some insurance providers ask if you've complied with regulatory guidelines (e.g., PCI-DSS, HIPAA, etc.) and/or had security audits. They want to get the best sense of the risk they are taking with your organization.

Although this was almost unheard of just a few years ago, many insurance firms are now requiring that they, or their appointed service, be allowed to do external and/or internal vulnerability scans. They want to confirm how many easy-to-find vulnerabilities you have that an attacker might take advantage of and ask you to fix the critical ones before they will offer a policy. They may also ask for the right to conduct additional vulnerability scans during the policy period and revoke the policy prematurely for noncompliance.

Underwriting and Approval

Once all the information is collected, it is sent to an insurance underwriter, who examines the collected information. The underwriter has already previously sent out the guidelines that were followed to start with, but they now take the collected information and try to form a decision about whether the applying organization can be insured, and if so at what pricing points.

They'll want to know a number of additional things. How much coverage you want? How much deductible are you willing to pay? Do you want ransomware coverage? And so on. Then the underwriter decides if they need more information to make a decision. If so, the insurance firm will ask the organization applying for insurance to respond with more information. Then, with the new answers, the policy goes back for a go/no-go decision. It's pretty normal to get some additional questions or even to be told that you have to do something (such as get MFA) if you want to get the policy.

I've heard from a few insurance brokers that it is getting harder for an insurance broker to give out a quote and get the client to approve it in time before the underwriter changes the requirements. The longer the customer takes to get the insurance policy quote approved, the stronger the chance that the quoted policy requirements gets cancelled or changed. Again, a lot of this is caused because of the increasing damage ransomware is causing and its financial impact of the cybersecurity insurance industry.

In the end, if the customer agrees on the terms and pricing proposed by underwriting and the insurance broker, the customer now has a cybersecurity insurance policy for covered events. If the cybersecurity insurance policy includes a recommended or required incident response broker, now is the time for the insured organization's cybersecurity leader, or primary contact, to reach out to the insurance company's incident response contact. Most insured customers wait until a cybersecurity incident happens to reach out, for the first time, to the incident response broker. And although that is fine, there can be some benefits to make a pre-incident call and introductions.

The insured firm needs to make sure all the relevant contact information, and policy, is available offline, because the online computer systems could be down and unavailable or not trustworthy to use. The insured organization's contact should introduce themselves to the incident response broker and ask about how a real incident response would likely go. Perhaps, it's even time for a simulated "tabletop" exercise to be accomplished. In talking to many people who have gone through ransomware incidents and to incident response brokers, all agree that having a pre-meeting between the two parties is useful to both sides. Unfortunately, less than 1 percent of insured organizations make a pre-incident introductory call. So, if you have cybersecurity insurance and have a required or likely incident response team/broker, give them a call.

Incident Claim Process

Now, let's suppose a cybersecurity event, ransomware in particular, happens to an insured customer. What does the response process look like?

Typically, there are one or more systems that first crash because they are starting to be encrypted. Initially, most people, if in front of the screen, start to see the system they are on have operational issues but are not sure what is going on. It's just some unexpected, strange, critical-looking error message. Then either the system they are watching or another they check on to troubleshoot the first system finally displays a ransomware extortion message.

The victim organization should contact the other needed incident responders in the organization and senior management as they begin to disconnect all systems from the network (wireless and otherwise). At some point, the insurance company's previously communicated incident response number will need to be called. Normally, this notifies the insurance company that an incident is occurring during the initial response call, or the insurance company will be called by the victim separately at a later time or date. The insurance company will have some maximum time within which the insured must notify them for the incident to qualify under the policy. This time limit can range from a day to weeks. The insurance company is strongly invested in their customer getting the technical help they need first to minimize downtime and cost. Having to notify the insurance company immediately during the initial few hours is not usually required. With that said, it can't hurt to get your insurance broker involved to repeat what types of items are reimbursable under the policy and what types of evidence and receipts may be needed to get expenditures reimbursed.

Initial Technical Help

When the incident response person or company is called, normally they will start to tell you what is going to happen when. Usually, they will get as much information as they can, such as how many computers are impacted and where, and if the strain of ransomware has been identified yet. Identifying the strain and version of ransomware is important to initial responders, since different ransomware programs and gangs have different attributes. Ordinarily, the victim organization's caller will be told about the other type of information needed and who else is needed to be on the next call. Then a time will be set for the next call. During the next call the initial recommended responses, as covered in Chapters 7 and 8, will be communicated. The "Stop the Spread" and "Stop the Damage" experts and recommendations will be in charge at this point. Additional people or teams will be called in as needed.

Eventually, the initial crisis risk will begin to lower. The maximum amount of damage will have occurred or begin to stabilize. Depending on what is happening, perhaps the ransom will start to be negotiated. At some point, the incident response will move from the initial phases into the next phase of recovery. The various compromised systems will begin to be ranked according to business impact (along with their dependencies), and efforts to begin initial restoration will begin. Systems will begin to be brought back online. New hardware and software are usually bought in and deployed. Encrypted data may begin to be decrypted if possible. Systems will be checked to ensure they don't have other backdoor trojans installed or simply rebuilt from scratch.

There will probably have been multiple check-ins by the insurance company to assess how things are going and start to access current and future expected expenses. Eventually, expense claims will be submitted to the insurance broker, questions will be asked, documents will have to be produced, and commitments made along with more discussion.

Some insurance payments may have already been provided (minus the agreed upon deductible), such as paying for the early incident responders and recovery expenses. Or the victim covers all expenses initially and gets reimbursed later on. Eventually, all receipts are submitted to the insurance company by the client, and some final reimbursement amount is agreed upon. This can easily be many months after the ransomware event happened. Key to this process is the customer understanding what is and isn't covered under their cybersecurity insurance policy and who pays what when. Ideally, the customer understood all the agreed upon included expenses well *before* signing the policy agreement.

What to Watch Out For

Cybersecurity insurance is often a good deal for organizations that are facing cybersecurity threats, like ransomware. They can often transfer excessive financial risk to the insurance firm. However, there are many "outs" that customers should look for and some to avoid anytime you see them.

Social Engineering Outs

There are cybersecurity insurance policies that specifically exclude or significantly diminish coverage for exploits involving social engineering. These types of policies should be avoided 100 percent of the time. This is because 70 percent to 90 percent of all malicious data breaches involve social engineering. It's slightly less so regarding ransomware alone (but it is still at over 50 percent according to most surveys). This means that a cybersecurity exploitation event likely will include social engineering as a root-cause exploit method. Allowing a cybersecurity insurance policy to disavow or weaken coverage because of social engineering is essentially accepting that you're not likely to have the best coverage when you need it.

Make Sure Your Policy Covers Ransomware

Some policies specifically don't cover ransomware. Survey after survey has shown that these days most organizations (over 50 percent) will get hit by ransomware each year. This means your organization will more than likely be hit by ransomware this year or next and having a ransomware exclusion would not allow you to have coverage, again, when you need it most. With this said, there are many organizations that cannot get coverage any other way, for any other cybersecurity risk event, other than to accept that ransomware will not be covered. If you think the risks of other cybersecurity risk events are fairly high and you want coverage for those, then it might make sense for these types of organizations facing those factors.

Employee's Mistake Involved

I've seen policies that denied coverage if an employee makes an inappropriate decision that leads to malicious compromise. At times, you may see a "carve back" provision for certain instances such as an employee willfully transferring money. You might also see some insurance policies that will stipulate that if the employee didn't execute the required "dual authorization" procedures before transferring money and it goes to a fraudulent account, it would not be covered.

In general, these types of carve-outs (for employee mistakes) are fairly rare, but I've seen them. There have even been some court cases, involving fraudulent payments (e.g., aka CEO fraud or business email compromise scams) where cybersecurity insurance firms were using the employee's mistake to avoid paying off on the policy even if an employee's mistake was not specifically and clearly spelled out in the policy as an exclusion. The vast majority of cyberattacks involve an employee being socially engineered. Any clauses mentioning employee mistakes as a reason to exclude payout should be avoided at all costs.

Does E&O Cover Employee Mistakes?

An organization's normal "errors and omissions" insurance might cover employee errors like the ones involved with social engineering and ransomware. Be sure to clarify what is and isn't covered and how much the coverage is for.

Work-from-Home Scenarios

Some rare policies only cover incidents that happen at the insured's primary place(s) of business. Make sure "work-from-home" (WFH) scenarios, so popular these days, are not a valid reason for exclusion. Most insurances cover WFH scenarios, and they are an increasing reason for the success of ransomware, but always make sure your policy covers your employees and business no matter where located.

War Exclusion Clauses

The Russian-delivered NotPetya ransomware event caused many billions of dollars of damages to firms and tens of billions of dollars across Ukraine and other nations. Many cybersecurity insurance firms are trying to deny coverage under the "Acts of War" exclusion. Most insurance policies have a clause essentially saying they do not cover acts of war. NotPetya has strongly been proven to have been created and released by a cyber offensive arm of the Russian government, which also attacked Ukraine kinetically at the same time using troops, missiles, and other weapons. Most countries and the United Nations have officially declared Russia's hostile acts against Ukraine, war. Since NotPetya is considered a cyber arm of the same act of aggression, many cybersecurity insurance firms are saying they do not have to pay.

On a good note, most cybersecurity insurance firms have paid despite there being a potentially strong claim to an "act of war" defense, and other cybersecurity insurance firms have further explicitly clarified that they do cover acts of digital cyber terrorism. Just make sure to read your policy carefully and ask questions about unclear terms or phrases.

Future of Cybersecurity Insurance

Besides the fallout in the cybersecurity insurance industry, with more and more insurance firms no longer offering the coverage, many of the remaining providers are ramping up their offerings. You've read about ransomware as a service (RaaS) in Chapter 1. The top tier of the cybersecurity insurance industry is essentially offering an offsetting risk management as a service (RMaaS).

They will not only offer tailored threat assessments and vulnerability scans during your policy registration and renewal process, but all the time in between! Because of their excellent incident response experiences they have been involved in, some progressive cybersecurity insurance firms are starting to offer or act like manage service security providers (MSSPs). They will ascertain your current risk; make security control recommendations; provide security awareness training, compliance assessments, and consulting services; and constantly monitor your cybersecurity risk status. If you need someone to read your logs or patch your computers, your friendly cybersecurity insurance company may be able to do that for you. Why go to one company to insure your risk and another to manage it when it can be done at the same firm? Figure 3.2 shows you the types of services offered by AIG's Cyber-Edge Risk Management Solution. Other firms offer similar end-to-end services.

CyberEdge Risk Management Solution

From our innovative loss prevention tools to educate and potentially prevent a breach, to the services of our CyberEdge Breach Resolution Team if a breach does occur, insureds receive responsive guidance every step of the way.

Risk Consultation and Prevention	Insurance Coverage	Breach Resolution Team
Education and Knowledge	Third-Party Loss Resulting From a Security or Data Breach	24/7 Guidance:
Training and Compliance	Direct First-Party Costs of Responding to a Breach	Legal and Forensics Services
Global Threat Intelligence and Assessment	Lost Income and Operating Expense Resulting From a Security or Data Breach	Notification, Credit, and ID Monitoring Call Center
Shunning Services	Threats to Disclose Data or Attack a System to Extort Money	Crisis Communication Experts
Expert Advice and Consultation	Online Defamation and Copyright and Trademark Infringement	Over 15 Years' Experience Handling Cyber-Related Claims

Figure 3.2   Example services offered by AIG cybersecurity insurance product from a marketing document

These new offerings are where the ransomware has the cybersecurity insurance industry. It is causing rates to go up and insurance options and coverage to go down. But it is also turning cybersecurity insurance firms into MSSPs and improving overall cybersecurity. Cybersecurity defense has always been about risk management; it is just now being managed from start to finish that way. The cybersecurity industry is having a positive impact on cybersecurity by encouraging more organizations to get and maintain stronger security. Not only does their insurance product help do this, but many times they can directly help the insured organization to have stronger cybersecurity practices.

To be clear, I don't know if the cybersecurity insurance industry can do computer security defense and risk management better than existing models. But I bet many C-level executives, who are focused on risk and risk transference as a primary defense, will see some benefit by having a single vendor, end to end, help manage their risk, especially if it translates to lower premiums and lower cybersecurity costs overall. I also don't know if this new "trend" originating from the most progressive cybersecurity insurance firms will become permanent and something seen as normal in the future. Cybersecurity defense has always been about risk management, and so the firms stringing it together from beginning to end might be on to something.

The critical lesson for organizations considering cybersecurity insurance is to make sure that they understand what is and isn't covered, and with what limits. You don't want any surprises if a ransomware event strikes.

Summary

This chapter covered cybersecurity insurance, starting with the basics of what it was and how it is changing because of the "success" of ransomware attacks. Every organization should consider getting cybersecurity insurance, if it makes a good risk versus financial decision. Every buyer of cybersecurity insurance should make sure to identify what is and isn't covered in their policy. Many buyers were burned because they either didn't understand the exclusions well enough or didn't understand how likely they were to occur. Ransomware is forcing the remaining cybersecurity insurance firms to better assess risks and that in turn is forcing customers and potential customers to have better cybersecurity.

Chapter 4, "Legal Considerations," covers the potential legal risks in paying the ransom.

Chapter 4
Legal Considerations

> ## This chapter and book should not be considered legal advice.
> It is the opposite of that. The author has not been to law school, does not have a legal degree, and does not have a license to dispense legal advice. What is said in this book and chapter is not legal advice. For legal advice, consult a lawyer.

In this chapter, we will discuss the legal consequences related to ransomware recovery and payments. No one wants to pay a ransomware extortion demand. Most, if not all, law enforcement agencies and many experts recommend not paying the ransom, as it only encourages future ransomware extortion events. Most, however, understand paying the ransom may be the best financial decision for a victim (organization) involved in a ransomware recovery event.

It's important to understand not only that paying a ransom but simply being involved in helping someone else to recover from a ransomware event may create legal jeopardy in some countries, states, or with regulatory entities. *Let me say that again: simply helping someone else recover from a ransomware event can result in legal consequences!* Most people, if they know of the legal jeopardy issues surrounding ransomware, think it applies only if you pay a ransom, but it also clearly applies to anyone helping to recover from a ransomware event where the victim is paying the ransom. More on this below.

Since most ransomware extortion payments are paid in bitcoin, it can be helpful to better understand bitcoin before discussing the potential legal issues related to ransomware.

Bitcoin and Cryptocurrencies

Ransomware usually asks for a ransom extortion payment to be made using bitcoin or some other cryptocurrency. As covered in Chapter 1, bitcoin was first publicly released in January 2009, by a (pseudo)anonymous identity given as Satoshi Nakamoto. Nakamoto released bitcoin to the world in a paper entitled "Bitcoin: A Peer-to-Peer Electronic Cash System" (`https://bitcoin.org/bitcoin.pdf`) along with a website and software that could be used by anyone to create and use bitcoin.

Pseudo Anonymous vs. Anonymous Identities

A truly anonymous identity is difficult to impossible to tie back to a specific owner, user, or group. It could be anyone or multiple people at the same time, and the same identity label could be reused by anyone at any time. No identity system could accurately vouch for the real identity of any specific holder of an anonymous identity at any one use or time. In contrast, a pseudo-anonymous identity means that only a single user (or subject/principal) can "own" or use the claimed identity. The identity is unique within the same identity management system. No one else can use the same identity. For example, I use rogerg for a logon name. The identity management system may know that rogerg belongs to real, verified person, Roger A. Grimes, but no one else knows that. They just see rogerg. The identity system could be forced to reveal the real identity tied to rogerg by a court order, of course.

It wasn't until December 2013 that the first ransomware program, CryptoLocker, started to ask for payment in bitcoin. Before then, various ransomware purveyors asked for payments to be sent to foreign post office boxes, wiring services, and money cards. Each of those methods made it harder to follow the money to a real identity of the crook, but not impossible. If the authorities cared enough to follow the money, they often were able to identify the receiver(s) and involve that collected evidence in official legal claims. Needless to say, this frustrated criminals.

The arrival of bitcoin and the other later-arriving cryptocurrencies made it easier in a way to follow the money, but a lot harder to impossible to see who got the money (more on this in a moment). Many people mistakenly believe that using bitcoin and cryptocurrency makes the money trail impossible to trace, but this is not always true. But because a cryptocurrency user's real identity can be unknown and difficult to impossible to determine, today most ransomware programs ask for payment in bitcoin, although a small percentage ask for payment in some other cryptocurrency or some other even more obscure method.

There are many reasons worth for understanding why criminals like to use bitcoin, blockchain, and other cryptocurrencies. Bitcoin and other cryptocurrencies use cryptographic routines, protocols, creations, and "proofs" to create, track, and validate value, transactions, and the digital identities tracked to each transaction.

In particular, when Nakamota released bitcoin, he (assuming the pronoun *he* for ease of writing) not only created bitcoin but created an underlying transaction distributed tracking ledger called *blockchain*. Today, blockchain can and is used separately with other cryptocurrencies and with other applications that have nothing to do with bitcoin or any cryptocurrency.

A blockchain is a distributed, decentralized ledger (i.e., database or list of records) for tracking and verifying individual or collections of transactions. Each individual transaction tracked may be stored in a separate transaction "block," or multiple transactions may be stored together within a single block. The number of transactions stored per block and what a transaction represents depends on the implementation. An individual block contains the transaction information (it can be any information as defined by the application, including just a hash of the required transaction information) and at least one cryptographic hash result, along with any other required information. Figure 4.1 represents a common blockchain format.

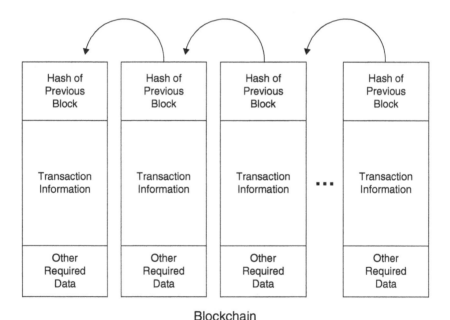

Blockchain

Figure 4.1 Graphical representation of a common blockchain format

A hash is a cryptographic result of any content manipulated using a cryptographic hash algorithm. The output result of a hash manipulation is known as a *hash result* or, confusingly, also known as a *hash*. A hash result is unique per unique input. Thus, if two analyzed inputs create the same hash result, the two inputs are very likely identical, and vice versa. Any different inputs will create different hash results. Hash results, or hashes, are used to cryptographically prove or disprove that two compared contents are either identical or not. Hashes are used throughout computers and digital transactions to prove or disprove the integrity of two different compared contents. Common hash algorithms are represented as SHA2, RIPEMD-160, NT, BCRYPT, etc. Blockchains uses hashes to verify the integrity of past transactions.

The "chain" of the blockchain refers to the fact that the hash of the previous block is stored in the next block, which is then hashed and stored in the next block, and so on. This makes each subsequent block "hooked" by hashing to the previous block in such a way that all blocks in the blockchain are cryptographically linked to each other. You cannot easily tamper with any block without also modifying every subsequent block (because the hash of the tampered block would change). It's a pretty strong (although not perfect) protection for preventing the tampering of previous transactions.

Bitcoin is the first cryptocurrency and also the first to use a distributed, peer-to-peer blockchain to keep track of transactions. There are a few different bitcoin blockchains (*forks*) where the individual value is stored for the involved blockchain, and transactions for the blockchain are tracked. Each bitcoin fork has its own separate blockchain that its participants use. The most common one used today with the most value (equivalent to hundreds of billions of dollars in today's pricing in August 2021) is associated with the BTC trading symbol. When most people say "bitcoin," it is this version they are usually referring to. It is also the cryptocurrency most ransomware gangs use to collect the ransom.

BTC was valued at $884 billion at the day of this writing (August 2021). You can track bitcoin's overall value at several places including https://bitcoin.info/.

Every bitcoin participant has a bitcoin blockchain "address." The address is the participant's public key from an associated asymmetric, private/public key pair. Ownership or knowledge of a particular private key allows the holder to conduct secure transactions on a blockchain. The participant's public key, which can be known by anyone, can be used to verify the private key user's transactions.

Every participant can have one or more addresses, but those addresses are the key to the participant's store of value on the blockchain. If the private key owner loses control of (or the ability to use) their private key (by losing or losing sole ownership of their private key), they cannot conduct future secure transactions, cash out value, or even prove their ownership of the existing value stored on the blockchain. If they lose their private key (i.e., address), their "money" is essentially gone. If someone else learns a victim's private key, they can steal the victim's cryptocurrency.

The participant's blockchain address is their identity on the blockchain. In bitcoin and most other cryptocurrencies, a person's real identity is not tied to the blockchain address in any way. This is why digital criminals prefer to use cryptocurrencies to ask for and receive ransoms. If they are careful, then it is extremely hard to impossible to tie a blockchain transaction to anyone's real identity.

Any participant can send or receive bitcoin value using the participant's bitcoin address. Each transaction is recorded using the participant's address into the blockchain. Every participant can download part of or the entire blockchain. At this time, the BTC blockchain is many, many gigabytes in size. But any participant can load a bitcoin client and instruct it to download the entire blockchain to their local computer/device. Each transaction on the blockchain can be viewed or verified by any participant.

Different cryptocurrencies and applications work in different ways, but they all usually have the feature that allows any participant to view part or all of the blockchain and to verify transactions.

For More Information on Bitcoin and Blockchains

Any reader interested in learning more about bitcoin, block-chain, and how transactions are recorded, tracked, and veri-fied, for bitcoin and other popular cryptocurrencies should check out *Investigating Cryptocurrencies: Understanding, Extracting, and Analyzing Blockchain Evidence* by Nick Furneaux (`https://www.wiley.com/en-us/Investigating+Cryptocurrencies%3A+Understanding%2C+Extracting%2C+and+Analyzing+Blockchain+Evidence-p-9781119480563`).

Where blockchain becomes useful to investigators is that any participant, including investigators, can see what transactions and value went to what address. Thus, any ransom paid is paid to a particular blockchain address, and everyone, including the investigator, can see where, when, and how much. Most ransomware extortion demands will include text that indicates what cryptocurrency and blockchain address must be used to pay the ransom. Figure 4.2 shows the bitcoin address displayed by NotPetya from Figure 1.2 in Chapter 1.

Figure 4.2 The bitcoin address used by NotPetya

Although NotPetya was wiperware (e.g., designed solely for data destruction) and not ransomware, the typical ransomware extortion instruction looks very similar. Sometimes the ransomware extortion instruction tells the victim to instead email the ransomware gang on some predefined email address or chat channel to get the details, but somewhere along the way the victim gets a blockchain address to send the value to. It is how the ransomware gang gets paid.

Ransomware gangs will often have multiple blockchain addresses, although increasing the number of addresses adds complexity to their operations. It would be like any regular person having more than one or a few bank accounts. You can do it, but it often starts to add more complexity than it's worth to your financial life. Some ransomware gangs will have a unique bitcoin address for every ransomware victim or affiliate, but most only use a few addresses they share among all victims. And some have only a single blockchain address shared to all victims or all victims within a particular period of time or geographic location. If you can get the addresses tied to a particular ransomware demand or shared address used by a ransomware gang, you can track the ransoms paid to that gang and possibly when they "cash out" their ill-gotten goods.

There are many organizations, including specialized blockchain tracking companies, such as Chainalysis (`https://www.chainalysis.com/`) and Elliptic (`https://www.elliptic.co/`), law enforcement agencies, cybersecurity insurance companies, etc., that specifically track ransoms paid to particular ransomware addresses. You can read stories about "x" amount of ransom was paid by "x" number of victims in "such-and-such" period of time.

Any one person, including you, can follow and research individual ransomware payments made on blockchains as long as you know the payment address(es). This is because all transactions can be tracked on most blockchains, including the ones used by ransomware gangs. Here's an example of cryptocurrency tracking company, Elliptic, following the bitcoin ransoms paid by Colonial Pipeline and other Darkside ransomware victims (`https://www.elliptic.co/blog/elliptic-follows-bitcoin-ransoms-paid-by-darkside-ransomware-victims`). Figure 4.3 shows a graphical representation by Elliptic of the ransom paid via bitcoin to the Darkside ransomware group.

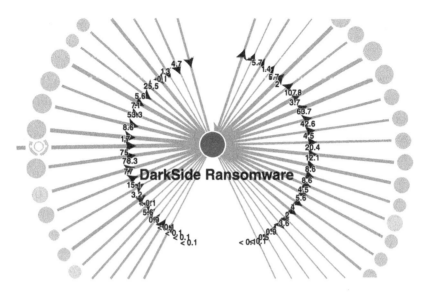

Figure 4.3 Elliptic's graphical representation of the ransom paid via bitcoin to the Darkside ransomware group

Ironically for the ransomware gangs, the cryptographic protection that makes the blockchain "secure" and makes transactions difficult to tamper with also means that who (by address) gets what can be tracked with fairly great accuracy. The great security of a blockchain can be an identity undoing for a criminal, if law enforcement or investigators can learn what real identity is using a particular blockchain address. For example, the bitcoin money movers for the Clop ransomware gang were identified and arrested in June 2021 (https://www.bleepingcomputer.com/news/security/ukraine-arrests-clop-ransomware-gang-members-seizes-servers).

If law enforcement or an investigator learns the private key associated with a particular blockchain address, they can simply take the participant's address (and the stored value) as their own. This also happens from time to time. You will read stories where law enforcement was able to stop or re-claim money sent to a ransomware gang. For example, with the Colonial Pipeline ransomware incident, the

US FBI was able to recover $2.3 million in paid ransom (https://
fintechzoom.com/fintech_news_cryptocurrency-news/u-s-seizes-
2-3-mln-in-bitcoin-paid-to-colonial-pipeline-hackers/).

Of course, ransomware gangs don't like to have their transactions tracked even when their real identities are not known.
As covered previously in Chapter 1, ransomware criminals are
known to move their cryptocurrency transactions into intermedi-
ate addresses, where the incoming transferred value can be shuffled
and "lost" among a bunch of other unrelated incoming transactions
and then transferred out, using one or more transactions, into other
waiting blockchain addresses. There are many services, known as
laundering, *mixing*, *fogging* or *tumbling*, that do as their primary or
partial business. They usually take a substantial percentage fee of
the transactions for the digital money laundering.

Ways Cybercriminals Can Cash Out Their Ill-Gotten Gains

The article "Bitcoin Money Laundering: How Criminals
Use Crypto" summarizes common ways cybercriminals
using bitcoin can cash out their ill-gotten gains. You can
find the article at https://www.elliptic.co/blog/bitcoin-
money-laundering.

It is common for ransomware thieves to use bitcoin fogging
as a way of providing additional protection to themselves. Law
enforcement and trackers can often identify foggers because of
the large number or amount of seemingly unrelated transactions
being transferred into a common address and then a bunch of different transactions (in both size and amount) coming out the other
side. Occasionally, a fogger slips up, gets identified by law enforcement, and ends up arrested, as seen in the example "Feds Arrest an
Alleged $336M Bitcoin-Laundering Kingpin" (https://www.wired
.com/story/bitcoin-fog-dark-web-cryptocurrency-arrest/).

Bitcoin and other cryptocurrencies have both advantages and disadvantages for ransomware criminals to use. The advantages clearly outweigh the disadvantages, but law enforcement and defensive mitigations are trying to narrow the gap. There are even repeated attempts by many to outlaw bitcoin and other cryptocurrencies that are heavily associated with illegality, including ransomware. Those parties are calling for a more heavily regulated type of cryptocurrency that would make it harder for criminals to use. It is unclear if these types of initiatives will gain support or if they would be effective in decreasing ransomware if they did become law.

Can You Be in Legal Jeopardy for Paying a Ransom?

It's a rarity in the realm of victimhood that trying to best recover from criminal damage could put the victim and their helpers in legal jeopardy. But that's exactly what is possible in some countries, including the United States. On October 1, 2020, the US Department of the Treasury's Office of Foreign Assets Control (OFAC) released a memo (`https://home.treasury.gov/system/files/126/ofac_ransomware_advisory_10012020_1.pdf`) specifically addressing the threat of potential legal issues for people and organizations who pay ransomware ransom and their helpers. Figure 4.4 shows the beginning of the OFAC memo.

DEPARTMENT OF THE TREASURY
WASHINGTON, D.C. 20220

Advisory on Potential Sanctions Risks for Facilitating Ransomware Payments[1]

Date: October 1, 2020

The U.S. Department of the Treasury's Office of Foreign Assets Control (OFAC) is issuing this advisory to highlight the sanctions risks associated with ransomware payments related to malicious cyber-enabled activities. Demand for ransomware payments has increased during the COVID-19 pandemic as cyber actors target online systems that U.S. persons rely on to continue conducting business. Companies that facilitate ransomware payments to cyber actors on behalf of victims, including financial institutions, cyber insurance firms, and companies involved in digital forensics and incident response, not only encourage future ransomware payment demands but also may risk violating OFAC regulations. This advisory describes these sanctions risks and provides information for contacting relevant U.S. government agencies, including OFAC, if there is a reason to believe the cyber actor demanding ransomware payment may be sanctioned or otherwise have a sanctions nexus.[2]

Figure 4.4   Start of OFAC memo stating that paying ransomware could be illegal for the victim to do

US law enforcement has always officially recommended that no one pay the ransom. After all, it only encourages cybercriminals to do more ransomware. But never before did any law enforcement agency, in the United States or elsewhere, imply there could be legal consequences for the victims of ransomware who pay the ransom or for anyone who helps them (even if not at all involved in paying the ransom). In the United States and other countries, it has always been illegal to send money, help, or other things of value to the listed "banned" countries and individuals. This is what the OFAC memo is referring or reminding people of. It explicitly states the following (using selected statements from the memo):

> "OFAC has designated numerous malicious cyber actors under its cyber-related sanctions program and other sanctions programs, including perpetrators of ransomware attacks and those who facilitate ransomware transactions . . . Facilitating a ransomware payment that is demanded as a result of malicious cyber activities may enable criminals and adversaries with a sanctions nexus to profit and advance their illicit aims . . . U.S. persons are generally prohibited from engaging in transactions, directly or indirectly, with individuals or entities ("persons") on OFAC's Specially Designated Nationals and Blocked Persons List (SDN List). . .OFAC may impose civil penalties for sanctions violations based on strict liability, meaning that a person subject to U.S. jurisdiction may be held civilly liable even if it did not know or have reason to know it was engaging in a transaction with a person that is prohibited under sanctions laws and regulations administered by OFAC."

The memo is pretty inclusive, stating that even computer people/organizations only providing recovery and forensic services could have legal liability, too. The OFAC memo states the following:

> "This also applies to companies that engage with victims of ransomware attacks, such as those involved in providing cyber insurance, digital forensics and incident response, and financial services that may involve processing ransom payments (including depository institutions and money services businesses)."

So, any company providing even recovery services could get in legal jeopardy by simply trying to help the victim company recover from a ransomware attack, even if none of the parties had reason to know the ransomware group they were dealing with was on a banned list. It's pretty frightening. To be clear, the US government and OFAC are simply restating what has already been the law and is just clarifying that, yes, it does also apply to ransomware incidents. Simply providing the reminding "clarification" sent shockwaves through the communities where it applies (which is any organization that could be hit by ransomware, involved with recovering from ransomware, and their legal counsels).

Innocent Parties

Most interpretations of the OFAC memo think if a vendor is not involved in any manner in assisting with processing of ransom payments (e.g., solely providing recovery/restoration services), there is no potential legal jeopardy for that vendor even if the victim ultimately pursues payment with an OFAC sanctioned entity directly or via another entity.

The idea that ransomware groups could be on a banned list isn't some futuristic worry. The memo lists many examples of ransomware groups or people who are on the banned list, including the following:

- Evgeniy Mikhailovich Bogachev, the developer of Cryptolocker
- Two Iranians for providing material support to a malicious cyber activity and identified two digital currency addresses used to funnel SamSam ransomware proceeds
- The North Korean Lazarus Group, behind the WannaCry ransomware, and two subgroups, Bluenoroff and Andariel

Other countries and even individual states in the United States have proposed legislation that would ban paying the ransom, for example:

https://www.csoonline.com/article/3622888/four-states-propose-laws-to-ban-ransomware-payments.html. Many regulatory agencies with the ability to levy fines have also recommended against paying ransomware extortions.

All of this begs the question, "Can you (a US organization) be punished for paying a ransom?" The short answer: yes.

The US government doesn't go out of their way to provide "clarification" lightly. Someone is sending a legal reminder for a reason. And if you show this memo to any lawyer, they will reach the same conclusion: that serious legal jeopardy can result from paying a ransom or helping to recover from a ransomware event if it was related to the payment.

There are some offsetting points, although neither is very impactful from a legal point of view. The first is, I do not know of a single entity who simply paid a ransomware ransom or helped recover from a ransomware event that was legally fined or prosecuted. There have been cases where individuals who helped the ransomware gang get paid and were seen more as agents of the ransomware purveyors, that were charged with crimes. But I'm unaware of any ransomware victim or helper of that victim, with no alignment to the criminals, who have been charged with a crime or fined for paying a ransom or helping someone recover from a ransomware event. Second, I don't think it would look great for any legal entity, even if allowed, to prosecute a victim or their helpers for trying to best recover from their situation, especially if they did not know the organization or person they were paying were on a banned list. This latter point is especially important because the use of cryptocurrencies often makes identifying the receiver hard to impossible.

Those are two important, potentially offsetting, defense claims, but they really don't mean much in the legal world. There's always a "first" for every prosecution under a particular law, and what looks "fair" is not what the law is only concerned about. Law students spend most of their time studying court case decisions where the seemingly "fair" outcome was not what happened.

Author's Perspective on the "Fairness" of Law

I took two law classes in college as part of my accounting degree, and I remember a good rule of thumb I used when taking exams when I didn't know the right answer to a case law question. It was to pick the case outcome that seemed the least fair to any reasonable, non-law, objective, person who read it. I got As in all my law courses. It seemed to me that a big part of legal education is to teach law students that "fair" isn't always what it first seems.

Consult with a Lawyer

Ahead of time, you should consult with a lawyer about these issues so that if your organization gets hit by ransomware, your lawyers will have consulted all the needed legal resources and developed an informed opinion to guide your organization's ransomware responses. You don't want to be hit by a ransomware event and then have to be asking for legal opinions under a very tight time schedule. With that said, most organizations hit by ransomware have not done so ahead of time. If hit by ransomware, get rapid but good legal advice.

Try to Follow the Money

Even though OFAC states ". . .even if [victim] did not know or have reason to know it was engaging in a transaction with a person that is prohibited under sanctions laws and regulations administered by OFAC [victim can still be liable]," it can't hurt to see if a particular ransomware group that is requesting ransom is on one of the known "banned lists." As stated earlier, there are businesses that offer this type of service, including blockchain tracking companies, like Elliptic (www.elliptic.co). Some cyber insurance firms and underwriters, like CFC Underwriting (www.cfcunderwriting.com), offer this service as part of their cybersecurity insurance policies and services.

Get Law Enforcement Involved

Getting law enforcement involved is a double-edged mitigation, and the decision to do so should be left to senior management and legal. Usually getting law enforcement involved is a good thing. They typically offer good advice and recommendations. However, law enforcement has the legal right to do many things, potentially against your wishes, if they want, such as seize assets, investigate people, forbid transactions, etc. When you invite law enforcement to get involved in your cybersecurity incident, you are inviting a risk that they could force a particular decision not wanted by the victim or their organization.

But there is a particularly good reason for inviting law enforcement in the United States to get involved. The OFAC memo also states the following:

> "Under OFAC's Enforcement Guidelines, OFAC will also consider a company's self-initiated, timely, and complete report of a ransomware attack to law enforcement to be a significant mitigating factor in determining an appropriate enforcement outcome if the situation is later determined to have a sanctions nexus. OFAC will also consider a company's full and timely cooperation with law enforcement both during and after a ransomware attack to be a significant mitigating factor when evaluating a possible enforcement outcome."

For US organizations, involving US law enforcement agencies and/or the US Cybersecurity Infrastructure Security Agency (CISA) can help with an organization's case only if they come under legal threat for paying a ransom.

Get an OFAC License to Pay the Ransom

US victims can also apply for an OFAC "license" to try to get approved to pay a ransom, although OFAC states there is a "presumption of denial." You'll have to let your lawyers tell you what path and actions to take if you get hit by a ransomware incident.

Do Your Due Diligence

The best advice anyone can give you is to get a good legal opinion on the matter and do your due diligence. Although I don't know of any organization or person prosecuted simply for paying a ransomware extortion payment (with no other illegal ties or involvement with the ransomware organization), you don't want to become the first "test case." Don't be the organization that becomes the first to be prosecuted or penalized for paying the ransom. Don't become a headline. Do your due diligence.

Your Ransom Payment May Be Tax Deductible

Some US tax experts think US organizations paying the ransom, legally, may be able to deduct it on their taxes (https://www.securityweek.com/hit-ransomware-attack-your-payment-may-be-deductible).

Is It an Official Data Breach?

Not every ransomware incident becomes a data breach. Not even every ransomware attack involving data exfiltration is an "official" data breach. The data stolen may not have been one of the regulatory defined data types (e.g., PII, PHI, etc.) or covered under another obligatory protection contract. But most organizations fall under some sort of data governance/privacy laws or contracts that require public and private reporting when defined protected data is breached. Part of any ransomware incident is to determine whether the incident constitutes an official breach that must be reported to someone outside the organization and handled in the prescribed, required manner. Let your lawyers make that determination if your organization is possibly covered under one of these data breach reporting laws or contracts.

Preserve Evidence

If there is a chance that involved resources could be used as part of a forensics investigation, a legal matter, or regulatory finding, you should preserve all evidence. When in doubt, preserve all evidence. This means, at the very least, making forensic copies of all hard drives (and possibly memory) of all involved resources. Doing this is the right thing to do in most cases, even if legal and regulatory issues are not going to be involved. Many ransomware victims asked questions later that they could not answer because they had destroyed the original evidence in their zeal to quickly recover. Ransomware encryption keys are sometimes found in computer memory. You don't want to wipe out the chance to recover your data without having to pay a criminal for the key.

Legal Defense Summary

In summary, to lessen the risk of getting penalized for paying a ransomware extortion payment or for being involved in a recovery, do your due diligence.

If you're a ransomware victim:

- Get your legal team engaged in this issue (if possible, ahead of time) so they can do the research and give you a well-researched opinion on how to handle legal exposure from a ransomware event.

- If hit by ransomware, immediately get your legal team involved.
- Let your legal team make all outside contact with others regarding the incident so communications are more likely to be covered under legal privileged communication laws.
- Try to determine whether the ransomware group is on a "banned" watch list.
- Involve the appropriate law enforcement agency and follow their guidance.
- Consider getting an OFAC "license" if you plan to pay a ransomware extortion demand.
- When in doubt, consider not paying a ransomware extortion demand.
- Determine whether you need to preserve evidence, and if unsure, preserve the evidence.
- Determine whether an official data breach event has happened, and if so, how to respond.

If you assist a victim with ransomware recovery or payment:

- Get good legal counsel to examine the ways and methods to reduce your legal exposure, including the necessary contract language.
- Get a good understanding if the victim has done their legal due diligence regarding the ransomware event to mitigate your own risk exposure.
- Do not assist with ransomware recovery or payment if due diligence is not performed by the victim.

Summary

Chapter 4 discussed the potential legal ramifications if an organization or person assists with ransomware recovery or payment. Much of the chapter is focused on the legality of paying a ransom and using bitcoin in general. There are other legal questions your legal team needs to answer such as if an official data breach has happened, and if so, what needs to be done to address it. Chapter 5 discusses what should be in a ransomware response plan.

Part II

Detection and Recovery

Chapter 5

Ransomware Response Plan

In this chapter, we discuss how to create a detailed ransomware response plan, including why do it at all, when to do it, and what it should include. Many of the items summarized here will be covered in more detail in the later chapters.

Why Do Response Planning?

Why should any organization create a ransomware response plan? In one short sentence: to save time and money. Since at least 2020, well over a third to over a half of all surveyed organizations have been successfully exploited by ransomware in a given year. This means the likelihood of any organization being successfully attacked in a given year by ransomware is pretty high. Somewhere around half of organizations recognize the initial ransomware attack before it has been able to encrypt all the targeted data, although some organizations still end up paying because of the data exfiltration threats.

Organizations that aggressively and specifically prepare for ransomware attacks have a better chance of preventing ransomware, have a better chance of more quickly recognizing ransomware, and may be able to recover far more quickly and at lower cost than those organizations that do not. Creating and practicing a ransomware plan likely means faster detection, faster response times, lower damage costs, faster back to operation times, and less legal liability.

When Should a Response Plan Be Made?

When should you make a ransomware response plan? Now, before ransomware has successfully exploited your environment. If you don't have a ransomware response plan, start to create one with a goal of having one as soon as possible. There is almost no other threat with the high risk of compromising your environment that will cause as much damage. If you don't have a ransomware response plan, time is of the essence. Begin now. I can assure you that every ransomware victim without a ransomware response plan in place when they got exploited wishes they had a plan in place before the event. Decisions made ahead of time, when more thoughtful analysis can be applied, are more likely to produce beneficial outcomes than those made under duress for the first time. If nothing else, a ransomware response plan is a great enterprise-wide education tool. At its best, it's specific, prescriptive, guidance that supports and improves on your more general business continuity/disaster recovery and incident response plans.

What Should a Response Plan Include?

A ransomware response plan needs to have the key people, policies, tools, decisions, and processes necessary to respond to a ransomware attack. This section discusses what should be included in a ransomware response plan.

Store Your Ransomware Response Plan Offline

It is critical to keep copies of your ransomware response plan offline but accessible to all the people who need to be involved in a ransomware response event. Assume your online data and systems are encrypted and normal communications (e.g., email, instant messaging, etc.) are down.

Small Response vs. Large Response Threshold

Not every ransomware event compromises large or mission-critical parts of the organization. Many ransomware events are caught before the biggest damage has been done. A single, compromised device, unless it disrupts mission-critical operations, often will not lead to a full response. Ransomware caught by antivirus/EDR before it's had time to execute will usually not lead to a full ransomware response event. Perhaps a few compromised machines will lead to a quick check to see whether more computers are compromised, but the full ransomware team is not needed unless the initial check confirms more compromises. What is the necessary threshold that would be require so that the full ransomware response plan is initiated? Every plan should include the threshold that must be met before the entire ransomware response, according to plan, needs to happen. No need to go big for small events.

Key People

Your ransomware response plan needs to identify, ahead of time, all the people and teams that will need to be involved in a ransomware response event. Recommended roles include the following:

- Team leader
- Senior management

- Legal representative
- IT personnel
- IT security personnel
- Ransomware subject matter expert
- Help desk
- Incident response
- Public relations (for internal and external communications)
- Outside consultants, as needed
- Law enforcement, as needed
- Cybersecurity insurance contact person, if involved

In smaller organizations, many of these roles could be represented by one person or filled by external resources. The objective is to identify all the roles and people needed, ahead of time, and let them know about the ransomware response plan, its objectives, and how they need to plan to set aside time to review, approve, and practice it. Ensure that everyone is aware of the role they might play, the responsibilities they may have in the event of a ransomware incident, and their need to participate in future practice sessions.

Communications Plan

This is a critical part of the plan. It's no surprise that many of the worst outcomes have been described as due to poor communications. So, plan ahead. The first communications objective that needs to be decided on is how everyone will access the ransomware response plan if it is needed. Assume every device in the environment is compromised and/or out of commission. Is the ransomware response plan printed out and physically stored at each participant's home? If so, can you ensure that each participant gets updated copies any time it is updated? Is it stored on another online storage site not connected to the organization's main environment that all participants can be guaranteed to be able to access if the organization device they normally use is down?

Should Your Ransomware Response Plan Be Stored Online at All?

It is known that some ransomware gangs often spend time wandering around victim networks, looking for useful information to both read and exfiltrate. They might come across your ransomware response plan. So, it makes sense for you to remove any online copies of the plan so that your adversary doesn't learn how you plan to respond to their attack. If you don't store it offline only, make sure that it is not easily accessible to the ransomware gang, such as by using encryption with the decryption keys stored offline.

How will the team members be notified of a ransomware event? Again, your network and normal communication channels may be down. I suggest you plan on using phones if you have no better method. Get everyone's phone number listed in the plan or collected in a separate document (and keep them up-to-date).

Keep the Plan Updated

A ransomware response plan will need to be updated on a regular basis and/or as needed. At the least, contact information will need to be updated as people and roles change. Procedures, processes, and tools may need to be updated. Plan on your plan being regularly updated. Whose responsibility is it to ensure that it gets done? How is it done? Don't make a great plan and then leave it alone until it's needed. Great incident response plans are "living" documents—cared for and updated.

Is separate meeting space needed? Most teams will be able to meet in the regular business space their organization uses normally. But I have been involved in malicious hacking events where the normal meeting space was compromised in a way that made it risky to use. In some of the cases, the IP phone system or remote meeting software was compromised so that the attackers could monitor the ongoing meetings. If this is a concern, set up a safe, external, meeting area; or just assume all meetings will be held remotely using a safe and secure communication method.

Many incident response plans, including ransomware response plans, define alternate physical meeting spaces or instruct everyone to connect to one of the defined initial responders to learn what the communication's method is going to be. Then, everyone can be on the same page and using the same recommended communication's tool.

It is likely that a separate online communication's channel be established ahead of time so team members can send each other information and updates. It should likely not be your normal email system or devices. Choose an external, online communication channel everyone can use. For example, company-specific Microsoft Office 365 or Gmail accounts not accessed using the normal corporate methods can be used as alternate communication channels. Many response teams go so far as to buy new devices and network equipment that all team members must use for a response event.

Let Legal Be the Outside Communicator

Legal counsel should communicate to all external entities regarding the ransomware event to protect as much of the communications as possible with client-attorney privilege.

Public Relations Plan

A bad ransomware event will significantly impact operations. You will need to communicate to employees, customers, other stakeholders, regulators, and potentially the "public" through direct contact and media channels. You will need to decide what to communicate to whom and when. Get a public relations (PR) team involved in your plan ahead of time and get their input on how to handle communications for each audience. They should mock-up some rough templates for each type of audience. Legal counsel, of course, needs to review all communications (ideally beforehand as mocked up as examples) and work hand in hand with PR. They should plan on how to communicate if all the normal systems are down.

I've routinely seen ransomware victims take days to publicly acknowledge that anything has happened. A big part of this is that all their systems and normal communication methods are down, and they did not plan ahead for that happening. Oftentimes, the only clue to the outside world that something is wrong is the victim's lack of communications to anyone. No one from the victim organization is responding to emails. Sometimes even the phone systems are down. The website is often kicking out 404 ("Not Found") error messages, or worse, they contain taunting and ominous messages from the ransomware gang. Customers and people understand that communicating with them may not be your first-order priority in the middle of a bad ransomware event, but how much better would it be if some thoughtful initial communication messages were ready to send out if you needed them?

What information to confirm and when is a big piece of the puzzle. You want to be honest and transparent in what you communicate. You want to be timely (definitely meeting and perhaps exceeding regulatory requirements). You want to communicate enough, but not too much. Never lie, over promise, or paint as fact something that is not confirmed. At the same time, short, terse messages lacking real information are rarely comforting to external parties and may even seem like the victim is hiding something. Plan on communicating at least a few paragraphs of information in the initial response. Typically, that response should come from the organizational leader (i.e., CEO).

Since employee personal information and credentials are often compromised by ransomware, think about how to deal with that outcome, especially if the ransom is not paid. Some employees may feel that the organization didn't care about them enough and decided to sacrifice employee personal information in favor of profits. You'll need to reassure employees and counter any ransomware gang narrative to the contrary. If you didn't pay the ransom and employee information was stolen, explain why. If employee personal information is stolen, consider offering free credit monitoring services for a year, or some other goodwill effort that employees will respect.

Reliable Backup

Even though a backup alone will not usually mitigate all the damage caused by most ransomware programs, a reliable, thorough, tested, offline, up-to-date backup must be a critical requirement. Unfortunately, far more organizations believe they have good backups than actually have good backups. Your organization needs to confirm it has a good backup. It needs to be comprehensive.

This means to assume a worse-case scenario and that every mission-critical device in your environment is completely encrypted and is no longer functional and/or has secure integrity. This includes servers, workstations, infrastructure services, cloud services, storage devices, front-end devices, middleware, databases, web servers, and so on.

Most organizations that say they have reliable backups either don't have this sort of comprehensive recovery or have never tested a restoration at this scale. Don't let a widespread ransomware event be your only test. Confirm ahead of time that you have a backup and restoration plan that guarantees secure and reliable restoration in a timely manner. The backup must be up-to-date. How much data can you stand to lose or have to recreate? The backup must be protected, which means storing it truly offline or at least protecting it so that a ransomware gang cannot impact it.

Many victims are convinced they have a secure, reliable, and timely backup. However, they didn't understand that if they, the legitimate holders, had online access to their backup storage, so, too, can an attacker. There are a large percentage of victims who were utterly convinced their backups were safe and reliable and, when successfully exploited, learned this was not the case. Attackers will absolutely try to delete or encrypt backups just before the encryption routine is started on live systems. I've even known victims who had their backup encryption keys unknowingly changed by ransomware gangs so that when the victim tried to restore what they thought was a good backup, it would not restore.

Many cloud services and cloud storage services claim they can protect customers from ransomware attacks. Many can, but probably even more do not. Confirm that your cloud provider(s) can restore all data and services in the case of an impacted ransomware event.

Confirm you have a reliable backup. This means all organizations should actually perform a comprehensive test restoration in a simulated environment. This takes planning, resources, time, and often money. Doing a truly reliable, comprehensive, test backup and restore isn't easy or cheap. But if you care about having a chance that your data can be restored—perhaps you get hit by wiperware and not "just" ransomware—you need to ensure you can restore every potentially impacted system in a timely manner. Some people who pay the ransom still do not recover any of their data. Most victims don't recover all their data, even if they pay the ransom.

People who pay the ransom have a better chance of recovering more data than those who do not pay the ransom.

Regardless of the threat of ransomware, it has always been a requirement that organizations have a secure, reliable backup for any data restoration need. Prior to ransomware, having a good backup was needed just for regular disaster recovery events (e.g., weather, fires, flooding, equipment failure, etc.). The need for a restoration due to those events was fairly rare. Ransomware has changed the need and likelihood for the average organization to have to restore one or more systems. Your ransomware response plan should include how a reliable, secure, comprehensive backup and tested restoration is performed. More importantly, the restoration should actually be tested, at least once per year, if not more frequently.

Ransom Payment Planning

One of the most important decisions any organization can make ahead of time is whether or not to pay the ransom. No one wants to pay an extortion demand, although many organizations, rightly, see it as cheaper and faster to pay the ransom. Some organizations ethically refuse to pay a ransom. Others are regulatory or legally forbidden from paying a ransom. There is no guarantee that paying a ransom will result in any data recovery, much less total recovery. Most ransomware exfiltrates data and credentials so that a data restoration alone will not mitigate all the damage. So, with all of that said, will your organization ever pay the ransom? This is a question with a binary answer: yes or no.

There are many organizations that claim they will never pay a ransom that, once exploited, end up paying the ransom. So, the first step is to determine if your organization will ever pay a ransom. If the answer is that the organization will absolutely never pay the ransom, this needs to be factored into your planning and communications planning process. I've seen many individuals lauded for not paying the ransom, even if it caused longer downtime and far more resources versus what paying the ransom would have done. Just make sure that senior management agrees with whatever decision is made. It is usually not IT's ultimate responsibility to determine whether ransomware extortion should be paid. It's up to senior management and the legal team.

Critical Communication About Ransomware Extortion

It is critical that senior management and legal counsel understand a data backup will not likely mitigate all ransomware damage. Most people when they hear of ransomware think only of encryption threats. Explain to them that critical data and (employee and customer) credential exfiltration are likely to be involved. They need to clearly understand all the potential damages involved and then make their informed decisions.

It is common for organizations to be open to paying a ransom, if needed. They will determine whether they may or may not pay the ransom depending on the scenario. The key is to determine if paying the ransom ever, regardless of issues, is a possibility. If it isn't, then it needs to be communicated to everyone involved, and that decision will significantly impact remediation and the ransomware response plan.

If paying the ransom is a possibility, then deciding ahead of time what circumstances and facts will cause the ransom to be paid versus not is helpful, including the following:

- Is the ransomware involved known to provide successful decryption if the ransom is paid?
- Can the victim organization withstand data and credential exfiltration risk or potential outcomes without paying the ransom?
- Is it legal for the victim to pay the ransom? How can the victim confirm legality?
- What is the maximum amount of ransom that will ever be paid?

- How quickly can a victim organization raise the amount of money being requested?
- How will the ransom be paid?
- Will insurance cover the cost of the ransom?
- Will you use a professional negotiator or not?

Most of the experienced and knowledgeable ransomware recovery experts will tell you that every ransomware event is unique, but each ransomware gang has its modes of operation and requirements. Ransomware responders want to first establish what ransomware program and ransomware gang is involved. Some of the ransomware programs and gangs are highly unreliable even when the ransom is paid, and the experts will recommend the ransom not be paid. Most recovery experts will recommend paying the ransom if you want the quickest and lowest-cost recovery. Can you trust restoring encrypted systems as being safe after the recovery? Can you trust the ransomware gang to delete or not publish exfiltrated data and credentials? All of these types of questions and decisions need to be considered and answered ahead of time. You don't want to consider what your ransomware extortion policies are during the heat of a huge downtime event. Thinking about what you will and won't do ahead of time will make the response to a ransomware event slightly more predictable.

Cybersecurity Insurance Plan

Will your organization get cybersecurity insurance or not? For years, the percentage of organizations getting cybersecurity insurance was increasing. There were terrific benefits to both the victim company and the insurance industry for doing so. Sadly, the terrible "success" of ransomware has led to a drastic increase in premiums, higher deductibles, less coverage, and less options. Cybersecurity insurance may not be the financial benefit that it once was. Still, I recommend every organization consider cybersecurity insurance and decide ahead of time whether they wish to purchase it. See Chapter 3, "Cybersecurity Insurance," for more details.

If you get cybersecurity insurance:

- Make sure it covers ransomware.
- Store any cybersecurity insurance policy offline or away from a potential ransomware adversary easily accessing it if in control of your environment.
- Make sure you have the necessary contact information, in case of a ransomware event, saved for easy access.
- Figure out how it impacts your ransomware payment decision.

What It Takes to Declare an Official Data Breach

There are laws and regulations that have mandated requirements if an official data breach happens. Most organizations don't want to declare that an official data breach has happened if not required legally. It used to be easier for a victim to say a data breach did not officially happen when ransomware only, mostly, encrypted files (although even then how anyone said a data breach didn't happen for sure is questionable). These days the overwhelming percentage of ransomware exfiltrates data, and that clearly raises the odds that a data breach event did happen.

As covered earlier, not every exfiltration of data meets the legal definition of what has to be reported as an official data breach. The stolen data may not have been a covered and defined type of data that meets a data breach definition (e.g., PII, PHI, etc.) or is not covered under a contract requiring protection. There is also a chance that what was stolen wasn't that serious. I've had more than a few ransomware victims tell me what was stolen was either old or not crucial. Oftentimes, they sighed in relief because the truly critical and valuable data was not taken.

Decide ahead of time what factors will make your organization officially declare that a data breach has happened. If a data breach is detected/declared, what is the maximum amount of time that can go by before the victim organization is required to report it, and to whom must it be reported? Again, senior management and legal need to make this decision.

Internal vs. External Consultants

Who will you involve in a ransomware event? Will you handle it using all internal staff, or will you involve external resources? If you use external resources, then who will they be? If you have cybersecurity insurance, are you required to use the resources they dictate, or are the recovery resources just recommended? Will you use a single resource or use different groups for different involved technologies and services?

My recommendation is to ensure that whoever you involve has proven experience in successfully responding to ransomware events. Pick a ransomware response coordinator ahead of time, and let them have the necessary people required to minimize damage, considering budget constraints, of course. You don't want to respond to ransomware on your own or use an external group with a lack of experience. You want a proven leader who has been there and done that.

Plan for Compromise

Most ransomware response teams do not have unlimited budgets. Who is involved and what can be accomplished is usually limited by resource constraints and budgets. Even in the best-case scenarios, where the organization involved seemingly has an unlimited budget, there will be constraints (due to timing, availability, etc.). Ransomware incidents often test leaders to make the best decisions they can considering the constraints. Plan for compromises to be made. It's the rare plan put into action that doesn't run into real-world constraints.

No matter who you use as a recovery resource, connect with them ahead of time, before a ransomware event has occurred, to introduce yourself if you do not already have a relationship. Let them know about your ransomware response plan and how you see an incident going and the vendor's responsibility, if they are needed. Of course, many ransomware response experts will tell you how things will proceed, from their perspective, once you contact them. You may even want their input on your ransomware response plan to see if they would add, change, or delete anything.

Cryptocurrency Wallet

If you might pay the ransom, you will need to consider how you might pay it using cryptocurrency—most likely bitcoin. It can be difficult to convert cash into cryptocurrency quickly. Traditional methods include the following:

- Pre-establishing a cryptocurrency account and balance on a cryptocurrency exchange, before one is needed
- Establishing a cryptocurrency account on a cryptocurrency exchange, but only when needed
- Working with a cryptocurrency broker that is willing to sell cryptocurrency "on the fly" when needed
- Working through a broker or negotiator that specializes in ransomware payments who already has the necessary accounts and/or currency

Establishing a cryptocurrency account on a trusted cryptocurrency exchange, like Coinbase (https://www.coinbase.com), can take a day or longer. Moving non-cryptocurrency funds into a cryptocurrency account can take easily take three to five days. Oftentimes, the ransomware gang wants payment within one to seven days, so if you are establishing a cryptocurrency account for the first time, there may be a scheduling problem, and this is on top of whatever latency might have occurred in deciding to pay the ransom. You can decrease some of the wait time by pre-establishing a cryptocurrency account on a trusted exchange. Then you will only be waiting for any necessary change in the amount of cryptocurrency needed in the account.

You can buy cryptocurrency on the fly from someone (check out `https://localbitcoins.com/`, for instance). However, in general, the more quickly you can buy and sell cryptocurrency increases the risk of a fraudulent transaction and/or usually involves higher transaction fees.

Always Use Reliable Cryptocurrency Sources

Unfortunately, the cryptocurrency world is full of frauds and fraudsters. Users have lost many billions of dollars over the last five years. Previously trusted currency exchanges have stolen everyone's money dozens of times. Make sure to only use the top, established, and most trusted cryptocurrency exchanges and traders. Both scammers and victims abound.

If you have a cybersecurity insurance policy, discuss with your insurance broker how any ransomware payment would occur. Would it be their responsibility to help with the payment, or is it solely up to you and your incident response vendors? Some insurance policies provide services on your behalf, such as negotiating and paying ransoms, while others are reimbursement-only. With the latter, your organization is responsible for all the costs associated with recovering from the ransomware and can claim reimbursement after the fact. While cheaper, such an insurance plan requires the organization to keep more money and resources on hand to respond to a ransomware attack.

If you are handling the ransomware payment directly with the ransomware gang, you may need to establish a TOR (The Onion Router) browser (`https://www.torproject.org/`) and secure connection to the ransomware gang's address. Using a TOR browser and connection means you are connecting to the "dark web," which simply means having the ability to access websites and services not accessible on the normal web. While the dark web is full of unethical sites and services, simply connecting there doesn't require any technical protections beyond what you might take with a regular browser session, although connecting from an isolated computer/virtual machine will decrease risk.

Response

The biggest part of your ransomware recovery plan should, of course, be the actual recovery steps. You want to stop the initial spread, limit damage, recover from the event, and prevent it from occurring again. Each of these phases will be covered in detail in Chapters 7 through 11.

Your ransomware recovery response plan should integrate with your existing business continuity/disaster recovery (BC/DR) plans if they exist, fitting into and utilizing the existing policies, procedures, tools, and formats. A ransomware recovery plan is a subset of your normal BC/DR planning.

Checklist

It is always good to have a summary checklist ready to go, which covers all the key points that any participant can quickly reference. Here's a quick checklist example:

- ✓ Confirm ransomware exploitation
- ✓ Does ransomware event require a full incident response and activation of the ransomware response plan? If so, continue:
- ✓ Activate ransomware response plan
- ✓ Notify senior management and other participants
- ✓ Establish alternate communications as planned (if needed)
- ✓ Disconnect potentially involved devices from network, including wireless connections
- ✓ Minimize initial spread and damage (Chapter 7)
- ✓ Start PR communications plan

✓ Determine ransomware strain and research expected behavior (if possible)
✓ Determine the scope of the ransomware exploitation damage
   ✓ Locations, devices, data and systems involved, what's encrypted, data and credential exfiltration, etc.
✓ Contact cybersecurity insurance company, if involved
✓ Contact ransomware response recovery contact
✓ Look for backdoors and other malicious programs
✓ Determine initial damage extent and known consequences
✓ Have initial response meeting(s)
✓ Decide if ransom should be paid; if so, begin negotiations
✓ Begin recovery (Chapters 8 and 9)
✓ Back up encrypted files for mistake recovery/possible future decryption (optional)
✓ Determine initial root-cause infection vector and mitigate
✓ Prioritize system recovery based on business impact assessment/needs
✓ Decide if decryption is possible and desired, if so, begin
✓ Decide if backup restoration is needed, if so, begin
✓ Decide if system recovery or rebuild is needed, if so, begin
✓ If ransom was paid and decryption key received, test on isolated test system
   ✓ If test successful and if decryption using ransomware decryption key is desired, pay ransom, obtain the rest of the keys, and continue
✓ Remove backdoors and other malicious programs
✓ Restore systems to known clean or best trusted state
✓ Change all possibly stolen logon credentials
✓ Continue system decryption/recovery/restoration/rebuild
✓ Fully recover environment
✓ Conduct post-mortem analysis (what was done well, what was done poorly, what should be changed)
✓ Attempt to prevent the next attack (Chapter 10)

This checklist is not detailed, inclusive, or perfectly in order. Each ransomware recovery plan will be custom. Again, Chapters 7 to 11 will cover these steps in more detail.

Definitions

All technical terms and acronyms, such as ransomware, bitcoin, cryptocurrency, cybersecurity insurance, multifactor authentication, patching, phishing, spear phishing, etc., should be described in the plan to ensure all readers of the ransomware response plan have a common understanding of them. Never assume that anyone or everyone understands all terms and acronyms. Definitions can be placed at the beginning or the end of your plan, depending on your organization's preference.

Practice Makes Perfect

A plan isn't nearly as good if it isn't practiced. All involved participants and stakeholders should review the plan draft and recommend additions, changes, and deletions. After the final draft is approved, everyone should review and practice. In most cases, a "tabletop" exercise should be performed, where each participant performs their required role, in order, either in-person or remotely, to give everyone a good sense of the plan.

Some of the most critical roles and procedures should move beyond mere tabletop, mental exercises, and actually be practiced as close to the real processes and tools as possible. For instance, the backup person should do a thorough test restore to prove that a reliable, comprehensive, up-to-date restoration can actually be performed. Forensics tools should be used to ferret out possible malicious programs and actions. Did the contact information allow team members and stakeholders to be contacted in a timely manner, and so on? The more that a ransomware response plan moves beyond the tabletop exercises, the more reliable it can be. The plan should be practiced at least once a year or anytime it has been significantly updated.

Restrain Your Cowboys

Most organizations have one or more super-talented technical people who excel at particular technologies and problem solving. They often, even after agreeing to a plan, will try to solve a problem on their own in a crisis. Unfortunately, there are many cases of these "cowboys" or "cowgirls" creating additional problems, technically, legally, and PR-wise, which could have been prevented if they had just followed the previously agreed upon plan. Make sure all ransomware recovery plan participants understand the importance of sticking to the plan, or at least get approval from the team for any deviations they come up with.

Summary

You want to define all the major critical decisions, policies, tools, procedures, and people that need to be involved in a ransomware recovery event. Document all of this in a written document and make sure it is accessible in case of a ransomware event. Define ahead of time how team members will be contacted and have every involved stakeholder familiarize themselves and practice the plan. Having a comprehensive, practiced, ransomware recovery plan will likely result in a faster and cheaper recovery than waiting for an event to happen.

Chapter 6, "Detecting Ransomware," will discuss how to best detect ransomware after it has successfully penetrated your environment despite your implemented preventative controls.

Chapter 6
Detecting Ransomware

I f you can't prevent ransomware, the next best thing is detecting it quickly. Up to 85 percent of victim organizations had up-to-date antivirus programs (and other traditional defenses) and still got successfully exploited by ransomware. In this chapter, the best ways to detect ransomware are discussed in an attempt to stop it immediately or to mitigate its spread and damage.

Why Is Ransomware So Hard to Detect?

Many people are surprised to learn that ransomware is so successful in organizations with all the traditional defenses enabled. Most organizations hit by ransomware had up-to-date antivirus, firewalls, content filtering, and all the normal defense controls we are all told we need in order to successfully defend against hackers and malware. There are more than a handful of reasons why ransomware can be so successful in environments you would expect to be well protected. Later in this chapter, we discuss some of the reasons why even well-defended organizations are breached.

First, antivirus and endpoint detection and response (EDR) software has never been 100 percent accurate, no matter what the ads say. Nothing in the computer defense world is both easy and

155

100 percent accurate (more on this later). These days it is incredibly hard for any antivirus vendor to keep up with the many millions of new malware programs created each year. It's not that there are truly millions of completely new, unique malware programs being created each year; it's that the same malware programs are being reworked, obfuscated, and encrypted to appear different in each exploitation. So, traditional, signature-based antivirus scanners have a hard time keeping up. They have to wait for a new malware program to be detected, reported, examined, and then a reliable signature created. By the time this happens, most ransomware programs have re-encrypted themselves to create a new signature. There will always be a lag between release and reliable detection, one that ransomware gangs make the most of. As covered in Chapter 1, once ransomware is executed, it is constantly "dialing home" and updating itself to avoid antivirus detection.

Second, no defense is applied perfectly. It is difficult for defenders to get 100 percent application of any security defense in their environment. Simply pushing a critical patch out to every computer that needs it rarely results in 100 percent success the first time out. For a myriad of reasons, whatever defense it is that a defender is trying to apply, some small percentage of the involved computers will simply not apply the defense. It can be because the Microsoft Windows registry is corrupt, the device is offline, the device's storage space is full, there is some third-party program blocking the application, the user is intentionally preventing the application of the security control, and so on. No matter what a computer defender is trying to do, getting 100 percent successful application of that security control is very hard. And it's nearly impossible to do across all computer security controls. It's been this way since the beginning of computers. Hackers and malware love inconsistency. Ransomware often finds its initial foothold access on a computer missing one of the critical defenses.

Third, once active, many ransomware programs immediately begin searching for and disabling defensive protections so they can't warn of the attack. Some ransomware programs look for particular defensive programs that have been particularly good at stopping them, and others take the more general approach and try to disable any one of dozens of programs. In fact, unexplained disabling of defensive controls is one of the best signs of a ransomware infection, if you can filter the malicious disablements from all the legitimate activity.

Fourth, most ransomware programs are increasingly reliant on using scripts, built-in software and commands, and legitimate commercial tools to do their dirty work, after the initial foothold exploitation. For example, one of the most commonly used post-exploitation ransomware tools is Microsoft's own Sysinternals' Psexec program (https://docs.microsoft.com/en-us/sysinternals/downloads/psexec). Psexec, which has been around for decades, allows programs to be remotely copied and executed on Windows computers, which makes it a favorite of not only legitimate admins trying to use automated scripts but also ransomware gangs. It is tough for a defensive program to tell the difference between a legitimate script or program and a script or the same program used maliciously.

Fifth, most admins and users really don't understand their environments as well as they should. So, when something malicious pops up, they don't know about it and don't research it. This is something we will explore and remediate in this chapter.

Sixth, monitoring is not nearly as aggressive as it should be. Many studies, including the much respected Verizon Data Breach Investigations Report (https://www.verizon.com/business/resources/reports/dbir/), have long touted that the vast majority of exploited organizations would have noticed the malicious compromise if they had simply looked at their logs. Security event monitoring tools are capturing the malicious events, but no one is looking. . .or not looking hard enough.

It's important to understand that even though "well-protected" organizations do routinely get compromised, it's still beneficial to run all the traditional defenses, including antivirus software. Why? Because even though they are not perfect, they do prevent some portion of malware, ransomware, and malicious hackers. We all wear seatbelts in our cars even though most of us don't need them most of the time.

Detection Methods

It is important to understand traditional and aggressive detection measures that can help any organization better and more quickly detect a new ransomware exploitation. It is assumed that you are already doing all the traditional computer defenses, including using antivirus/EDR, firewalls, secure configurations, content filtering, reputation filtering, anti-phishing, monitoring, etc. As such, the concentration will be on detection methods that work particularly well on ransomware (and other malware and hacker scenarios). Some of the recommended detection methods are simply using existing defenses in an improved way, and others are not new. The idea of this section is to expose you to a cross section of different types of detections and let you pick one or more to implement in your environment.

Like any computer defense, there is a definitive usability versus security trade-off. The best ransomware defenses require more resources, concentration, and manual research. There is no easy, automated way to 100 percent detect ransomware. If there was, we would not have the severity of the ransomware problem we have today.

Security Awareness Training

The vast majority of malicious data breaches, including ransomware exploitation, occur because an end user was tricked into providing logon credentials or running a trojan horse program. In my research (`https://blog.knowbe4.com/phishing-remains-the-most-common-form-of-attack`), 70 percent to 90 percent of all attacks are due to social engineering and phishing. It is the number-one root cause for malicious exploitation by far. It only makes sense to educate admins and end users about different signs of ransomware so that when end users see something potentially malicious, they can report it and have someone research whether it is ransomware-related or not.

What signs and symptoms should admins and users look for? They should look for any of these that are covered in the following sections below. Admins and end users need to stay current on the most popular signs and symptoms of ransomware. These are routinely written about on computer security vendor blogs, including at KnowBe4 (https://blog.knowbe4.com). You can even do Internet searches for ransomware articles, such as https://blog.knowbe4.com ransomware, to get a quick list. Ransomware signs and symptoms evolve over time, so make sure your admins and end users know what to look for. Today's ransomware doesn't look like last year's ransomware. Stay up-to-date!

AV/EDR Adjunct Detections

As discussed earlier, it's always right to run up-to-date antivirus/ endpoint detection and response detection (AV/EDR). They do catch and prevent some percentage of malware and ransomware. Just as important is to realize that many times AV/EDR finds what might otherwise seem like nonrelated malicious (or legitimate) programs that are being used by ransomware. Today, most ransomware uses other malicious programs, scripts, and even legitimate programs to do their dirty work. Many times, the sign that you have a pending ransomware attack is simply finding a single malicious program or unexplained script in your environment. In most big ransomware attacks, someone noticed a related program ahead of the main attack but did not understand its significance. How do you get someone to understand that what looks like an unrelated program or script may be related to a larger ransomware attack? Educate them!

True Story

I once consulted for a company whose security team was congratulating themselves on detecting and finding a password hash dumping tool (i.e., passdump4) on one of their domain controllers. They were excited to have found it and removed it. When I asked them how it got there and who was using it, they acted surprised like they had never thought to ask the questions. Instead of congratulating themselves, they should have set off a huge alarm and triggered a thorough investigation, but they didn't. A few months later they learned they had been compromised by multiple advance persistent threat (APT) adversaries.

Detect New Processes

Detecting new processes is the best detective control possible, but also one of the hardest to implement effectively. All ransomware executes new, unauthorized, malicious processes. To detect ransomware (and really all malware and malicious hackers), all you need to do is detect all new, unauthorized processes and determine if they are legitimate or not. Easier said than done, by a long shot. If you can do this well, then you significantly reduce the risk of ransomware, all malware, and most malicious hackers.

The difficulty is few organizations really understand what processes are running on a single device, much less across every device on their network. And you have to understand what legitimate, authorized processes are running on every device (or at least every device at high-risk for malicious compromise) and alert on new processes. Then every new process must be researched to determine its legitimacy. Figure 6.1 summarizes the basic logical steps.

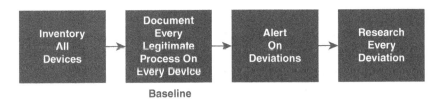

Baseline

Figure 6.1 Logical flow of process anomaly detection

The first step is to take an inventory of every device in the environment, or at least every device that can possibly be maliciously exploited. This means PCs, laptops, servers, network equipment, IoT devices, appliances, etc. The second step is to inventory the legitimate allowed processes on each device. This can be difficult to do and often involves different inventory software and steps to accomplish. How to account for future legitimate software and processes needs to be taken into account.

The third step is to install a monitoring process that can detect when a new, unauthorized process (or unauthorized "injection" to an existing allowed process) happens. Processes include executables, scripts, libraries, and anything else that can be classified as "active" code or content and be maliciously manipulated. The fourth step is for an incident response process to be created that quickly researches each newly detected, unauthorized process, to the point that it is determined to be either legitimate or malicious.

Anything new that can be used to hide, store, or launch maliciousness needs to be monitored and alerted on. For example, on Microsoft Windows, malware often installs itself in the Windows registry in such a way that it automatically gets relaunched if Windows gets rebooted. Or, it installs itself as a new scheduled task. There are literally dozens, if not hundreds, of ways for a malware program to install itself on Windows to ensure its persistence.

Microsoft's Sysinternals Autoruns program (https://docs .microsoft.com/en-us/sysinternals/downloads/autoruns) will reveal dozens of places programs, legitimate and otherwise, can modify to "auto-launch" themselves. If interested, the reader should download and run Autoruns to see those areas listed and populated. With Autoruns (and also Syinternals Process Explorer), inventoried items can be compared against Google's VirusTotal service to see if any listed found component has previously been detected as potentially malicious. There may be similar products for Apple, Linux, BSD, and other devices.

Any software or system you can buy that automates this process should be explored and considered. Later in the chapter, I'm going to show as an example, one way of doing this process, but it requires more manual deployment, monitoring, and research. If you can buy a software program (or realistically, programs) that can do the inventory, baselining, alerting, and research for you, or at least with far less manual intervention, you should.

There are many computer security programs that will do much of the work for you. I hesitate to give examples, because any list I give will be drastically incomplete. The following is a partial list of programs that specifically track individual processes (at least on some platforms) and will attempt to identify and alert on anomalous detections (in alphabetical order):

- Crowdstrike
- Cybereason
- Elastic
- FireEye
- Fortinet
- McAfee
- Microsoft
- Orange Cyberdefense
- Palo Alto Networks
- Sentinel One
- TrendMicro
- VMware Carbon Black

Many of these products are reviewed and compared at https://www.forrester.com/report/The+Forrester+Wave+Enterprise+Detection+And+Response+Q1+2020/-/E-RES146957. You can usually go to one of the listed vendor's websites and find the Forrester report, or a portion of it, for free.

The best programs do the inventory collection for you, alert on potential new maliciousness, and help with quick isolation. They conduct threat intelligence to keep on top of the new malicious processes, indicators of compromise, and malicious network origination points. They will often let you "walk" a single, original compromise and detail how it moved through your organization. They can be sophisticated and automated. Every company should use a product like this to help prevent and detect network maliciousness.

AV vs. EDR

Traditional malware detection is known as *antivirus* (AV) or *anti-virus*. New, more heavyweight anti-malware programs, known as *endpoint detection and response* (EDR), are popular these days. Traditional AV just used simple malware signatures (i.e., bytes that reliably appear in the malware program being identified) matching to detect and alert on malware. Today, even "simple" AV programs do a lot more than just signature comparisons, including sophisticated signature checking (i.e., replacing various bytes as needed to detect morphing malware) and heuristics (behavior analysis), and run malware in virtualized subsystems to look into executed programs where any encryption is removed. EDR software is often even more mature, inventorying and monitoring existing processes and connections. There is no hard and fast line of what an AV program does and doesn't do as compared to an EDR program. It depends on the AV and EDR programs being compared, but in general, the average EDR programs will have more accurate detection of hackers and malware over its AV counterpart. This is why you see more organizations moving from traditional AV programs to EDR. Obviously, AV vendors beg to differ, but clearly the market is now favoring EDR for the organizations that can afford it.

It's important to note that many organizations with these pro-grams get successfully exploited by malware. They aren't 100 percent accurate. Although, the bigger problem is usually that the programs did detect the new, unauthorized process or script but didn't auto-matically recognize the seriousness. If you want to truly defeat ran-somware (and other malware and malicious hackers), you need to aggressively inventory, monitor, alert, and research any and all new processes. To do this right, most companies would require at least a full-time, dedicated employee, and larger companies would require multiple dedicated employees. This is asking a lot, but if you truly want to defeat ransomware, it takes this level of commitment. If your organization cannot devote the resources it takes to do process detection 100 percent effectively, you should still try to do it the best you can.

Application Control May Be Cheaper in the Long Run

A strict application control program that stops all new installs and processes by default may be cheaper, easier, and more secure in the long run. But it also takes dedicated resources to accomplish.

Anomalous Network Connections

All ransomware establishes unauthorized network connections, both inside the compromised network and externally. Ransomware always "dials home," and where it dials home to is not a legitimate, authorized connection (although it often uses and points to general, public services like AWS, etc., making it hard to determine whether it is malicious or not). In most ransomware attacks, the ransomware gangs connect to the compromised network from nonlegitimate connections (e.g., not from legitimate customer sites).

On any enterprise network, most servers do not connect to every other server or to every workstation. Most workstations do not connect to other workstations. Most workstations do not connect to most servers. Domain admins (on a Microsoft Active Directory network) should not be connecting to most servers and workstations. There are legitimate and allowed network connections and connections that if monitored and known about would be considered anomalous by any competent observer.

Like detecting unauthorized processes, you want to inventory and document the legitimate, allowed network connections, and alert on the anomalous ones. Just like with process anomaly detection, network anomaly detection follows the same basic logical flow: inventory, baseline, alerting, research. Figure 6.2 summarizes the basic logical steps of network anomaly detection.

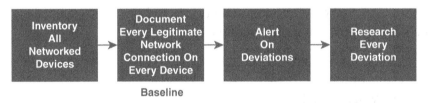

Figure 6.2 Logical flow of network anomaly detection

Most of the software products listed earlier in the "Detect New Processes" section monitor both anomalous processes and also anomalous network connections. There are also network traffic analysis products that specifically concentrate on network connection anomalies. Some of these include the following (in alphabetical order):

- Bro
- Cisco (specifically their Lanscope Stealthwatch product)
- Corelight
- Darktrace
- Flowmon Networks
- Juniper Networks
- Netscout
- Noction

Network anomaly detection is also known as network flow analysis, network behavior analysis, net flow, network intelligence, and other similar terms.

Every organization should understand its legitimate network traffic connections and alert on and research anomalous connections.

New, Unexplained Things

Any newly found, unexplained activity, process, or network connection that could potentially be involved in ransomware (or other malware or malicious hacker activity) should be investigated. This includes the following unexplained things:

- Collections or archives of data files
- Scripts or tools
- Newly installed drivers
- Changes in masses of files (e.g., location, attributes, permissions, encryption, etc.)
- Presence of a mass of files with common, but strange, file extensions (e.g., readme, ransom, etc.)
- Changes in backup jobs
- Changes in backup encryption keys
- Boots into Safe Mode
- Program crashes, operational interruptions, etc.
- Use of taskkill.exe, PsExec.exe, Wbadmin.exe, Vssadmin.exe, etc., if not routinely used

These are all common ransomware indicators of compromise (IoC). It is worth noting that there have also been some instances of ransomware installing legitimate drivers, which are known to be buggy, so they could then exploit the newly installed driver to gain additional access to the compromised system

and network. An example can be found at `https://news.sophos`
`.com/en-us/2020/02/06/living-off-another-land-ransomware-`
`borrows-vulnerable-driver-to-remove-security-software/`. Be
aware that even the most innocent-looking install can possibly
be used maliciously. Always research all newly installed, unexplained items.

What About Fileless Malware

Many malware programs, including ransomware, are known
to use "fileless" methods. This is supposed to mean the malware doesn't use traditional files to store and execute. Instead,
fileless malware uses the registry or some other obfuscation
method to store, hide, and execute itself. Many people wonder if traditional detection methods can as easily detect these
types of fileless malware. The answer is that fileless malware
has been around for decades (since at least the late 1980s on
PCs. . .the first PC virus, Pakistani Brain, was "fileless") and
is readily detected by most anti-malware scanners. Additionally, I've never seen a fileless malware program that didn't
then create one or more file-based malware programs that
could be detected. In short, fileless malware is not the huge
threat that many people and vendors make it out to be. It
does make malware detection more difficult, but not sub-
stantially so.

Unexplained Stoppages

The previous detection methods are mostly about detecting something new, be it a process, program, task, file change, or network
connection. However, unexplained stoppages are also common ransomware indicators of compromise and are becoming a good way
of quickly detecting ransomware. Any of the following unexplained
stoppages should be investigated:

- Antivirus or EDR software
- Firewalls
- Databases (often stopped to exfiltrate data)
- Email services (often stopped to exfiltrate bulk emails)
- Backup jobs (e.g., volume shadow copies)

It can be difficult to detect whether a newly stopped defensive process or service is due to malicious reasons. Stopped and restarted services happen all the time, the vast majority of which are not due to malicious causes. For example, simply rebooting a computer will stop and restart a service. Many services routinely stop themselves to do routine, legitimate maintenance.

The key is in determining and alerting on higher risk occurrences. One way to do that is to take a look at your application log files and determine what stops and starts are normal and frequently recurring, and then alert on the anomalous instances. Another way is to alert only on stops that aren't associated with a device shutdown. Or, alert only when a defensive service has been shut down (not related to a reboot) and is not restarted in the next 30 minutes. Even if the stoppage is not malicious, it deserves to be investigated.

Another technique is to use *keep-alives*. Keep-alives are packets, processes, or procedures that are routinely performed that should generate traffic to a defensive detection engine. The absence of these keep-alive packets indicates something is wrong with the involved service. For example, if your antivirus software scans all files once a day, every involved device can have the EICAR (https://en.wikipedia.org/wiki/EICAR_test_file) test file installed on it. The EICAR file is intended to test antivirus programs and make them detect or alert on it as if a real malicious file was detected. Any system containing an EICAR file should generate an antivirus warning event. The absence of the warning, for example if the antivirus software has been disabled, indicates an event that needs to be investigated. Many progressive computer security departments implement keep-alive events and will investigate services that don't regularly report in as expected.

Aggressive Monitoring

All of these detective controls require that administrators understand what is and isn't normal on their devices and network or have tools that do the same. Essentially, all organizations need to study ransomware IoCs and look out for those types of instances. Many of the most common ones are listed earlier in this chapter.

Good ransomware detection requires aggressive planning, research, and monitoring. It is because most organizations don't do this that ransomware is often successful. Don't be a ransomware victim. Learn what should and shouldn't be running on and connecting with other endpoints in your environment, and detect, alert, and research all anomalies. If you don't have the resources, buy software or services that can do it for you. Not doing so means your organization will be at increased risk of a successful ransomware attack.

It must be noted that having an aggressive understanding and actually doing the monitoring of processes and network connections isn't easy or inexpensive. This is true even when the organization needing it has the resources or tools to do it. It is because it is so resource intensive and/or expensive to do that most organizations, even big organizations, don't do this monitoring.

To be clear, organizations that cannot do it well are at significantly increased risk of a hacker or malware attack being successful. Organizations that can do it well are at significantly less risk of a successful attack. Many organizations, lacking the necessary resources to do process and network tracking well, buy what they think is the best combination of EDR and backup solutions and hope for the best. If possible, don't rely on hope to protect your organization. Have a good AV/EDR solution, a good backup solution, and also do process and network anomaly detection.

Example Detection Solution

This chapter ends by summarizing an example detection method that can be readily implemented by anyone using enterprise versions of Microsoft Windows. This solution involves using Micro-soft's AppLocker application control program, in audit-only mode, to detect and alert on new processes.

Microsoft's AppLocker has been in Windows since Windows 7/ Windows Server 2008. It replaced Windows XP's Software Restric-tion Policies. Today, it is seen as the "easier" cousin of Microsoft's Windows Defender Application Control, released in Windows 10. AppLocker can be configured and controlled by PowerShell, a local or Active Directory group policy, or a mobile device management service like Windows Intune. This example shows how to configure and deploy using local Group Policy.

The first step is to enable and configure AppLocker. To do so, at your Start ≻ Run prompt, type in **gpedit.msc**, and hit Enter. This will display the Local Group Policy Editor. In the editor console, navigate to Computer Configuration\Windows Settings\ Security Settings\Application Control Policies\AppLocker, as shown in Figure 6.3.

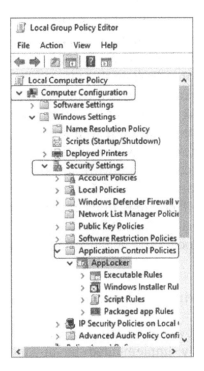

Figure 6.3   Opening AppLocker using Local Group Policy

This should result in a set of AppLocker "rule" options similar to those shown in Figure 6.4.

Figure 6.4 AppLocker rule types

Each of these rule types can be enabled separately, as shown in Figure 6.5, by clicking on and enabling the checkbox. For our purposes, each rule should be enabled in Audit Only mode versus Enforcement mode.

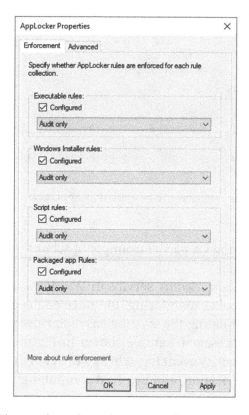

Figure 6.5 Enabling Audit Only mode in AppLocker

As Figure 6.6 shows, AppLocker will allow the administrator to create a set of "baseline" rules, which will allow all existing executables to execute without creating a security event. Anything currently installed will be allowed to run without creating a security event.

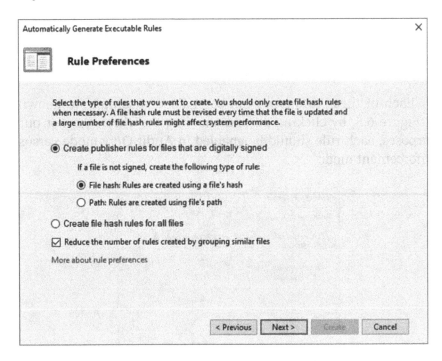

Figure 6.6   Baseline rules about to be created in AppLocker

Figure 6.7 shows a partial example of what the resulting baseline rules look like.

The *Application Identity* service in Windows must be enabled to enable AppLocker monitoring. But once enabled, any execution or installation violating the existing baseline rules will generate an 8003 warning message (example shown in Figure 6.8), written to the Windows security event log, which will detail the offending executable, device, location, and involved computer and user.

	Action	User	Name	Condition
Local Computer Policy				
∨ Computer Configuration	Allow	Everyone	Baseline Rules: MICROSOFT® WINDO...	Publisher
> Software Settings	Allow	Everyone	Baseline Rules: HTML HELP signed by O...	Publisher
∨ Windows Settings	Allow	Everyone	Baseline Rules: MICROSOFT(R) CONNE...	Publisher
> Name Resolution Policy	Allow	Everyone	Baseline Rules: MICROSOFT ® WINDO...	Publisher
Scripts (Startup/Shutdown)	Allow	Everyone	Baseline Rules: THE CURL EXECUTABLE ...	Publisher
> Deployed Printers	Allow	Everyone	Baseline Rules: INTERNET EXPLORER sig...	Publisher
∨ Security Settings	Allow	Everyone	Baseline Rules: WINDOWS INSTALLER - ...	Publisher
> Account Policies	Allow	Everyone	Baseline Rules: MICROSOFT ONEDRIVE ...	Publisher
> Local Policies	Allow	Everyone	Baseline Rules: MICROSOFT® DRM sig...	Publisher
> Windows Defender Firewall with Advanced	Allow	Everyone	Baseline Rules: WINDOWS® SEARCH si...	Publisher
Network List Manager Policies	Allow	Everyone	Baseline Rules: MICROSOFT (R) WINDO...	Publisher
> Public Key Policies	Allow	Everyone	Baseline Rules: Windows.WARPJITServi...	File Hash
> Software Restriction Policies	Allow	Everyone	Baseline Rules: ADOBE® FLASH® PLAY...	Publisher
∨ Application Control Policies	Allow	Everyone	Baseline Rules: setup.exe, _isdel.exe	File Hash
∨ AppLocker	Allow	Everyone	Baseline Rules: WpcUapApp.exe	File Hash
> Executable Rules	Allow	Everyone	Baseline Rules: XGpuEjectDialog.exe	File Hash
> Windows Installer Rules	Allow	Everyone	Baseline Rules: StartMenuExperienceHo...	File Hash
> Script Rules	Allow	Everyone	Baseline Rules: NarratorQuickStart.exe	File Hash
> Packaged app Rules	Allow	Everyone	Baseline Rules: CapturePicker.exe	File Hash
> IP Security Policies on Local Computer	Allow	Everyone	Baseline Rules: MICROSOFT EDGE signe...	Publisher
> Advanced Audit Policy Configuration	Allow	Everyone	Baseline Rules: WINDOWS DRIVE OPTI...	Publisher
> Policy-based QoS	Allow	Everyone	Baseline Rules: MICROSOFT EDGE WEB ...	Publisher
> Administrative Templates	Allow	Everyone	Baseline Rules: REMOTEFX HELPER sign...	Publisher
∨ User Configuration	Allow	Everyone	Baseline Rules: MICROSOFT WINDOWS ...	Publisher
> Software Settings	Allow	Everyone	Baseline Rules: FaceFodUninstaller.exe	File Hash
> Windows Settings	Allow	Everyone	Baseline Rules: scp.exe, sftp.exe, ssh-ad...	File Hash
> Administrative Templates	Allow	Everyone	Baseline Rules: WAVES MAXXAUDIO sig...	Publisher
	Allow	Everyone	Baseline Rules: INTEL® SOFTWARE GU...	Publisher
	Allow	Everyone	Baseline Rules: REALTEK HD AUDIO UNI...	Publisher

Figure 6.7 Partial example of resulting AppLocker baseline rules

Figure 6.8 Example 8003 AppLocker event log warning

In any environment deploying AppLocker as a primary new process detection tool, as shown in this section, all 8003 log message warnings should then be researched until the execution is determined to be legitimate or otherwise. In multicomputer environments, all 8003 log messages should be collected to a common database, and administrators or researchers are then alerted to begin the research.

There could be additional automation put around each 8003 event including sending a "form" email to the involved user asking if they meant to install the new, previously unexplained executable. Or, the involved executable could be sent to Google's VirusTotal or the user's anti-malware vendor for further analysis. The concept is the same no matter which tools you use. Figure out what should be running in your environment, detect deviances, and research.

In even a moderately sized organization, the number of new processes detected every day can be overwhelming. These can be minimized by not allowing regular end users to install new programs (by taking away their administrator or root accounts), but regular end users can still install plenty of new software. It can take hours of research to take down and determine what is and isn't legitimate. Many organizations use application control in blocking mode to slow down new installs and unapproved executions. Others use EDR software, most of which should have a lot of this functionality built-in, including the ability to determine what is and isn't malicious. But even the best EDR programs cannot beat the accuracy of a human being researching each newly detected deviation.

In the end, that is the ultimate decision that needs to be made. If a human being researches each newly executed and installed program, that will require lots of resources. If a program is used to do it, accuracy is likely to suffer at least a little. Sometimes resource and budget constraints force one option over another. The better choice would be to use an application control program in blocking/enforcement mode, but that requires resources as well.

Every organization, no matter how done, should strive to get a better understanding and control over the programs and network connections in their environment. It will take a lot of resources to do it no matter how you do it. But you should still do it. Doing so will reduce your risk of a successful hacker or malware attack. It is because most organizations do not devote enough resources to process and network anomaly detection that ransomware is so successful.

Summary

This chapter summarized various detection methods, such as end-user awareness, anti-malware detection, and detecting new processes, network connections, and unexplained stoppages, as a way to detect potential ransomware (or other malware or malicious hacker activities). Chapter 7, "Minimizing the Damage," will discuss the initial actions any defender should take when first realizing that a successful ransomware exploitation event has occurred.

Chapter 7
Minimizing Damage

I n this chapter it is assumed that you have detected a large-scale ransomware attack in your organization and are now just start-ing to respond. You have activated the ransomware response plan, initiated contact with the needed team members, and now need to assess the scope of damage and minimize it. This is the first 24 hours.

Basic Outline for Initial Ransomware Response

After activating the ransomware response plan, the first major task that needs to be completed is stopping the further spread and dam-age from the ransomware program(s). This is followed by determin-ing the initial scope of the ransomware involvement and damage. That is then followed by the first official team meeting to discuss what everyone has learned and then make the additional initial response decisions. Figure 7.1 shows the initial tasks graphically.

Everything in early phases of the ransomware response plan can typically be accomplished in 24 hours, although it may be longer depending on circumstances, resources, timing, and the aggressiveness of the response. Ransomware attacks are notorious for intentionally launching late at night, on weekends, and during holidays. Attackers want to maximize the potential for their program(s) to do the most harm and for the defensive response to take longer to happen and be less effective. The following sections look into each of these tasks in more detail.

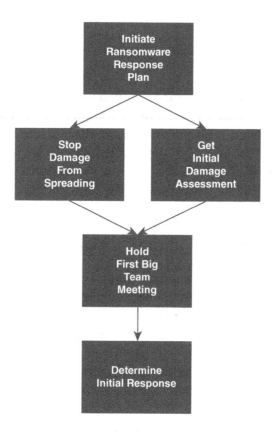

Figure 7.1   Basic ransomware initial tasks

Weighing Cost-Benefit of Mitigations

There is no one "right way" to respond to ransomware. Each victim will need to weigh the various recommended responses and mitigations and make their own risk assessments. What is right for one organization may not be right for another. So, when you read something like "Shutdown all devices" or "Shutdown all networking," for most organizations that is the right answer. For yours, it may not be. Each organizational leader needs to make what they feel is the right risk choice for their scenario and organization.

Stop the Spread

The first two tasks, stopping damage spread and getting an initial damage assessment, usually happen in parallel. Stopping the spread of the ransomware program(s) usually means assessing what types of devices are involved, where, and how they are impacted.

Stopping the spread of the ransomware program(s) and its damage involves trying to do two different mitigations—one, to stop the spread and any possible additional damage on devices known to be currently exploited; and two, trying to stop the spread to additional devices not already compromised.

The initial damage assessment is going to reveal one or more devices that have been definitely impacted by the ransomware. On at least one or two impacted devices you're going to quickly see if you can determine what is wrong. What does the ransomware message say? Take a picture. Try to have the initial responder do some quick forensics checks. Do the files truly look encrypted or is it just scareware? Can any unencrypted files be seen? You are looking to see if you can get a general sense of what is happening.

Power Down or Isolate Exploited Devices

After the initial assessment, in most cases, you are going to want to power down or isolate all impacted devices to prevent future damage and spread. You may even want to power down or isolate additional, seemingly unimpacted devices to prevent them from becoming exploited or damaged.

One of the biggest decisions to make in a ransomware response event is whether to power down or just isolate impacted computers. Many guides and experts argue for isolation only. They are concerned that powering down devices will cause them to lose valuable forensics evidence and this is true. Powering down devices may even remove ransomware encryption keys that are located in memory.

Some ransomware response advice takes a middle approach, such as the advice from the Cybersecurity & Infrastructure Security Agency (CISA) found at `https://www.cisa.gov/sites/default/files/publications/CISA_MS-ISAC_Ransomware%20Guide_S508C.pdf`. The CISA advocates only powering down devices that you can't disconnect from the network but leaving powered up any device where networking can be disabled. The thinking is that powering down any device, whether roughly or smoothly, erases potentially valuable evidence that is in volatile memory. This is a valid concern.

The "power everything down" approach is more worried about devices that may be in the middle of additional encryption or damage, and by shutting them down, it saves the most amount of data and services possible. The "power everything down" makes the most sense if you determine that what you are really facing is a "wiper" event, where the malware programs are out for as much unrecoverable destruction as possible. Events on the ground, as you learn them, will lead to one approach versus another.

The reality is that the differences from either approach, powering down or remaining up, in most ransomware scenarios are usually not that significant from a pure damage point of view. Usually by the time the initial incident response is occurring the majority of the damage has already occurred. Still, a quick response and powering down devices is likely to result in less damage, if that is possible, and forensics evidence collection is not a primary concern. Sometimes the ransomware attack has been noticed in the early stages before the majority of the damage has been done. Ultimately, it is a judgment call of the ransomware response team leader.

When in doubt, isolate devices, but leave them up and running. Many, if not most, ransomware response experts recommend this strategy. Leaving them up and running preserves crucial forensic evidence, often assists in recovery, allows them to more easily be manipulated later, and most of the damage that is going to occur has already occurred. When in doubt, "chicken out" and leave them running (but isolated).

If you decide to power down, don't do graceful shutdowns unless you know for sure that doing an ungraceful shutdown will cause worse unrecoverable damage that can't be undone. You want to weigh the potential damage from doing a "soft" shutdown versus what the malware program could do if you don't power the system down right now. Your goal is to minimize overall damage.

Disconnecting the Network

Everyone agrees that disconnecting everything that could be impacted from the network as soon as possible should be done, understanding that you will not be able to perform remote tasks like forensics to those impacted devices until the networking is restored. You should disconnect all possible networks, including the following:

- All Internet ingress and egress connection points
- All wired and wireless connections
- Potentially short distance networks like Bluetooth, NFC, etc., if they can possibly allow ransomware or damage to spread

Prior to Network Disconnection

The ransomware team members should have already established a new connection method as agreed upon in the ransomware response plan, which will not be impacted by the network disablement.

Disconnect at the Network Access Points

One of the best ways to disable network connections is to disable networking at the involved network access points and not on the individual devices. This is because, if done correctly, it can quickly disconnect all devices from the network in the shortest amount of time and can more easily allow re-connecting, with future restrictions, as needed. If you disconnect networking on the local device itself, then usually that networking cannot be re-enabled without physically visiting the impacted device again (although physical assessment of every device is often required anyway).

Disabling networking using network aggregation points, such as routers, switches, or VLANs, more readily allows selected devices, ports, originations, and destinations, to be disabled and re-established as needed. Once you understand how the ransomware programs are acting and establishing network connections, you can re-open the network in a more fine-tuned manner to permit remote forensics or recovery, while blocking the malware from communicating.

If networking cannot be disabled using network aggregation points, disable networking on each device, making sure to disable both wired and wireless connections. How you do that varies by operating system and implementation. If you cannot disconnect devices using network access points and you also plan to power them down, then disconnect networking on each device before you power them down, if it can be done quickly and safely. That way when you bring devices back online, they have networking already disabled by default and will not automatically allow networking traffic to happen before you are ready.

> # Practice Makes Perfect
> No matter how you plan to disable networking, this step needs to be carefully thought out and practiced ahead of time. You don't want to be thinking about and wondering what you need to do and how in the middle of a ransomware event. Instead, know exactly what you're going to do and how you're going to do it so that in the middle of an emergency response, you've "been there, done that!"

In the best possible scenarios, defenders have a network inventory plan with a list of all networking connections on all devices and network access points. Defenders can then use that list to disconnect the networking connections as quickly as possible, making sure they include all available network access points and devices. They have the network access points listed ahead of time, the commands needed to disable networking on them, and possibly even an automated script to accomplish the global network disconnection process quickly.

Suppose You Can't Disconnect the Network

There are scenarios where shutting down the entire network is not an option. Nearly every organization hit by ransomware initially feels this way. Shutting down the entire network seems implausible to most victims, at first, but not shutting down the network (or all potentially impacted devices) means taking the risk of additional spreading damage and service disruptions. Most organizations don't think they can shut down their entire networks. However, most of those organizations would be better off, from a risk perspective, if they did.

There are rare organizations that truly cannot shut down their networks without causing worse damage, where the risk of shutdown far outweighs the risk of additional ransomware damage. I'm talking about organizations that run missile defense systems, industrial control systems where a sudden shutdown causes real physical damage, and so on. I've consulted with companies where shutting down the network, despite the increased risk, is not an option. For those rare situations, still try to disconnect as many unnecessary network connections and services as you can. You'll just have to be more granular and prioritize. In these instances, consider shutting down these types of nonessential network connections, if possible:

- Internet ingress and egress points, or limit connections to just a few devices
- Any nonessential devices
- Connections to nonessential storage devices
- Any active "sync" connections, such as Microsoft Exchange ActiveSync, Microsoft OneDrive, Dropbox, iTunes

Ransomware gangs often have everyone's login name and password, including the most powerful accounts on devices and networks (e.g., Administrator, Domain Admins, root, service accounts, etc.). Disable privileged accounts and/or change their passwords to prevent hackers, scripts, and malware from using them if known and used.

The key to both powering down devices and disconnecting the network is to prevent existing malware programs and active hacker connections from doing more damage on existing compromised devices and from spreading to additional devices. Devices and networks should not be brought back up or removed from isolation until proven.

Initial Damage Assessment

You are trying to quickly determine what devices and services are involved, how bad they are hit, what locations are involved, and whether data and credentials were stolen. You don't need to be 100 percent accurate, but you do want to be as accurate as you can be with the initial assessment. Here are the types of things you want to assess and report on:

- OS platforms involved
- Locations
- Types of devices
- Types of roles (e.g., servers, workstations, database servers, web servers, infrastructure services)
- Exploit pattern
  - Do impacted systems seem random, or is there a relationship between impacted systems?
- Storage devices—servers only, network drives only, mapped or shared drives only
- Local storage only or cloud stored data and services
- Cloud storage involved
- Cloud services
- Portable media involved, like USB devices
- Impacted backups
- Email servers involved
  - Have emails been eavesdropped on
  - Are there any malicious email "rules" copying emails to external email addresses?
- Data exfiltration
  - Does it appear as if data or credential exfiltration is involved?
- Attacker environment familiarity
  - Does the attacker seem to know people's names and roles?
- Malicious files
  - Are you finding malicious scripts, other malware programs, unexpected large archive files (e.g., gz, zip, arc, etc.)?
- Notices and information from ransomware attackers

What Is Impacted?

You need to determine what devices and services are impacted. Start making a list (e.g., spreadsheet) of confirmed impacts, likely impacts, and confirmed devices and services that are not impacted.

Knowing what isn't impacted is as important as knowing what is. Also, even if a device or service isn't currently, directly impacted, consider the likelihood that it could have been involved or might be impacted in the future. For example, if an attacker has impacted your Active Directory domain controllers, could they have done that without also having the necessary access to impact every workstation, other services (e.g., DNS, DHCP, etc.), or capturing people's personal passwords as they went to personal websites. You want to understand what was definitely impacted, what could have been impacted but is not 100% confirmed, and what does not appear to be impacted. It's not always easy or straightforward. Oftentimes, computers are showing critical errors, but those errors are related to connection problems with other computers that have been compromised, and the machine showing the error is uncompromised (although still impacted).

Ensure Your Backups Are Still Good

It is essential that you locate your backups and verify their integrity. The integrity of the backups and their ability to be restored needs to be 100 percent. Many victims have done cursory checks and thought their backups were good, only later to find out they had been corrupted. This is one of the most important steps to verify with 100 percent accuracy, as much of the additional ransomware response depends on whether the backups are reliable. If the data in the cloud has been corrupted, can you get back known, clean copies? If the cloud data has been impacted, notify your cloud vendor and/or ensure what data you can get restored. You may need to stop backups temporarily during the attack so that corrupted files don't get accidentally backed up over known clean copies.

Check for Signs of Data and Credential Exfiltration

What is the ransomware attacker claiming they have exfiltrated? Did they send "proof of life" (i.e., a stolen data sample)? Check logs for signs of intruder presence. If you have data leak prevention

(DLP) systems, check to see if there are signs there. Can you find any large file archives? During this initial phase, the first task at hand is to confirm whether your data and/or credentials have been exfiltrated. Some ransomware groups will lie about their data exfiltration capabilities and try to bluff you. You want to confirm or disprove the data exfiltration claims. With that said, most ransomware groups claiming they have exfiltrated data and/or credentials have actually done so. If data exfiltration has occurred, does what was stolen indicate that an "official" data breach needs to be declared?

Check for Rogue Email Rules

Many email servers and clients, especially Microsoft Office 365, Microsoft Exchange, and Microsoft Outlook (but also Apple Mail, Gmail, Thunderbird, etc.), allow rules, forms, or filters to be created that can be used by attackers to maliciously eavesdrop on or perform other rogue actions like forwarding copies of messages or deleting messages to hide signs of malicious activity. It can never hurt to see if there are any rogue rules, forms, or filters. Microsoft created a PowerShell script to check for all custom rules and forms in Office 365 instances, here: `https://github.com/OfficeDev/O365-InvestigationTooling/blob/master/Get-AllTenantRulesAndForms.ps1`. This script, from whitehat hacking forum SensePost, checks for rules and forms in Microsoft Exchange environments: `https://github.com/sensepost/notruler`. I do not have scripts for Gmail and other environments, but a decent scripter should be able to write one if needed.

What Do You Know About the Ransomware?

What is everything you know about the ransomware and ransomware gang? Do you know the ransomware program being used, including version? Are there any public reports on how negotiations with past victims have gone? What is the demand? How does the ransomware gang demand payment? What is the initial timeline countdown they are giving? What is the cryptocurrency they are demanding payment in? What cryptocurrency wallet addresses are they using? Is it one address or more?

If you have encrypted data, is there a chance that the data can be decrypted without the backups or without the ransomware decryption keys? Some ransomware program's encryption routines fail for a myriad of reasons. They think they have succeeded, but the data is not encrypted for some reason. You may be able to try some quick decryption websites to see if the decryption keys for the ransomware you're facing are available there. For example, try `https://www.nomoreransom.org/en/decryption-tools.html`.

The key thing you need to discover about the ransomware program is the name and version if that can be ascertained. This information is very valuable in determining the next steps.

First Team Meeting

After the initial damage is mitigated and prevented from spreading, it's time to have the first official team meeting with all the relevant team members to learn the basic facts of the attack. If you plan to have external consultants involved, this first big meeting is a good time to have them involved. Depending on their role, they may want to lead this meeting and get the answers to the questions they need to know to be helpful and efficient.

Again, the key questions you want answers to are these:

- What are the ransomware demands and known details?
- Has additional damage been prevented?
- Are devices powered off or left on?
- Is networking disabled and if so how?
- Extent of damage (e.g., platforms, locations, roles, numbers, types of involved devices)?
- Do we know how long the ransomware program has likely been dwelling in the environment?
- Do we know how ransomware likely infiltrated the environment?

- Are there additional malware programs found beyond "just" the ransomware program(s) (this is often the case)?
- What is the impact to the business?
- Does it look like data and/or credentials were exfiltrated?
- What ransomware program is involved, and version, if known?
- Is backup safe and verified as good?
- What are dates and times on the latest backups (for each device and role impacted)?
- Who currently knows about the ransomware attack or service disruption? Have there been any unexpected leaks?
- If cyber insurance is involved, has the insurance broker or carrier been notified?
- Who is currently involved in the ransomware incident response, and what are they currently doing?
- What are the top unknowns?
- What are the worst things working against incident response?
- What are the best things working in the team's favor?

Of course, any other relevant details should be shared at this time. It is important to assess what does and doesn't look like it is involved. Different types of services and roles will need different types of incident response experts to resolve.

Determine Next Steps

Now that you know the scope of the damage as well as the strain of ransomware you are dealing with, you can make a more informed decision as to what your next actions will be. Key initial decisions include the following:

- What systems need to be brought back up, in what order, first?
- What are the initial additional steps that need to be performed?
- Does anything else need to be done to stop the spread of damage?
- Based on encrypted or damaged data alone, can the damage be recovered without paying the ransom and/or getting a decryption key?

- If data or credentials have been exfiltrated, what does that mean to the incident response? Will a ransom be paid to prevent the release of stolen data and information even if backups are good?
- Will the ransom be paid? If so, will a professional negotiator be involved?
- Will impacted systems be repaired (i.e., just known malware removed), completely restored from known good copies, or rebuilt from scratch?
- Who is needed on the internal teams? What is their location and expected hours of work?
- What logon credentials will need to be changed and when?
- What other recovery specialists need to be brought in? What are their timing, rates, budgets, etc.?
- What is the public PR response? Who else needs to be notified?
- Critical paths? Project plan?
- Additional meetings needed? Who are the necessary stakeholders for these meetings, such as specialists, senior management, or a general team meeting?
- Next meeting times and dates?

Pay the Ransom or Not?

Do you pay the ransom or not? That is a huge answer that needs to be determined. Again, it may be that the ransom is paid even if the data can be recovered from backups simply because of the risk from additional data exfiltration exposure. Much of the work done in the future relies on that answer.

Keep in mind that most ransomware victims, even the ones that pay the ransom, do not recover all their data. However, victims obtaining the ransomware decryption keys tend to recover more data on average.

Recover or Rebuild?

If you recover systems (i.e., decrypt data, remove known malware, change logon credentials, etc.), can they be completely trusted? Or do you have to rebuild everything from scratch, reusing nothing from before? The safest, least risky option is to completely rebuild from scratch all impacted systems. This is the only way to guarantee that previous compromised information cannot be used to more easily compromise you again. It's the only way to ensure that there is not some hidden, additional, backdoor program lurking somewhere that the attacker can use to compromise your environment again.

> ## Recovery versus Rebuild
> Rebuilding everything from scratch is a type of recovery. But in this book, the term recovery is used to describe recovery methods that include everything less than a complete rebuild or replacement.

With that said, most ransomware gangs can be trusted to not re-exploit victims who have paid the ransom. Not all, but most. If ransomware gangs got paid and re-attacked the same victims again, as word of this practice spread, far less victims would ever pay the ransom. It is in the criminals' own best interests not to attack the same victim again (if the ransom is paid).

Knowing this, many victims decide that the cost and time to rebuild everything from scratch can result in significant, expensive, painful downtime. Even though they know not rebuilding increases risk that something malicious was left behind by the attackers, many victims decide to accept the risk and just do recovery. Every victim needs to decide for themselves, do they do simple repair recovery and trust the attackers that nothing else is amiss or completely rebuild things from scratch? This is not always a binary decision. Some victims decide to rebuild some impacted systems and to recover or not touch others. It's all up to how the victim organization has been impacted, resources, timing, and risk acceptance.

Organizations considering getting cybersecurity insurance in the future may want to consider rebuilding. Some insurance companies will not insure a previous victim unless they have rebuilt their environment from scratch. The rebuild versus risk decision is graphically represented in Figure 7.2.

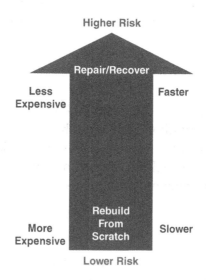

Figure 7.2   Rebuild vs. repair recovery risk decision

Overall, if you've done these initial response tasks well, your organization and team are starting to feel confident in the information collected and the agreed-upon future path. Stress and uncertainty levels are always going to be high. But a successful initial ransomware response with a lot of documented knowns and critical decisions already made should help to make both less than they otherwise could be.

Be Calm in the Storm

Calm people usually make better decisions. It can be difficult to be calm in the middle of a big ransomware event that has caused massive service disruption. However, if you are a leader, try to project an air of confidence and calm (even if you don't feel that way). There will already be lots of stressed people around you. If you project outward calmness and confidence, you will calm those around you more. If you act excited, stressed out, and unconfident, you will just accelerate those same feelings in others. You will ratchet up people who are already stressed and potentially stress others who were not already stressed. And vice versa. If you project calmness and confidence, you can be a calming influence on everyone. A good, practiced ransomware response plan can have a calming effect.

Summary

This chapter covered the initial ransomware response tasks, including stopping the damage from spreading, collecting initial information, having the initial team meeting, and deciding on next steps. Chapter 8, "Early Responses," discusses the next steps.

Chapter 8
Early Responses

This chapter covers what to do after initially stopping further damage from ransomware. It includes examining what is currently known about the ransomware, additional major decisions that need to be made, and additional early actions. In general, this chapter covers the second phase of the ransomware response but does not include most recovery tasks.

This chapter assumes the ransomware response plan has been initiated and that the ransomware program has been identified and prevented from spreading further or causing more damage. The on-site damage you already have is assumed to be the maximum damage you will have.

What Do You Know?

Now is the time to, again, write down and document what is known about the ransomware attack including the following:

- What resources are impacted?
- What resources seem unimpacted?
- What are the commonalities of the resources that have or haven't been impacted (e.g., location, OS, role, network, shared services, accounts, etc.)?

- What assets are still up and operating normally, if any?
- What networks are still up and operating normally, if any?
- Are there assets or networks operating at partial levels?
- What are the current project teams, in-process task threads, and likely future tasks?
- Who currently knows of the incident?
- Who has been contacted and is aware of the incident?
- What is the current communications plan? What are you still waiting on to be communicated to whom?
- Do you know if any data has been exfiltrated? Do you know if any data has been exfiltrated, including emails, logon credentials, or employee or customer information?
- What malicious executables have been identified?
- Have you or anyone in your organization reached out to the ransomware gang? Has the ransomware gang reached out to you? If so, what was communicated or requested?
- How much is the ransomware extortion request?
- What is the method of payment?
- Have the backups been verified as reliable?
- What is not going according to plan and why?
- Biggest outstanding issues and challenges?
- Other outstanding questions?
- Any other notable data points?

These items should be well documented and the remaining outstanding issues prioritized. Update the project plan, listing critical paths in the incident response that are still outstanding, in prioritized order. List the major remaining questions that need to be answered. Summarize findings and communicate what is known with the team. Allow the team to update and correct current understandings.

Get on the Same Page

Too many times I've asked a victim organization incident response team an important question at this stage only to get conflicting answers from different team members. Simple questions, such as "Have you contacted the ransomware gang yet?" often get contradicting answers from multiple individuals. Not only is it embarrassing, but it means the group is not effectively communicating, working on the same information, or "rowing in the same direction." Make sure all major information is known and shared among all team members, especially before making crucial decisions or working with outside groups. One way to do that is to instruct all team members to communicate with a central contact point, who collects, aggregates, and routinely distributes all known, critical information. Perhaps known information can be shared to a "wiki" or spreadsheet that is accessible by all. Team members can be instructed to check the wiki hourly to see the latest updates.

A Few Things to Remember

There are a few important things to remember that many victims get wrong or misunderstand the importance of at this stage of the response.

- Encryption is likely not your only problem.
- Reputational harm may occur.
- Firings may happen.
- It could get worse.

I'll cover each in more detail below.

Encryption Is Likely Not Your Only Problem

Many victims focus on the local, logical damage done by the ransomware's encryption process. It's important to remember that more than 70 percent of all ransomware can also exfiltrate data and/or business/employee/customer data and credentials. A quick Internet search can usually provide whether or not the currently identified ransomware strain/gang you are dealing with is known as commonly participating in data exfiltration. If the ransomware strain/gang is known for exfiltrating data, you must assume they have done so within any organization exploited by it. Ransomware response leaders must remind stakeholders of this risk during the initial phases of the incident. Many people saying the word *ransomware* tend to focus only on the encryption part and forget other factors may be involved.

Third-party legal liability may also play a factor. According to past cybersecurity insurance statistics, third-party payouts factored into nearly a third of all cybersecurity insurance claims. Third-party liability covers damages to downstream stakeholders and customers who were impacted by an upstream cybersecurity incident. At the bare minimum, this can include perceived or real damages from service/product interruptions, data privacy issues, regulatory defenses, and media liability.

Many ransomware victims have been sued for data privacy issues. It is the biggest reason why a ransomware victim organization is sued. Two examples of such actions can be found at https://www.fierce-healthcare.com/tech/following-ransomware-attack-scripps-health-now-facing-class-action-lawsuits-over-data-breach and https://grahamcluley.com/irish-hospital-sued-by-cancer-patient-after-ransomware-attack/.

Although it's less common, downstream impacted individual customers have also sued over service and product delivery interruption issues. An example of such action can be found at https://healthitsecurity.com/news/class-action-lawsuit-filed-after-allscripts-ransomware-attack. There are even claims, later successfully refuted, that ransomware attacks are causing deaths that would have otherwise been avoided such as in the case of an attack on a hospital covered at https://www.hipaajournal.com/hospital-ransomware-attack-results-in-patient-death/. Here is another: https://healthitsecurity.com/news/us-fertility-sued-over-ransomware-attack-health-data-exfiltration.

While it may seem that a majority of the lawsuits appear to be healthcare-related, victims in industries of all types are sued (https://abc11.com/colonial-pipeline-gas-prices-shortage/10821125/), including cloud service providers (https://www.securitymagazine.com/articles/93857-blackbaud-sued-after-ransomware-attack), stockholders (https://www.cyberscoop.com/fedex-shareholder-suit-notpetya/), and a transit authority (https://www.cbc.ca/news/canada/british-columbia/translink-ransomware-attack-lawsuit-1.5887462).

Any ransomware victim organization holding the private data of others should assume legal liability is high until time proves otherwise. That's why all organizations hit by ransomware need to make sure their legal counsel is involved in all ransomware recovery operations and communications. Someone suing an organization hit by ransomware is for sure going to request that all email and other communications related to the ransomware event be shared with the prosecution. Privileged communications between the organization and legal counsel will likely be harder or impossible for the prosecution to obtain.

Reputational Harm May Occur

Even if your organization does not get sued by customers or third parties, there is likely to be some amount of reputational harm. Most victim organizations are able to weather the initial reputational harm, recover, and go on to have increased revenues. This is not always true. There are organizations that literally cease to exist. The ransomware attack takes them offline, and they never become a "going concern" again.

Some organizations recover initially, but the reputational harm lingers, sometimes for years. Ask Equifax, victim of one of the largest data breaches (https://en.wikipedia.org/wiki/2017_Equifax_data_breach) in recorded history. To this day, there are potential customers and breach victims that refuse to do business with them. Financially, they are doing better than before the breach, but who knows what they could be doing today if they hadn't suffered one of the worst breaches in history. To be clear, I don't think Equifax was doing computer security significantly worse than most other potential victims, but media narratives can be very hard to counteract.

Firings May Happen

Organizations suffering financial and reputational issues like to assign blame, even if that blame is misplaced. If a ransomware event occurred because of a decision you did or didn't make, your job could be on the chopping block. If your company was part of the victim organization's security defense, they could easily decide to go with a competing vendor. Downstream customers could easily decide to use other vendors and services.

Be Careful of Accepting Blame

If someone is pointing to a decision you did or didn't make as the reason why a cybersecurity incident happened, be cautious in "courageously" accepting blame. Many people might see proactively accepting personal blame as the ethical, "right thing to do." I assure you, any lawyer would caution you against doing so. Accepting blame is more likely to get you fired than to get you celebrated as someone who takes responsibility. This is not to say that you should deny any accountability forever if your direct decisions or actions are found to be directly involved; just be careful about any proactive acceptance of blame, at least without talking to a lawyer first. Accepting blame might make you more likely to be held professionally and personally liable in lawsuits, and the prosecution's lawyers would love to get documented evidence of you accepting blame for the incident during the judicial discovery process.

It's always a good idea to do a "post-mortem" on why the ransomware attack was successful, what could have been done better to prevent it, and how the ransomware response went. If blame is going to be assigned, oftentimes a good post-mortem assessment shows there's plenty of it to go around. Usually it is not just one person's mistake that leads to the compromise.

It Could Get Worse

Many ransomware victims assume what they currently know about is everything, including all compromised resources, damage, and stolen data. For example, they believe, after having been reassured multiple times, that their backups are safe and ready to be used in restoration. Many times this is not the case. The people giving the initial assurance were unaware that the backups were faulty, encrypted with unknown encryption keys, or have been corrupted for weeks to months.

Based on the initial assurances, some victims have refused, or even taunted, the ransomware gang, believing they have everything under control. Sometimes this is true, but sometimes the victim didn't realize the extent and length of the compromise, and the ransomware gang comes back more voraciously, angrier, and with higher demands.

Do Not Disrespect a Ransomware Gang Under Any Circumstances

Some victims have unknowingly or knowingly disrespected the ransomware gang so badly that the ransomware gang takes it personally and causes the victim maximum damage now or, if unable to implement now, in the future. There is no benefit to taunting a cybercriminal, ever! Now is not the time to let an overly confident ego get in the way.

Many victims think what they know about is the worst of it. I've had many victims tell the ransomware gang they would not pay the ransom only to learn that the ransomware gang has far more control over their network than they thought; or the ransomware gang reveals they also have the victim's most valuable confidential data, and they ask for double the original ransom.

I've seen ransomware gangs retaliate by causing more damage, including attacking customers, employees, and initiating large, distributed denial-of-service (DDoS) attacks. Ransomware gangs will sometimes use every tool at their disposal to cause the victim organization unbearable operational interruption, financial losses, and reputational pain. Some ransomware gangs start out with the most pain possible, and others rachet up the pain only if the victim refuses to pay the first ransom request.

It's a good rule of thumb to assume there are factors you don't yet know and that the attackers may hold additional cards they have yet to play. Always proceed conservatively and with caution.

Major Decisions

There are a handful or so of major decisions that must be made at this point that drive other remaining decisions and actions. Some of those major decisions are discussed in more detail in the following sections.

Business Impact Analysis

At some future point, you will be bringing your impacted business assets back online. You should already have a business impact analysis (BIA) done, and if not, quickly perform one. In most cases, the BIA will state the various mission-critical systems that must come back up, in order, depending on operational and financial objectives. Make a numbered list starting with the needed dependent systems that must be recovered first.

Most applications and systems have multiple supporting dependencies, such as the network, IP addressing, DHCP, DNS, security systems, authentication systems, databases, middleware, front-end systems, etc. Figure out which systems need to come up first (don't forget email, help desk, phones, etc.) and all the dependencies that must first be brought to a known clean state in order for the relying systems to come up. Core infrastructure will always be among the first systems that need to be restored.

In most ransomware scenarios, you will not know what logon credentials are compromised. Assume all credentials not protected by multifactor authentication (MFA) are compromised. This means all the non-MFA passwords to your network equipment, infrastructure, and computer security equipment must be changed in order to even think about relying on them again. Start with the basics and then move up your dependency chain until you can get the main priorities and applications back online.

There may be times when a lower-priority system can be brought back online before a higher-priority system, with far less work. If you can work on multiple recoveries at the same time, it may make sense to recover the "low-hanging fruit" earlier than its BIA priority might suggest, if for nothing else than as an emotional morale booster.

Determine Business Interruption Workarounds

For some part of the ransomware incident, one or more systems will not be operational or fully operational. How will the business conduct business while the primary systems are out? "Workarounds" should have been documented in existing disaster recovery/business continuity plans already. For example, it may mean taking customer requests by phone and using paper to record new transactions. It may mean breaking out paper credit card forms, writing in credit card numbers, or using physical credit card embossing machines. Can your company's business be conducted using an alternate application, such as an existing mobile or cloud-based alternative? All the alternatives should have already been worked out in existing preparation plans, but if not, now is the time to brainstorm and test alternatives.

Did Data Exfiltration Happen?

Have you been able to rule in or out data exfiltration? If it seems the ransomware gang exfiltrated data, what data? Since more than 70 percent of ransomware gangs now exfiltrate data, in light of evidence to the contrary, assume critical data has been exfiltrated. Many times, the gangs were able to download data, but it isn't the most damaging, worst-case scenario. If they claim to have data, have they sent "proof of life"? Are there classes of data that, if stolen, would make you pay the ransom for sure? If data exfiltration has happened, do you need to decide whether an official data breach has happened?

Can You Decrypt the Data Without Paying?

In a small minority of scenarios, it may be possible to decrypt encrypted data without paying the ransom extortion demands. Even though fairly rare, it can't hurt to see if one of these scenarios applies:

- Ransomware is buggy and didn't encrypt files.
- Ransomware decryption keys exist on a website that the victim knows about and can use.
- Ransomware gangs publishes all of their decryption keys.
- Ransomware master key was recorded during the encryption process by some monitoring program.
- Decryption keys can be found in memory of the impacted devices.
- Law enforcement has control of the ransomware decryption keys (this is another example of why contacting CISA or the FBI can be a good thing).

The following sections go into more detail on the individual scenarios.

Ransomware Is Buggy

There are examples of ransomware simply not encrypting files for a myriad of reasons. Sometimes it's because the ransomware program had one or more bugs and simply did not work. Sometimes, the exploited device had a defensive system that stopped the encryption. Other times there was some security or configuration setting that prevented the ransomware program from being successful. So, always check and confirm that the files the ransomware claimed were encrypted are really encrypted.

Ransomware Decryption Websites

There are websites on the Internet, like https://www.nomoreransom. org, which hold one or more ransomware decryption keys. Some of these sites, such as No More Ransom, are more reputable than others. Many of the websites are very old, not current, and haven't been updated with recent decryption keys for years. Oftentimes, the ransomware they cover hasn't been used in years.

The best thing most victims can do is a quick Internet search on their ransomware strain name along with the search string "decryption keys," and see if any viable sites come back. Better yet, let a trained ransomware response professional do the search. Some of the websites ask for or require that the victims upload their encrypted files. If so, make sure any uploaded files are not confidential, as you cannot trust the site you upload files to. Other websites ask for cryptocurrency addresses, which are then linked to the ransomware the website is tracking.

Example websites offering to help with decryption include the following:

- https://godecrypt.com/
- https://www.avast.com/ransomware-decryption-tools
- https://geeksadvice.com/remove-gujd-ransomware-virus/
- https://howtofix.guide/how-to-decrypt-djvu-ransomware-files/

There are many dozens of them on the Internet.

Ransomware Gang Publishes Decryption Keys

In some instances, the ransomware gangs themselves will release the keys. Many times, they claim they are going out of business, willingly or unwillingly, and publicly release their master keys. It has happened more than a few times, including as indicated in these news stories:

- https://www.bleepingcomputer.com/news/security/avaddon-ransomware-shuts-down-and-releases-decryption-keys/
- https://www.zdnet.com/article/fonixcrypter-ransomware-gang-releases-master-decryption-key/
- https://www.secureworld.io/industry-news/shade-ransomware-shutdown-decryption-keys

Sniff a Ransomware Key Off the Network?

There is the possibility that a defender can capture the network packets between an impacted computer and the ransomware's command-and-control (C&C) servers, allowing them to capture one or more encryption keys. An example of how someone might do it using Wireshark is at https://sensorstechforum.com/find-decryption-key-files-ransomware/.

Sniffing encryption keys off of networks is possible, but since most ransomware programs use HTTPS, all the traffic between the victim device to the C&C servers is encrypted. To sniff the traffic, the network packet analyzer must be installed on the victim's computer, or the network architected in such a way to see "inside" the HTTPS-protected packets. Even then, it's not an easy process.

The problem is that most of today's ransomware programs use a different encryption key for each encrypted file or folder, and those keys are encrypted by another master key (or set of master keys). It's difficult or nearly impossible to catch the master key. Thus, any encryption key you sniff is only going to work with one file or folder, and the average compromised device has more than 100,000 files. That's a lot of keys to sniff and use in a decryption process over and over.

Still, if you're looking for one particular key for a particular important file or folder, it may be something to consider. For most victims, it's too much work to recover even one system. On top of that, remember, data exfiltration is a major threat, and data encryption is not your only worry.

Recovery Companies Who Lie About Decryption Key Use

There is a real problem of "ransomware recovery" companies that claim to recover ransomware-encrypted data without paying the ransom, many of whom are lying. Many of these companies claim to have a special, elite ability to recover encrypted files without paying the ransom, but all they are really doing is paying the ransom, getting the decryption keys, and making the victim pay significantly more than they had to. This phenomenon is well covered in this excellent exposé found at https://www.newyorker.com/magazine/2021/06/07/how-to-negotiate-with-ransomware-hackers.

These companies are used by enough victims that I sometimes wonder if it's being done by accident because the victims are unaware or willfully on purpose for some other hidden agenda. Surely, some ransomware victims just aren't aware that the company they've come across that promises to help them with ransomware is a sham company—at least in how they propose to recover encrypted data.

Perhaps there are also companies that have publicly "officially" decided for one or more reasons not to pay the ransom, but really want or need to when it happens. Maybe it's forbidden by the CEO, board of directors, or an industry regulator, etc. Possibly the victim finds themselves unable to recover the data any other way, and they decide that despite their initial promise not to pay the ransom, that they need to secretly pay the ransom in order to get the best outcome. Working with a sham firm gives them coverage or even plausible deniability if it gets discovered.

If You Get the Decryption Keys

If you get the decryption keys, don't directly use them on production data on a production system during the first test. Instead, back up the encrypted data and restore to another system—a virtual machine (VM) is useful, because it can be easily isolated and reset if needed. Then attempt the initial recovery there.

Don't Give Trust Easily

Be aware that ransomware decryption programs may be buggy or contain malware themselves. Trust nothing that you yourself did not create, especially software from attackers. Back up data to be test decrypted and run in a VM, until the decryption process is known to be a safe and effective restoration program and process. There have been many reports of a ransomware gang's decryption process not working. There have been even more reports of a "decryptor" downloaded off the Internet not working and even reports of decryptors containing malware or intentionally causing more damage. Many experts recommend never restoring on original computers. They want all restoration done to alternate computers or virtual machines. This minimizes risk and potentially saves forensics information on the original impacted computer. If you do that, you'll need to backup the original computer's data and restore it to an alternate computer with a hardware and software configuration that will align and work with the restored data (and programs).

Save Encrypted Data Just in Case

The data you decrypt may not successfully decrypt all the way for one reason or another. Not all ransomware gangs are known for their bug-free, flawless code. Even if you decide to skip decrypting the data altogether, you may want to save a copy of the encrypted data just in case the ransomware gang, law enforcement, or another recovery group releases the decryption keys in the future.

If you can decrypt the encrypted data without paying the ransom, this is great! Document your success and share with team members immediately. However, there are still other reasons that may cause a victim to pay the ransom even if they can recover the data without needing to pay the extortion demand. The ability to successfully decrypt the data and deciding whether to pay the ransom are two different phases in ransomware recovery, although they are often related.

Determine Whether the Ransom Should Be Paid

Factors to consider when deciding whether to pay the ransom have been covered in previous chapters, but at this point in a response effort the decision may not have been made. Now is the time to decide if paying the ransom will be done or not. The decision will end up creating a distinctly different set of actions moving forward.

Not Paying the Ransom

Many organizations (estimated at 40 percent to 60 percent of victims) decide not to pay the ransom for one or more reasons. This is a great decision in many scenarios, and ultimately if most organizations made the same decision, ransomware would not be the major problem it is today. Unfortunately, because so many victims pay the extortion demand, one individual decision (i.e., possibly your decision) does not impact whether or not future ransomware incidents will occur. The decision to pay or not pay the ransom should be made solely on the factors involved for each victim.

If the victim has the ability to pay the ransom and is considering not paying, they should confirm whether:

- They can rebuild or recover the systems and data using an alternate method; or can survive without the data.
- All needed backups are confirmed as safe and reliable if the victim hopes to restore the impacted systems.

- They have confirmed the estimated timing of how long it will take to restore all corrupted systems from backup, or how long rebuilding will take.
- Data or credentials have been exfiltrated that cause problems for employees or customers.
- They have considered the reputational or legal harm that might result from not paying the ransom.
- They have considered possible additional damage or demands that may be coming once the ransomware gang is told they will not be getting paid.
- They considered that a future attack from the same ransomware gang may occur undoing their current incident recovery efforts (i.e., paying the ransom usually means the same ransomware gang will not attack the same victim in the future).

These questions are not trying to convince any victim to pay or not pay the ransom. Paying the ransom is up to each individual victim. These questions and considerations, however, highlight some of the factors that could be missed or overlooked and that might lead a victim to pay a ransom even if they were not initially inclined to pay. Decision-makers need to be aware of them.

If you don't pay the ransom, document the decision along with how the data and systems will be recovered, and tell the team.

Paying the Ransom

If a victim is considering paying the ransom, the following factors should be considered:

- What is the initial requested extortion amount?
- How long was the victim initially given to pay the ransom?
- Does the ransomware gang have a history of providing the required decryption keys after getting paid? Did the decryption keys and/or program work to fully recover the encrypted data?
- Is it legal for the victim to pay the ransom?
- If cybersecurity insurance or law enforcement is involved, do they approve paying the ransom?

- Does the victim have the full ransom amount to pay, or can the ransomware amount demanded be negotiated down to meet the ability of the victim to pay?
- How long will it take for the victim to get ransom extortion amount in a payable form?
- How are communications with the ransomware gang performed?
- How is the ransom to be paid? Which cryptocurrency? Usually it will be bitcoin (e.g., 97 percent of all ransomware victims who paid the ransom were asked to pay in bitcoin).
- What are the involved cryptocurrency addresses, and where is the payment to be made?
- Will a professional ransomware negotiator be used?
- Will a cryptocurrency exchange be involved? If an exchange is involved, what is the lag time between transferred payment and the cryptocurrency being available for use?
- Will a cryptocurrency account or wallet need to be set up?
- Will a TOR browser need to be set up to communicate on the dark web?

When the ransomware amount has been successfully negotiated, ask for proof that the decryption keys will work. At this point, the ransomware gang may ask for a smaller payment ("to show mutual trust"). When done, the ransomware gang provides one or more keys to decrypt some of the data.

If data exfiltration has also occurred, proof of life of the exfiltrated data should be required. If data exfiltration did happen, the victim needs to re-affirm with the ransomware gang that their stolen data must be successfully deleted upon the payment of the ransom (especially when that is one of the primary reasons for why the ransom is being paid). Some ransomware gangs will ignore this request, but it can't hurt to express the importance to your organization and why it's paying in the first place.

If paying the ransom, usually it will be paid in cryptocurrency. If paid in cryptocurrency, whoever is doing the actual paying should confirm the details of the payment, especially the account/key to which the payment is made. Payments made to the wrong account usually can never be reversed. There are cases of victims paying the ransom to the wrong account and losing that money forever. It's not like the ransomware gang member is going to take less money because the victim made a mistake. It's best to re-confirm the payment details provided by the attacker, make a small test payment to the attacker, and have them confirm it. You should then have two or three people confirm the payment details entered during the larger payment before it is committed.

Record any ransom payments, tests, and involved details. Communicate with the team. Make sure any paid ransoms are recorded and communicated as such to the victim's tax and financial people. Paid ransoms are often tax deductible.

Recover or Rebuild Involved Systems?

Another major decision is whether impacted systems are completely rebuilt from scratch or just recovered. As covered in Chapter 7 and summarized in Figure 7.2, rebuilding is far less risky from a cybersecurity point of view but is usually slower and far more expensive to perform than just simple recovery. With recovery, the ransomware programs are removed, passwords are changed, and other malicious modifications are searched for and removed, if found. Even though it's the riskiest option, most ransomware victims choose recovery over rebuilding and accept the remaining risk for most involved devices. Many ransomware victims did not appropriately understand the risk involved with not rebuilding, and others are simply forced to rebuild because of time, money, and other resource constraints.

Determine Dwell Time

How long was the ransomware program inside of your devices and/or environment? Knowing this answer can have significant impacts on your decision to recover or rebuild. The longer the dwell time, the greater the risk. Ransomware often looks for and steals passwords it can find while dwelling. Assume any password typed or any stored in a password manager or browser, during the ransomware's dwell time, is compromised. Shorter dwell times, such as minutes or just a few hours, means the ransomware gang and their malware likely did not discover as much confidential information. Many malware programs do an initial, cursory check for passwords (sometimes only in the first 15 seconds) and then immediately encrypt the devices they are on. They either don't exfiltrate data or don't look around as much to determine what to take, if anything. Shorter dwell times mean lower risk.

Determine Root Cause

It is important that great effort be expended to see if it can be determined how the ransomware program gained its initial access. This can often be done by looking at log files and logons to look for unauthorized activity. The unauthorized activity is going to be related to one or more malicious programs and/or scripts and usually involves unauthorized logons. Looking at the various timestamps for the newly installed programs and scripts and the related logons often points to when the malicious program first appeared and where. That finding can often lead to a root cause.

As covered in Chapter 2, "Preventing Ransomware," most ransomware gains initial root access using social engineering methods, followed by unpatched software, followed by password guessing (or the attacker knows the password and doesn't need to guess) against remote admin services. Defenders can look into their logs to see if they can spot the potentially malicious activity. If no root cause can be found, defenders should assume the most popular three methods (as listed at the beginning of this paragraph) were used.

It's important that the defender try to figure out what root-cause exploit the ransomware used, because if that vulnerability is left open and the ransom is not paid, the current, involved ransomware gang is likely to use the exploit again. It's important for all three of the most common ransomware root exploit methods to be mitigated to prevent the current and future potential ransomware attacks.

It is common for ransomware victims to be so caught up in recovery efforts from ransomware that when faced with the possibility of determining the root cause, they don't care or focus on determining the root cause of their current ransomware attack. It could be my anecdotal experience, but the first-time ransomware victims who flout trying to best understand how they were attacked seemed more likely to be hit again. Usually, the second and third times are worse.

Point Fix or Time to Get Serious?

Ransomware victims seem to go one or two ways during recovery. Some victims want to recover as quickly as possible with the least amount of computer security self-reflection. They simply want to get back up and operating, back to status quo. Others seem to take the attack as a wakeup call and opportunity to take a look at their overall computer security posture. The latter group tends to redefine and improve their computer security posture and become more long-term resilient. For example, the former group will reset all their passwords. The latter group moves from passwords to multifactor authentication. The former group tries to do patching better on just the software systems involved. The latter group improves all of their patch management. The former group turns on Windows logging. The latter group buys endpoint detection and response (EDR) software and buys a security incident event monitoring (SIEM) service or product. The former does the bare minimum to get back up and running. The latter takes the opportunity to do serious risk assessment and looks to fix a whole lot of broken or weak practices during the recovery.

It would be disingenuous of me to say that both strategies have scenarios where they work equally well. The latter strategy of seriously examining your organization's overall cybersecurity is the preferred method. Want to keep malicious hackers and malware out of your environment long-term? You'll have a better chance with a more encompassing strategy.

It, of course, is likely to be more expensive and time-consuming in the short-term. Fixing a broken environment with a lot of weaknesses and building a strong culture of cybersecurity strength takes time, resources, and money. Organizations performing more holistic assessments and fixing all their weaknesses are far more likely to avoid another ransomware incident and fare better against malicious adversaries in general. If you get exploited by ransomware, use the event to improve as much cybersecurity as you can.

Early Actions

There are many additional responses that need to take place regardless of the prior decisions. Here are some of the big ones that need to take place at this phase of the response.

Preserve the Evidence

In most recovery scenarios, it is crucial to preserve the evidence. This often means taking forensics copies and memory snapshots of the impacted devices before they are recovered or rebuilt. Doing so can be a crucial step in recovery, can assist with legal issues, and can help determine the root cause of the ransomware exploitation.

Remove the Malware

If everything possibly impacted by the ransomware event is not rebuilt from scratch and you are recovering impacted assets, the ransomware and any involved programs, scripts, and tools need to be identified and removed. How you do this depends on your existing or newly purchased cybersecurity software. Most ransomware programs have a particular common name or pattern of names that can be readily identified. Those can be removed manually or using an anti-malware scanning program like EDR.

Because systems will likely still be disconnected from the network at this time and may be powered off, each potentially impacted device will have to be connected to, and the scan run. If local USB key devices are used, make sure the USB devices are "write-protected" so USB-infecting malware can't infect the USB key and spread the infection to other computers.

If the network was disconnected using network access control points and the devices still powered on, you may be able to run the scan remotely by locking down the network connectivity so that only the scanned devices can communicate with just the scanning computer and other supporting network infrastructure (e.g., DNS, DHCP, Active Directory, etc.). You want to prevent all other connections.

Search for all related malware files, scripts, and tools. Look for strange, unexplained files on impacted hosts, servers, domain controllers, and storage disks. Run anti-malware detection tools in their most sensitive, "paranoid" detection mode. Check network connections for strange, unexplained network connections. Of course, if you don't know what is normal, you will have a hard time recognizing abnormal processes and connections.

Note: When in doubt, if you can't completely gain confidence that you have removed all potential malicious programs, scripts, and tools, rebuild from scratch whatever you cannot confirm as being clean. Rebuilding is the preferred method anyway for pure risk reduction.

For Windows Computers

I'm a big fan of Microsoft's free Sysinternals Tools (`https://www.sysinternals.com`). I especially like Process Explorer, Autoruns, TCPView, and Process Monitor, for forensic analysis. Process Explorer and Autoruns have the ability to send any running process for a malware check to Google's `VirusTotal.com` website, where it can be scanned by more than 70 different antivirus products. TCPView is a quick and easy way to correlate running executables to the network connections they make. There are better tools, but these are both free and pretty easy to use. If you don't have any other more sophisticated forensics tools, these work in a pinch for Microsoft Windows systems.

Change All Passwords

You have to assume that any used or stored passwords available during the ransomware program's dwell time are compromised. At some future date, you will need to change all involved passwords, including network logins, email passwords, system accounts, daemon accounts, privileged users, web servers, web services, etc. Any passwords used by employees for any reason, whether stored or manually typed in, need to be changed. Any passwords stored in a browser, or a password manager will need to be changed. All system, network, privileged accounts, and email passwords need to be changed after removing *all malware*, but before re-connecting to the Internet.

The passwords must be changed after removing all malware, tools, or scripts that could steal and exfiltrate passwords. You don't want to change passwords only to have malware exfiltrate the new passwords. Once all malware, tools, and scripts have been removed, change the passwords. Start with the elevated accounts, services, daemons, etc., and then those accounts can be used to automate and quicken the recovery. Users should have their passwords cancelled and forced to set new ones as they come back onto clean systems.

Summary

This chapter covered the major decisions and tasks that need to be accomplished right after stopping the initial damage and spread (covered in Chapter 7). It includes deciding on what systems and dependencies need to be recovered first and when. It includes determining whether data can be recovered without paying the ransom, whether the ransom will be paid or not, root-cause analysis, data exfiltration issues, determining dwell time, malware removal, and changing all passwords. Chapter 9, "Environment Recovery," covers how to recover an environment in more detail.

Chapter 9
Environment Recovery

In this chapter, we discuss how to recover your IT environment from a ransomware attack. It is assumed that you have stopped and removed the ransomware threat and any other related malicious executables. This chapter dovetails with the material you learned in Chapter 8. You have either paid the ransom or not, and you have recovered what data you could either way. The ransomware program and attackers are no longer a threat. In this chapter, we will cover how to recover or rebuild your network and various popular platforms.

This chapter assumes your whole environment, or a large part of your environment, was impacted, and you're doing a full environment recovery. If the ransomware event was only a partial impact, you will want to modify your plan appropriately.

Big Decisions

There are still two major decisions to make, both of which were introduced in previous chapters. Decisions still need to be made now in order to continue going forward. The two big decisions are recovering versus rebuilding and determining the order in which to proceed.

Recover vs. Rebuild

Recovery versus rebuilding was covered in Chapter 8, but I'll cover it here again because it's often a decision that is faced over and over and not just once at the beginning of the response.

The first decision is whether to recover the involved compromised devices, potentially involved or confirmed as compromised, or rebuild from scratch. As covered previously, rebuilding from scratch is the safest answer from a security standpoint, but also likely the most costly in terms of resources and time. Recovery means removing current and potential likely future attack vectors from a compromised device so that you have a reasonable amount of reassurance, without having to rebuild every impacted device from scratch.

The recover versus rebuild decision can be made on a per-device or per-application basis. It's not a binary choice; it isn't all or nothing. For example, you can decide to rebuild from scratch network devices and client workstations and recover Microsoft Active Directory and DNS. Choose the option that has the best combination of assurance versus cost for your situation.

Retain Evidence

As stated in previous chapters, most victims should do their best to maintain forensic evidence before the recovery/rebuild process. It not only helps in legal issues, but it allows a better chance of recovery and reconstruction of the root cause of the incident. In most cases, this means doing forensic copying of hard drives and memory before recovering or rebuilding.

In What Order

You have to decide in what order to recover or rebuild involved IT resources. All passwords should have already been reset (after all malware and unauthorized access has been eliminated). Your business impact analysis should determine what applications and services to recover or rebuild and in what order. If you have no other plan, consider using the following list as a general priority template and starting guide to create your own custom plan:

- Network infrastructure
- IT security devices/applications/services
- Virtual machine hosts
- General backup/restoration services
- High-priority/Tier 1 client computers/devices
- Email or other primary communication software/services
- Highest-priority/Tier 1 applications/services
- High-priority/Tier 2 servers and clients
- Medium-priority/Tier 3 servers and clients
- Low-priority/Tier 4 servers and clients

Tiers

Numbered tiers refer to priorities of assets that indicate the preferred order of recovery. Depending on the environment, Tier 1 assets may be underlying infrastructure services (e.g., DNS, Active Directory, DHCP, etc.), or be infrastructure services plus the most valuable and critical services and data used to benefit the organization. Tier 1 means "recover these first!" Tier 2 is the second most important assets and data, and so on.

Restoring Network

Gather all environment documentation possible, including IP addresses, host and domain names, networks, VLANS, etc. Have available any documentation necessary to recover your environment.

Every involved service should be documented as to what network traffic they output or consume so that monitoring of those services can be done, with abnormalities generating immediate alerts and investigations. All investigations should be completed to their end before the service can be broadly deployed in the production environment.

Lab Testing

If you are unsure what network traffic a particular device, service, or application generates or consumes, consider restoring the asset into a lab environment with local process and network monitoring enabled. Start with a new install that has nothing to do with your environment, and document what ports and services are used. Then restore, to the lab environment, the configuration and implementation of what you intended to restore in the production environment, and again, document processes and network connections. Research all processes and network connections to confirm legitimacy and to establish expected baselines.

When starting with the network infrastructure, start by assuring that the physical network devices that make up the network (i.e., routers, switches, Wi-Fi access points, cable modems, WAN devices, etc.) are secure. The passwords should have been changed. Maybe admin logins have been converted to multifactor authentication (MFA) for increased assurance. Perhaps network device firmware has been restored to a known good copy, configuration settings have been restored from a known good copy, or the devices were newly configured from scratch. You want to ensure that nothing that could be malicious is running on the network equipment.

Next, start bringing back up the devices/software/services that provide Internet Protocol (IP) connectivity (i.e., IP address device management). These may include Dynamic Host Configuration Protocol (DHCP) services and Domain Name System (DNS) servers/

services. They may also include virtual local area network (VLAN) and/or software-defined network (SDN) configurations, devices, and services.

Restore IT Security Services

Next, bring up all the critical IT security systems. You want to have all the logging and monitoring at their highest levels of detail and the people in charge of these services heavily participating and monitoring captured events and traffic, looking for any signs of maliciousness. Pay particular attention to the methods used by the ransomware gang during the latest attack, as they are oftentimes likely to be the same methods used to regain control of an impacted network. Victims paying a ransom may be at less risk of exploitation from the same ransomware gang, but it is no guarantee that you won't be exploited again.

Reenabling the Internet

A crucial decision is when to reenable Internet access. Enabling Internet access means outside attackers may be able to make their way back into the environment if all malware and malicious connections were not removed and if passwords were not changed. All early Internet connections should be heavily monitored and reviewed to check for malicious traffic. Be ready to shut down all (or partial) Internet access, again, if a malicious network traffic connection is detected.

Restore Virtual Machines and/or Cloud Services

Virtual machine hosts, like VMware ESXi and Microsoft Hyper-V, can be brought back up. In most environments, they are likely to be supporting infrastructure, applications, and services. Ensure that the VM host software is safe and all admin passwords have been changed. You may reenable cloud infrastructure services at this time, as well.

Restore Backup Systems

Restore your backup and restoration services, again, using safe implementations and changed passwords. Future backup jobs and data should be protected against unauthorized manipulation. You want to restore or rebuild your backup and restoration services before you begin to restore clients, servers, and applications, in case you need to back something up first in those restoration processes. You can't get everything else to a safe and secure state without first doing the same to your backup and restore services.

Restore Clients, Servers, Applications, Services

Finally, clients, servers, applications, and services can begin to be restored, beginning with the highest-priority items first. All clients, servers, applications, and services should have already been prioritized from Tier 1 (highest priority) to Tier 4 (lowest priority). Restore highest-priority assets first and lowest-priority assets last. It is allowable for lower-priority assets to be restored ahead of higher-priority assets if timing and resources allow. Sometimes, it can take weeks to months to restore a high-priority asset, and a lower-priority asset can be done in hours to days, while waiting for the higher-priority asset to be restored.

Lower-Priority Assets Recovered First?

To be clear, restore high-priority assets first every time. If you're waiting around and have some free resources, it's okay to show easier wins. It might seem to go against logic (i.e., restoring lower-priority systems when higher-priority systems need to be restored), but if something can be done quickly without interfering with the higher-priority recovery at the same time, the success of doing it can help grow confidence in the recovery team. This is one of those "in-the-field" lessons, not shown in most project management books, that can be learned only in "battle."

Conduct Unit Testing

During the process of restoring/recovering the necessary servers and clients, you should do individual, small tests. These "unit tests" should be done before starting the wider restorations. Document ahead of time all expected involved processes and network traffic. Create test input and document expected output that is expected from the input. Make sure to include inputs of all possible types to test all the processes of the system being tested. You will, of course, need your subject-matter experts involved to create test input, run processing, and review the output.

Once testing is done, then restore/recover a single instance of the service or application you plan to restore into the production environment. Input test data and document if the expected output (e.g., database records, services, reports, etc.) occurs. If the real output does not match the expected output, then step back and resolve the issues. Once all processes and network connections are confirmed for legitimacy from the initial production test, begin to deploy more widely. Have IT security monitor all restorations (the test and the wider implementation) for any signs of maliciousness. Document outcomes and report to the team.

Rebuild Process Summary

You may decide to rebuild one or more clients or servers. The following is the general process:

1. Make a copy (i.e., hard drive and memory) of the existing system first (optional) in case the rebuild process does not go as planned or for forensics purposes.
2. Collect the necessary instructions, security credentials, software, drivers, and license keys needed for the rebuild process.
3. Rebuild, if needed, hardware and firmware devices/drivers.
4. Rebuild core asset to secure base configuration.
5. Ensure all critical patches are applied.

6. Add new software and services as desired from incident response recommendations.
7. Add custom configuration settings, add service accounts, etc.
8. Restore or re-create data.
9. Connect back into network, if not already done.
10. Do unit testing.
11. Approve for wider deployment.

The term *rebuilding* implies a complete rebuilding from the "bare metal" on up. Traditionally, this might mean formatting a hard drive, installing a clean copy of the operating system, patching, and then starting the software and data restoration process. These days, many devices and operating systems allow a faster, logical rebuilding where all or most of the software is rebuilt as if the computer was fully rebuilt without actually going through all the rebuilding steps. If considering these "quasi-rebuilds," determine whether the quasi-rebuild is safe to use in the rebuild process.

For example, some hackers hide their malware in the "slack space" or unused portions of a storage disk (or even in firmware or video memory). A quasi-rebuild may not restore these usual areas to their known clean copies. If a quasi-rebuild process leaves these areas untouched, it is possible for the malware to "live through" a rebuild. Do quasi-rebuilds only if you are sure malware remnants won't be left around that can be used to more easily allow the hacker or ransomware to re-establish their dominance. Examples of areas used by hackers or malware that are not rebuilt during quasi-rebuilds include the following:

- Unused, unallocated disk sectors
- Unused disk partitions
- BIOS, UEFI, and firmware
- Controller card memory
- Windows registry areas
- Email rules, filters, forms, etc.

When in doubt, erase or rebuild potentially problematic areas.

Watch Out for Malicious Email Rules

Hackers have used malicious email rules and rogue forms for decades to hide maliciousness and backdoors. In many of today's email services, users can use rules, filters, forms, and scripting to customize the way their email client acts upon certain events. They were intended to improve the end user's experience. But hackers have long used them for malicious means. Unless someone looks for unauthorized email rules and removes them, they are likely to "live" through a rebuild. I know of users who have rebuilt all software, implemented new hardware, and changed their passwords, only to have the hackers easily come back into their environment. Sometimes the methods the hacker used were traced to malicious email rules and forms. You can find more details in my one-hour webinar at `https://info.knowbe4.com/webinar-10-ways-hacked-email` where I discuss this sort of attack along with demonstrations of a few related attack tools. You can also find an article I wrote on malicious email rules and forms at `https://blog.knowbe4.com/check-your-email-rules-for-maliciousness`.

These quasi-rebuild processes can range from something akin to a true rebuild to something closer to a partial restoration. For example, Microsoft Windows has three quasi-rebuild methods: Refresh, Reset, and Restore. On its support site at `https://support.microsoft.com/en-us/windows/how-to-refresh-reset-or-restore-your-pc-51391d9a-eb0a-84a7-69e4-c2c1fbceb8dd`, Microsoft describes each this way:

- **Refresh** your PC to reinstall Windows and keep your personal files and settings. Refresh also keeps the apps that came with your PC and the apps you installed from the Microsoft Store.

- **Reset** your PC to reinstall Windows but delete your files, settings, and apps—except for the apps that came with your PC.
- **Restore** your PC to undo recent system changes you've made.

These are on top of the ability to restore files and folders that were backed up using built-in or third-party backup applications. The safest option is probably a Reset, where Windows is restored to the state it was delivered from the vendor on the first day.

For Apple computers, most users would hit Command+R during startup to go into the Apple macOS recovery mode. You will eventually see an option to *Restore from Time Machine*, *Install macOS*, and *Disk Utility*. You can restore from any Time Machine backups that were taken, re-install the MacOS, or delete or erase a particular disk. The Restore From Time Machine option is useful if you can identify a point in time before the ransomware was placed on the system, while Install macOS installs a new version of the operating system, and any Time Machine backups can be used to manually restore specific files or directories.

Rebuilding Linux computers requires either a data restore from a backup program or the vendor's distribution (i.e., distro) series of commands for doing so (e.g., fdisk, mkfs, mount, etc.). The commands vary per the distro and version. You can find one example of a manual Linux rebuild process at `https://documentation.com-mvault.com/commvault/v11/article?p=57175.htm`.

Most other devices have similar types of rebuild processes. Some devices call a rebuild back to the base OS a *hard reset*. In contrast, a *soft reset* may be a simple reboot without rebuilding anything or simply removing some recently installed applications or recently changed settings. Research your device's rebuild and recovery instructions if unsure.

Recovery Process Summary

Recovery implies not restoring an impacted system back to its original configuration and base. A recovery looks for and removes potentially malicious files and configuration settings, and then trusts that the recovery efforts keep the environment safe. The general recovery steps are as follows:

1. Make a copy (e.g., hard drive and memory) of the existing system first (optional) in case the recovery process does not go as planned or for forensics purposes.
2. Collect the necessary instructions, security credentials, software, drivers, and license keys needed for the recovery process.
3. Look for and remove malicious files and configuration settings.
4. Ensure all critical patches are applied.
5. Add the new software and services as desired from incident response recommendations.
6. Add custom configuration settings, add back in service accounts, etc.
7. Add or re-create data.
8. Connect back into network, if not already done.
9. Do unit testing.
10. Approve for wider deployment.

The series of steps is similar whether the system is recovered or rebuilt. The difference in a recovery is you're looking for maliciousness and, if found, removing it before restoring the asset to its place and function in the environment. How you look and what you look for varies based upon computer platform and service. Two examples of recovery are detailed in the following sections:

• Recovering a Windows computer
• Recovering/restoring Microsoft Active Directory

Recovering a Windows Computer

When looking to confirm that a Windows computer is not harboring any maliciousness, here are some common areas of malicious manipulation to check for:

• Auto-startup areas (there are dozens)
• Services

- Programs
- Files and folders
- Registry settings
- `\Windows\System32\drivers\etc\hosts`

Run a trusted anti-malware service in its most detailed mode where it checks every file using every signature. You might be surprised to learn that most AV programs run in their default modes don't check for everything they are capable of doing. Consider downloading and running Microsoft's Sysinternals utilities:

- Process Explorer (`https://docs.microsoft.com/en-us/sysin-ternals/downloads/process-explorer`)
- Autoruns (`https://docs.microsoft.com/en-us/sysinternals/downloads/autoruns`)

Both utilities can interface with Google's VirusTotal.com and scan included files and processes by more than 70 different antivirus scanners. Both utilities do a great job of showing you the places malware, especially active malware, can hide, although you may have to do more research to determine if what they enumerated is a legitimate or malicious program. You cannot always trust VirusTotal to be 100% accurate.

Should You Use Safe Mode?

Some forensic investigators always boot Windows into Safe Mode before doing analysis. This can help to remove malicious software that may be lurking in memory, which, if active, could hide its presence from investigators and investigative tools. However, some ransomware and malware intentionally modify the Safe Boot process, so you cannot be assured that malware isn't still hiding. Booting into Safe Mode will absolutely change many of the normal programs (and even potentially prevent malicious programs) from loading, which would then *not* be discovered by tools like

Autoruns and Process Explorer. If you don't boot in Safe Mode, you increase the risk of malware hiding from forensic investigators slightly. If you do, there's a far greater chance that normal forensic tools, like Autoruns and Process Explorer, will not report malware because they are not loaded and active. If given the choice, I recommend that you do not boot Windows computers into Safe Mode unless you have already identified malware and need to boot into Safe Mode to remove those malicious programs.

When in doubt as to whether a recovered computer is clean or not, rebuild it from scratch instead. No need to take an elevated risk. Recovering and rebuilding are both a lot of work. But the differences are inconsequential compared to the work required due to another successful ransomware attack.

Recovering/Restoring Microsoft Active Directory

Recovering or restoring Microsoft Active Directory (AD) to a known good state is a common task for organizations running Microsoft Windows computers. Active Directory can be provided online by Azure AD or on-premises by traditional Active Directory services running on domain controllers (DCs).

If AD is down, it is usually because the ransomware programs have encrypted one or more domain controllers or at least the primary DC containing the most vital flexible single master operation (FSMO) roles. The best bet is to restore a primary DC from a known, good backup. This can done using a few methods, including the following:

- Restore a full backup of a primary DC(s) with the FSMO roles to an existing DC and promote it to become the primary DC.
- Build a brand new DC, install or transfer (if a fully functional AD DC still exists) the FSMO roles to the new DC.
- Use Azure Site Recovery (if enabled) to a stable recovery point.

If data restoration doesn't work, you may need to rebuild a new AD from scratch. Some ransomware victims choose to rebuild from scratch to minimize risk and to take the opportunity to remove legacy AD objects they had long been trying to remove but could not otherwise justify the downtime. But now that ransomware has them down anyway, they use the security justification to build AD the way it should be built for the current operation (and remove legacy remnants).

Usually restoring AD means the other underlying network services (e.g., network infrastructure, DNS, DHCP, etc.) have been recovered first. If a partial restoration is desired, you will need to review the existing AD and its most critical security-related objects (e.g., users, groups, and group policy objects) looking for malicious modifications or additions.

The most common AD modification related to ransomware is adding new members to privileged groups (such as Enterprise Admins, Domain Admins, or local Administrators). Remove all unneeded members from elevated groups.

Here are other guides that can help with restoring AD during a ransomware recovery event:

- Backing Up and Restoring an Active Directory Server (https:// docs.microsoft.com/en-us/windows/win32/ad/backing-up- and-restoring-an-active-directory-server)
- AD Forest Recovery – Perform initial recovery (https:// docs.microsoft.com/en-us/windows-server/identity/ad-ds/ manage/ad-forest-recovery-perform-initial-recovery)
- Back up and restore Active Directory domain controllers – Best practices (https://docs.microsoft.com/en-us/azure/backup/ active-directory-backup-restore#best-practices)
- Surviving a Ransomware Attack with Azure Site Recovery (https://dokumen.pub/surviving-a-ransomware-attack-with- azure-site-recovery.html or https://1lib.us/book/11369256 /4fc00a?id=11369256&secret=4fc00a)

The last document is a great practice lab document detailing how to simulate ransomware attacks and use AD site recovery to recover from a ransomware event. It's a great document to read and learn from.

Refer to recovery guides for other device, network, and platform types. At all times, especially during the initial recoveries, IT security should be strongly monitoring processes and network connections looking for malicious activity. If the victim organization did not pay the ransom, the ransomware gang will be looking for a way back into the environment. Any malicious program or backdoor or unchanged password can allow the attackers back into the environment.

Summary

The overall processes and steps for recovering an environment from a ransomware attack were covered in this chapter. Recovering the network infrastructure, IT security, virtual machine hosts, cloud services, backup systems, clients, servers, applications, services, and conducting unit testing on each before the wider deployment into production were all covered. Microsoft Windows recoveries and rebuilds were covered in a bit more detail along with Microsoft Active Directory, since they are commonly involved in ransomware recoveries.

In Chapter 10, "Next Steps," you will learn what victims need to do to prevent and mitigate another ransomware attack. The chapter will focus on some needed overall paradigm shifts as well as specific tactics that will benefit any cybersecurity defender.

Chapter 10
Next Steps

A ransomware attack is a wake-up call. It means you have at least one serious weakness in your computer security defense and, more likely, many others. This chapter discusses ideas that victim organizations may want to consider in the aftermath of a ransomware attack. This chapter focuses on some needed overall paradigm shifts and some specific tactics that will benefit any cybersecurity defender.

Paradigm Shifts

Eighty percent of ransomware victims suffer multiple attacks (https://blog.knowbe4.com/80-of-ransomware-victim-organizations-experience-a-second-attack). A bad ransomware event causing serious operational interruption is a chance to relook at your whole cybersecurity strategy. Most cybersecurity defenders are defending inefficiently, concentrating on the wrong things, and not putting the bulk of their efforts into the right places. This section discusses likely paradigm shifts needed in most ransomware victim's computer security defenses. You may be one of the few victims who already do these things, but if not, read on. This chapter reinforces some of the ideas and recommendations presented in Chapter 2, "Preventing Ransomware," and adds more.

Implement a Data-Driven Defense

Imagine two armies, one good, one bad, locked in a multidecade war. The bad army is constantly winning battles on the right flank and has done so for years. In real-world battles, the good army, after noticing a weakness on the right flank, would amass more troops and resources on the right flank to counteract the enemy's continued success. In fact, in a real war, the good army would continue to amass additional resources on the right flank until it became impenetrable or they would ultimately lose the war.

But, in the virtual war that is being conducted against today's corporate computers, upon learning that the right flank is constantly being defeated, defenders inexplicably amass defending troops nearly everywhere else. They put more troops and resources on the left flank and the center. They sometimes even stack troops up vertically because they have heard of some theoretical attack from the air that they might one day have to defend against. Everyone involved can see that they are losing because of the battle occurring on the right flank, they complain about it, and then they respond by doing everything else but addressing the attacks on the right flank threat.

In a real war, if you couldn't get the generals to fight on the right flank, you would replace those generals. Unfortunately, in the computer world, those replacement generals are just as likely to concentrate on anything but the right flank, just as their predecessors did. If you think this sounds like a terrible way to conduct a war, you are right.

If you don't like the war allegory, imagine a homeowner who lives in a house that intruders constantly break into by using a window next to the door. In response, the homeowner buys more locks for his door because he's heard that most home burglaries happen because doors don't have enough locks. Or, he's heard that traditional locks aren't smart enough and don't have enough technology in them, so, despite the best direct evidence that the window is the problem, the homeowner upgrades the wrong defense. Home burglars and hackers alike appreciate such a lack of appropriate focus.

Most readers will recognize parts of their companies in these allegories. It would seem the most natural thing in the world, to fight the things that are causing you the most harm, but most cyber-security defenders do not put the right defenses in the right places in the right amounts against the right threats.

> ## Magnum Opus
> The ideas and concepts recommended in the book *A Data-Driven Computer Security Defense*, which I also wrote, should underlie all defenses. The book is available at https://www.amazon.com/Data-Driven-Computer-Defense-Way-Improve/dp/1092500847.

There is a myriad of reasons why cybersecurity defenders don't concentrate on the biggest threats. First, there are tens of thousands of threats. In 2020 alone, there were 18,103 new vulnerabilities to patch (https://cyber-reports.com/2021/02/21/highest-number-of-vulnerabilities-disclosure-reported-in-2020/). And although it was a record year for vulnerabilities, as Figure 10.1 shows, thousands of new vulnerabilities every year is a trend that has persisted for a long time.

The number of threats is on top of all the many tens of thousands of human adversaries and tens of millions of malware programs, which could be trying to break into your organization every day. It's an avalanche of threats.

Second, there are lots of vendors and stakeholders vying for the defender's attention. Every computer security company wants to convince defenders that their product is the answer to all security prayers. Many intentionally increase the fear level around the problem that their product mitigates because it's easier to sell things when defenders are fearful. The outcome of this avalanche of competing narratives is that defenders are overwhelmed by the number of different types of threats and don't know which they should be concentrating on the most. The problem isn't helped with every

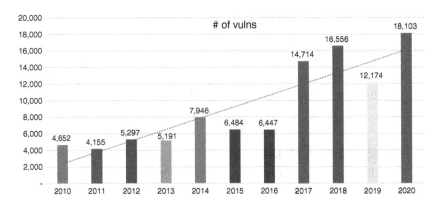

Figure 10.1 Number of newly publicly announced vulnerabilities by year

computer security guide and regulation they read or are forced to comply with telling them they have to do more than a 100 different security controls, perfectly, all at once. What specific threats and risks are the biggest is often lost in the goal to do it all well at once. It is the lack of focus on the most likely and harmful threats and risks that causes inefficient computer security defending. So, how to fix? I'm glad you asked.

Focus on Root Causes

The single best thing any computer security defender can do is to focus on the root causes of the initial exploits that allowed ransomware (and other hackers and malware) to get onto their devices and into their environments, so they can be used to deploy the right mitigations to prevent the next attacks. As covered in Chapter 2, there are nine different root causes that account for all hacker and malware attacks. I'll repeat them here:

- Programming bug (patch available or not available)
- Social engineering
- Authentication attack
- Human error/misconfiguration
- Eavesdropping/MitM

- Data/network traffic malformation
- Insider attack
- Third-party reliance issue (supply chain/vendor/partner/watering hole attack, etc.)
- Physical attack

Figure out which root causes are the most likely threats in your environment and mitigate them first and best. Every time malware or hackers are discovered and removed from your environment, try your best to find out how those things got into your environment. What let them get onto the devices where they were found? Find and focus on root causes. Ransomware is not your problem. It is an outcome of your real problem.

Rank Everything!

Computer security defense is full of unranked lists. You will constantly be handed large lists of unranked things and told to go fix or implement them. Don't blindly accept unranked lists anymore. Instead, force those lists to be ranked according to how much doing that thing will improve your defense and do the most impactful things first.

When someone tells you to go do something, ask yourself if it is the best use of your time, or is there something else that would matter more to your computer security defense? If so, fight (respectfully) to do the other thing.

Here's an example. The National Institute of Standards and Technology (NIST), which I love, released the following ransomware guidance draft document for review: "Preliminary Draft NISTIR 8374, Cybersecurity Framework Profile for Ransomware Risk Management" (https://csrc.nist.gov/CSRC/media/Publications/nistir/draft/documents/NIST.IR.8374-preliminary-draft.pdf). It listed eight specific recommendations to prevent ransomware exploitation. In order, they are as follows:

- Keep systems up-to-date and run update reviews periodically.
- Only allow applications that have been pre-authorized by cybersecurity or IT professionals.

- Restrict the use of personal devices on corporate networks.
- Promote the use of standard user accounts rather than accounts with administrative privileges whenever possible.
- Avoid using noncorporate applications and software, such as personal email, chat, and social networking clients, on corporate devices.
- Be careful with unknown sources. Do not open files or click on links from unknown sources unless a scan has been executed beforehand.
- Block access to ransomware sites, using cybersecurity solutions that block access to ransomware sites already identified as such.
- Always use antivirus software and configure it to automatically scan emails and flash drives.

The number-one way ransomware exploits devices is social engineering. The last three controls possibly mitigate social engineering, although really the fifth, which is security awareness training, is the one most likely to have the greatest impact on ransomware risk reduction. Ignoring that it doesn't address multifactor authentication (MFA) and good password policies, which are also a good way to prevent ransomware attacks, it lists the recommendations most likely to decrease the most risk last. Ransomware attackers love when we do this. If the list was "data-driven" and risk-ranked, it would move those three recommendations up to the top and put the sixth recommendation first.

Get and Use Good Data

Ask the right questions. If you don't have the data to answer the question, try to get the data. Value your organization's specific threat experience more than reports about other people's experience. Many times, the data is there, but no one is collecting it or analyzing it. Other times the data isn't there, but it would not be hard to collect the data. Start to use data and metrics to drive cybersecurity solutions. Don't accept "gut feelings" and anecdotal experiences as primary drivers. Instead, collect as much good data as you can and use that data to drive projects and solutions.

Heed Growing Threats More

All cybersecurity threats go through ebbs and flows, from less popular to very popular to less popular again. Threats often chase emerging technologies, sometimes lagging them and sometimes leading. Use your threat intelligence data to determine how often different threats and risks are occurring and are successful in your environment. Take notice of growing threats as they often become the newest, biggest problems. Our response to emerging cyber threats is usually reactionary, so the sooner we see a growing problem and start to address it, the better.

Row the Same Direction

Once you have identified the biggest threats against your environment, communicate that understanding to everyone in the organization. You cannot have an efficient cybersecurity defense unless everyone knows the top problems and is asked to participate in mitigation. Step 1 is making sure everyone knows the top problems. Step 2 is sharing what is going to be done to mitigate those issues.

Step 3 is continuing to communicate the top threats, over and over, until the top threats are no longer the top threats, and you begin to focus on a new top threat. Focus on the top threats no matter what they are, and change focus as top threats change. Strangely, in the computer world there is this idea that you can't tell people the same thing over and over and over. For instance, if phishing emails are your top threat (which is likely these days), most organizations will send out a cybersecurity newsletter or announcement warning end users about it but then feel that they can't share the same threat and warning next time. Instead, they pick another subject such as malformed digital certificates attacking banks in a foreign country and warn about those. They have absolutely no impact on the threats facing the organization, but the communications department feels they have to share something different each time, lest their readers get bored.

It's insane! Once you have identified what the top threat is, it is incumbent on the risk reduction team to discuss it over and over and over again so that everyone is focused on the top problem(s). Anything else is inefficient and, to reference earlier allegories, focusing on left flanks over right flanks or doors instead of windows. It is this lack of focusing on the top root causes that allows malicious hackers and malware to be as successful as they are. Fight back. Focus, focus, focus.

Focus on Social Engineering Mitigation

For more than 30 years, the top threats have been social engineering and unpatched software. As covered in Chapter 2, password issues are also a top threat (covered more later in this chapter). You should focus on what are your organization's top threats. If you don't know what the top threats to your environment are, focus on social engineering first, unpatched software second, and password issues third. Everything else should become secondary to your focus on mitigating those issues. Most organization's computer security risk would be best and most efficiently reduced by focusing on those three issues first and foremost.

Most organizations could reduce the most risk by focusing on social engineering mitigation the most. This includes implementing all the policies, technical controls, and training to best fight social engineering.

Comprehensive Ebook on Fighting Social Engineering

As covered in Chapter 2, I prepared a comprehensive ebook for my employer, KnowBe4, which covers every single thing I could think of to mitigate social engineering. You can find KnowBe4's Comprehensive Anti-Phishing Guide at https://info.knowbe4.com/comprehensive-anti-phishing-guide.

Track Processes and Network Traffic

It is clear that ransomware often dwells for months without being detected in most environments. Every organization should do more to inventory, track, and alert on anomalous computer processes and network traffic. The best defense would be to implement application control programs that refuse to allow any unapproved process to run. Doing so would significantly reduce the risk of malicious attacks in an organization.

Unfortunately, implementing enforced application control can be difficult, requires a lot of resources, and may end up causing too much discontent from management and end users if not done well (and it's often not done well). In these cases, using any program, such as application control or endpoint detection and response (EDR), that tracks processes and network traffic can be a good thing. The key is to investigate any and all new processes and network traffic connections until you have proved them to be legitimately necessary or otherwise. This is not easy to do. But our inability to do process and network traffic connection anomaly correlation well is a huge reason why ransomware is so successful. If you want to stop ransomware from running rampant in your organization, be proactive, and do process and network traffic anomaly detection.

Improve Overall Cybersecurity Hygiene

Most organizations could significantly reduce their risk of attack by ransomware (and other malware and malicious hackers) by improving their overall *cyber hygiene*. The term *hygiene* is used as an allegory to how bathing, dental, diet, and overall personal hygiene are seen as one of the best indicators of long-term health in humans. The following are some common cybersecurity hygiene recommendations.

Use Multifactor Authentication

Multifactor authentication requires that a user input at least two different types of proof of ownership of a digital identity to authenticate themselves to a particular access control system. MFA comes in many forms, including hardware devices, software programs, and phone applications. Although someone using MFA can still be hacked and any MFA solution, itself, can be hacked or bypassed, using MFA significantly reduces some common forms of hacking. For instance, if someone tries to phish your password, but you're using MFA in addition to the username and password, you're not going to be tricked by that very common social engineering trick. You should use MFA to protect systems containing confidential data when you can. Unfortunately, probably less than 2 percent of systems and websites allow MFA to be used to log on. But when you can, if you use MFA, it significantly reduces some forms of malicious hacking and malware, including ransomware attacks.

Be aware that using MFA does not mean you can't be hacked or that an environment protected by MFA won't be compromised by hackers and malware. It just reduces the likelihood. All MFA users should be educated about the type of MFA they are using and how that MFA method can be hacked and bypassed.

Hacking Multifactor Authentication

The book *Hacking Multifactor Authentication* discusses MFA in detail, how it can be hacked, and what admins, developers, and users can do to make it more secure. You can find the book, which I also wrote, at https://www.wiley.com/en-us/Hacking+Multifactor+Authentication-p-9781119650805.

Use a Strong Password Policy

There are a few major types of password attacks, including the following:

- Password guessing
- Password theft

- Password hash theft
- Asking a user what their password is
- Unauthorized password resetting or bypass

> ## Everything You Want to Know About Password Attacks and Defenses
> I cover password attacks and defenses in detail in a one-hour webinar that is available at https://info.knowbe4.com/pesky-password-problem.

Based on my experience, I understand password attacks and defenses better than most, and here is the password policy I recommend:

- Use MFA when possible.
- Where MFA is not an option, use password managers to create unique, long as possible, random passwords for each website or security domain.
- Where password managers aren't possible, use long, simple passphrases.
- Use at least 12-character or longer passwords, use 16-character or longer passwords if worried about password hash guessing, or if account lockout is not enabled everywhere, it can be used.
- Change all passwords at least once a year, and change business passwords every 90 to 180 days.
- Enable account lockout wherever possible.
- Don't reuse the same passwords between any website or service.
- Don't use common passwords (e.g., 123456, password, or qwerty, etc.)

All computer security defenders should follow these password policy recommendations as closely as possible to decrease cybersecurity risk. The following are articles (most are written by me) on password threats, defenses, and policies:

- What Your Password Policy Should Be and Why, And Other Password Frustrations (https://www.linkedin.com/pulse/ what-your-password-policy-should-why-other-roger-grimes)
- Q&A Regarding Password Policy (https://blog.knowbe4 .com/qa-with-data-driven-evangelist-roger-grimes-on-the- great-password-debate)
- What is the Right Password Policy? (https://blog.knowbe4. com/what-is-the-right-password-policy)
- Why Doesn't MFA Stop All Hacks? (https://www.linkedin .com/pulse/why-doesnt-mfa-stop-hacking-roger-grimes)
- Best Password Managers - Wired Magazine article (https:// www.wired.com/story/best-password-managers/)
- Can Your Password Manager Be Hacked? (https://www. linkedin.com/pulse/can-your-password-manager-hacked- roger-grimes)

Secure Elevated Group Memberships

Every operating system and network has one or more built-in elevated groups. In Microsoft Windows, the local elevated groups are Administrators and Power Users (the latter is being deprecated). On Microsoft Active Directory networks, it is Administrators, Domain Admins, Enterprise Admins, and Schema Admins (and two handfuls of other privileged groups). On Apple, Linux, and BSD computers, it's root.

Do your best to limit the number of permanent members in any elevated group. The fewer people who have elevated memberships, the lower your cybersecurity risk. The best authentication and access control systems aggressively manage who belongs to these groups, minimizing permanent membership and adding members only as needed, only when needed, and only for as long as needed. All uses of elevated membership should be heavily monitored and restricted as to where they can be used. For instance, members of

Domain Admins should only log on to domain controllers. Any Domain Admins log on to a non-DC is considered an elevated risk and unnecessary. Give out individual elevated permissions and privileges when that can be done instead of giving someone membership to an elevated group that always contains far more privileges and permissions than the person needs to do the immediate task at hand.

Improve Security Monitoring

Most organizations would have noticed ransomware exploitations sooner had they been paying attention to unusual events in their security event logs. All organizations should define events that could indicate malicious events or at least merit additional investigation and then alert on and respond to those events.

Secure PowerShell

Microsoft PowerShell is often used by hackers and malware to do malicious things. PowerShell is Microsoft's preeminent scripting language, and disabling it completely can often cause operational disruption or at least slow down legitimate tasks. Instead, put PowerShell into restricted mode or another mode that requires that the PowerShell script be signed by some entity you trust.

By default, there are five PowerShell execution modes:

- **Restricted:** The default. No automated scripts can be run. PowerShell can be used only in interactive mode by a user typing in commands.
- **Unrestricted:** No restrictions; all Windows PowerShell scripts can be run.
- **AllSigned:** Only scripts signed by a trusted publisher can be run.
- **RemoteSigned:** Downloaded scripts must be signed by a trusted publisher before they can be run.
- **Undefined:** No execution policy has been set.

Ensure that your PowerShell environment is set to Restricted or one of the modes requiring signed code. The following are two more related links covering securing PowerShell:

- https://docs.microsoft.com/en-us/powershell/ module/microsoft.powershell.core/set-strictmode?view= powershell-7.1
- https://winaero.com/change-powershell-execution- policy-windows-10

Secure Data

The vast majority of ransomware is looking to exfiltrate your data. Anything you can do to prevent the data from being exfiltrated should be explored. Data protection options include the following:

- Programs specifically designed to prevent unauthorized data exfiltration
- Encrypted databases (especially field-level encryption)
- Data wrappers
- Virtualized data viewing
- Containerized data
- Data leak prevention tools
- Conditional access

One example of conditional access is Microsoft's Controlled Folder Access. Working with Microsoft Windows 10/Microsoft Windows Server 2019 and later, administrators declare which folders are protected by Controlled Folder Access protection and then define which trusted applications are allowed access. Any non-declared program, like ransomware, would not be able to access the data. Although it does not prevent all ransomware from being successful, it does currently prevent many forms. The following are two relevant links:

- https://docs.microsoft.com/en-us/microsoft-365/security/ defender-endpoint/controlled-folders?view=o365-worldwide

- `https://docs.microsoft.com/en-us/microsoft-365/security/ defender-endpoint/enable-controlled-folders?view=o365-wo rldwide`

It's important to note that preventing data encryption or exfiltration will likely not be enough to stop the average ransomware program or gang from being successful. Encryption of operating system and other types of non-data files will still corrupt an environment and likely cause operational issues, but at least it will make it harder for ransomware gangs to exfiltrate data. I expect data-focused protection systems like this to become more numerous and popular in the future.

Secure Backups

Protect your future backups against ransomware. Ransomware often deletes Volume Shadow copies, deletes online backups, stops backup jobs, and uses other methods to corrupt them. Make sure to use this 3-2-1 method of backups:

- Make sure there are **three** copies of all data (original plus two backups).
- Store them on at least **two** different types of storage media.
- Store **one** backup copy on an offsite/offline location so that an attacker cannot corrupt or delete it.

Many backup solutions allow MFA logons, so add that option if it is available. Out of all these backup recommendations, the most important is to store one truly offline. If you can get to your "offline" backup in an online method without requiring anyone to do something physically to make the data "online," it's not an "offline backup."

It's worth noting that many "cloud services," such as Microsoft Azure, Dropbox, Google Drive, Microsoft OneDrive, etc., are not as vulnerable to ransomware in the same way as traditional computer-based storage. Files stored on a cloud service with "anti-ransomware" features can be a godsend if ransomware hits. Ransomware still often impacts cloud-stored files, but the cloud services are often quite aware of the prevalence of ransomware and offer fairly easy data recovery. Look into whether your cloud vendor(s) offers easy recovery from ransomware events (including what is protected). In a world full of rampant ransomware, using a cloud-based storage provider may make more sense than ever before.

Summary

This chapter recommended some general paradigm shifts and specific tactical responses that if implemented, will significantly reduce cybersecurity risk in your organization. This includes implementing a data-driven computer defense, focusing on root causes, ranking threats, getting good data, heeding growing threats, rowing in the same direction, focusing on social engineering, using MFA, using a strong password policy, securing elevated group membership, improving security monitoring, securing PowerShell, securing data, and securing backups.

In Chapter 11, we will discuss the things that a victim should not do when faced with a ransomware attack.

Chapter 11
What Not to Do

M ost of this book has been about what to do in case of a widespread ransomware attack. In this chapter, each section will explicitly discuss what not to do to help you avoid common mistakes and misconceptions.

Assume You Can't Be a Victim

Many ransomware victims assumed before the attack that they could not be victims. They thought only the worst-secured organizations got attacked. They read in the media about all the companies that were terrible at patching or for years had not noticed that ransomware was in their network. If everyone but you is being attacked, it can lead to a premature conclusion that you must be doing something right and can't be attacked. Don't make that mistake.

Most victims didn't think they could even be a target of ransomware. "Why would they attack us?" is a common refrain. The answer is they want money, and your cryptocurrency is worth the same as anyone else's. Most organizations have relatively average security, which is to say not very great security. Most organizations do some computer security things very well, most things average, and many other things fairly poorly. All an attacker has to do is find one weakness such as finding one employee who can be tricked into clicking on an email phishing attack, one unpatched application, or one password logon portal left unprotected. The defender has to be perfect. The attacker needs only to be persistent.

Never assume you can't be attacked. If you haven't been successfully attacked by ransomware, it can always become a bad day. . .or month.

Think That One Super-Tool Can Prevent an Attack

Never think that one tool or any combination of computer security defense tools can prevent a ransomware attack. You will often have many vendors that claim their defense methodology is the one that can prevent all ransomware attacks. If that were true—that any one tool could prevent all ransomware attacks—the world would be beating a path to the vendor's door, and the vendor would not have to be asking people to buy their solution. No matter what the vendor is promising, it is likely that a ransomware attack was successful against one or more of their customers.

Assume Too Quickly Your Backup Is Good

A lot of ransomware victims assumed too early after the attack was launched that their backups would save them. After all, they had been attesting to good backups for years. Their backup software had been used to restore files and folders before without a problem. The IT person had even attested to the solid, reliable backups when asked. They said that the backups were offline and untouchable to hackers. How could you get any more assured than that?

Turns out having very reliable backups is harder than it seems. Most people, when they say they have good backups, mean they have tried restoring some files, folders, or even an entire computer or two. Almost no organization that performs backups has tried to restore every server and workstation at once, like ransomware can take out. Even when the backups are safe and reliable, the speed at which the restoration happens, when spread across dozens and dozens of computers, can be estimated to take years, even thousands of years, to complete. This is also assuming that the hacker hasn't somehow deleted or corrupted your backups. If you can get to your backups online, so, too, can the attacker.

To ensure that you have a reliable and secure backup, it must be tested, at least annually, in a way that a ransomware incident might require. That is to say, test restoring dozens and dozens of servers and computers all at once, or sequentially, to a test restore environment and measuring both how long it takes and whether it was reliable. Many times, restoring a bunch of systems ends up with a bunch of corruption because rarely are all systems backed up at the exact same time. And this causes synchronization errors. Some servers and services can be troubleshot and resolved, and some have to be rebuilt.

If you really want to be assured you have a good and reliable backup, you should hire a penetration tester to see if they can get at your backups, and if so, what can they do to them (i.e., delete, corrupt, etc.), and do an entire environment test restore at least once a year from offline or super-protected backups. Most victim organizations don't do this or won't do it even if told to do it because of the cost. It's expensive, so, unless you do your backup restoration testing thoroughly, never think it's solid and reliable until proven.

Use Inexperienced Responders

A ransomware attack is not the time to use inexperienced responders. You want experienced people who have done a ton of ransomware incident response. You want people who have been there and done that. Different ransomware programs and gangs do different things. Some do data exfiltration, some don't. Some claim to do data exfiltration but really don't. Most who get paid the ransom provide the decryption key(s), but some don't. Some provide the decryption key, but the decryption keys don't really work. Some claim they will not attack you again but do. Some try to slip in more ransomware using the decryption program. Some will take one-quarter of the originally demanded ransom; some require half or three-quarters. Some routinely look for cybersecurity insurance policies to find out the maximum reimbursable ransom that will be paid by the insurance company, though most don't. Some claim that they will take only Monero cryptocurrency but will take bitcoin nevertheless and charge an increased fee. Some will give you days to respond, some weeks. The scenarios can go on and on.

Knowing who you are negotiating with on the other side is an important part of ransomware response. Experienced ransomware incident responders, especially ones familiar with your ransomware variant, are worth their weight in gold, and vice versa. Inexperienced responders and negotiators can make things far worse than they need to be.

Give Inadequate Considerations to Paying Ransom

Many victims vow ahead of time they will never pay the ransom. Be careful in letting your ego or social ethics get in the way. More than likely not paying the ransom means more expense, longer recovery, and a significantly greater risk of current and future damage. That's a lot to trade off simply because you're morally against paying a ransom.

Some organizations refuse to pay the ransom because they know they have a good, reliable backup with which to restore the encrypted data. Remember, most ransomware attacks involve data and credential exfiltration, and the attacker may attack your employees and customers and blame you for it.

If you're not paying the ransom simply because you believe that paying the ransom only encourages ransomware attackers, you're right. Paying or not paying, however, will not change the economics of ransomware overall. Somewhere between 40 percent and 60 percent of victims are paying, and because of that, your individual decision of whether to pay is not going to change the hacker's motivation.

Lie to Attackers

I've read about victims lying to ransomware attackers about things small and large. In general, if the ransomware gang knows you are lying to them, it's not going to be a positive outcome. Assume your ransomware gang has been in your environment for months, reading your emails, looking at financial statements, reading documents, and learning the "crown jewels" of your organization. Don't lie to them about who's who. They usually already know. Don't lie to them about your revenues, cash flows, or ability to raise cash. Usually, they have a pretty good idea before they've launched the visible portion of their attack. Although you shouldn't lie, you also don't have to be overly forthcoming with information. Don't go out of your way to tell the attacker anything that can be used to their advantage.

Conversely, sometimes the ransomware gang has something critically wrong. I've read many times about a ransomware gang overstating the financial ability of an attacked victim to pay a particular ransom. You need to look at it from their perspective. They have read your financial statements without a knowledgeable eye about the differences between organizations. They may not know that Example Technical, Inc., is but a small subsidiary of much richer Example Worldwide, and that the parent company is not about to pay a much larger ransom for a smaller subsidiary.

If the attacker truly has something wrong, be gentle and informational in your correction. Don't yell at them or insult them with your response. Treat them as you would a child or shareholder who gets something wrong. There is no benefit to insulting your attacker.

Insult the Gang by Suggesting Tiny Ransom

Many victims are shocked to see the dollar value the ransomware gang is requesting. I'm not sure what the victim expected, but it's obvious that the victim's representative had a much lower figure in mind. Oftentimes, the counteroffer from the victim is far lower than the originally requested figure from the attacker. I've seen victims come back with extortion payment figures less than 1/10th of what was requested. Except in super unusual circumstances where the ransomware gang can be convinced that they made a terrific mistake in assessing the victim's net worth, ransomware gangs will rarely go lower than one-quarter to one-half of the originally requested amount. Suggesting something one-tenth or less of the originally requested amount is going to be seen as an insult and may result in harm to an already sticky relationship. Even if you plan to pay far less than the originally requested ransom, don't start negotiations by requesting that the ransomware gang accept a very tiny amount of the request as your first response.

Some master negotiators suggest replying with tiny amounts as a way to reframe the conversation. It's a common master negotiator tactic, but it works only in scenarios where the requestor has very few alternatives like real-world human hostage taking. A real-world human hostage taker, even if they are involved in a dozen kidnappings, has very few opportunities to get money. Basically, they have to take what they can get, because the risk of a new transaction is very hard to do.

Ransomware gangs, however, have plenty of other potential victims and almost no chance of being punished. Each transaction is low risk, the next transaction is low risk, and the one after that is also low risk. The ransomware gang's negotiators don't have to take it or leave it. They have nearly zero incentive to agree to a drastically reduced ransomware payment. Doing so could lead to a reputation where they are always offered far lower ransoms than they requested, and no ransomware gang wants that reputation.

Pay the Whole Amount Right Away

Conversely, never pay the whole requested ransomware amount right away upon first request. I've read the transcripts of many ransomware victim negotiations where the ransomware gang asked for an amount and the victim immediately agreed to the full amount right away. It's okay to do that, but you increase the risk that the attacker will come up with an excuse to ask for more money. Perhaps the ransom you pay only frees up some of the decryption keys. Most ransomware gangs are located in foreign countries where negotiations over large amounts of money are expected. It's okay to come back offering to pay a quarter or one-half of the originally suggested amount. You won't be insulting them, and you also won't be making them think they should have asked for more.

Argue with the Ransomware Gang

Let me say this again. Don't insult the ransomware gang. You would be surprised how many victim organizations end up insulting the ransomware gang they are talking to. I get it! You're being extorted by a criminal gang that is trying to steal money from you. You're insulted! You're angry! But you have very little power in getting the best outcome of a ransomware attack if you begin by insulting the criminals.

If you want the best possible outcome, be friendly, and be nonadversarial. Vent negative emotions to your team. Be calm, even, and mild-mannered when conversing with the ransomware gang.

Apply Decryption Keys to Your Only Copy

When trying the decryption process or keys for the first time, don't apply it directly to the encrypted server, workstation, or data, if that copy is your only copy. It is not unheard of for decryption processes or keys to end up corrupting the encrypted data due to a mistake. You don't want to screw up your only copy of the data. So, back up the encrypted data, restore it to a safe place, and try your decryption process there.

Not Care About Root Cause

To stop further ransomware and hacker incursions, you must mitigate all the ways they can get into your environment. Many ransomware victims are too busy trying to recover from a ransomware incident to give much thought to how it began. It may seem daunting or impossible to figure out how the ransomware got in. But with some review of log files and a little research, usually some good, educated guesses can be made. Many times I've seen, victims ask the attackers how they got in after the ransom was paid. Sometimes the attackers are honest and tell them. Other times they will say they aren't sure, that they just bought the access or a password off some other group. It can't hurt to ask. Victims who do not learn the initial, root-cause method of the ransomware attack are more likely to fall victim to the same sort of attack, especially if they did not pay the ransom.

Keep Your Ransomware Response Plan Online Only

Assume that your entire online environment will be down in a ransomware event. How will you access your ransomware response plan if it is all online? Make sure the plan is stored off the network and/or in paper form, in such a way that all critical team members can easily access it if needed during a ransomware event.

Allow a Team Member to Go Rogue

It is not unusual for a ransomware response team member to "go rogue" during a ransomware attack. This means that the otherwise well-meaning team member tries to be "helpful" by doing additional things on their own. Examples include the following:

- People talking to the press or other impacted stakeholders before external communications should happen or by people not authorized to do so.
- Multiple negotiators. The primary negotiator doesn't know that other negotiations are happening by other parties.
- Calls to other outside experts who have not signed an NDA.
- Decryption or recovery attempts on production systems that end up destroying evidence.

These are almost never helpful and put the victim organization at increased risk of liability, especially when an official legal representative should be making all outside calls, emails, and contacts about the ransomware event.

Accept a Social Engineering Exclusion in Your Cyber-Insurance Policy

I'm a fan of cyber insurance, even if it isn't as good of a bargain as it was years ago. Still, make sure your cybersecurity insurance policy does not have an "out" (i.e., policy exclusion) for events caused by social engineering or employee error. These are becoming more common. Because social engineering is the most common method of attack, allowing a policy exclusion like this is essentially saying that you do not want full policy coverage for the most likely type of attack. A well-educated, quality insurance broker should be able to identify the various needs of your business and help find policies or carriers who can meet those needs. For instance, the exclusion and sublimits of a policy are usually very different for each organization, so a broker who understands your business can help ensure adequate and tailored coverage.

Summary

This chapter was a quick rundown of some common errors and issues that any potential ransomware victim should avoid. The general themes are don't insult ransomware gangs, test decryption, find the root cause of the attack, and follow the ransomware plan.

In Chapter 12, we will discuss the final topic, the future of ransomware.

Chapter 12
Future of Ransomware

The previous chapters discussed how to handle today's ransomware threats. This chapter will discuss the future of ransomware and the possible defenses against it.

Future of Ransomware

For as long as I've been doing cybersecurity, I've been asked if I believe cybersecurity incidents will be better or worse in the coming year. Every year I predicted it was going to be worse, and I've never been wrong. The last few years have been particularly tough because it's pretty bad out there, and it's hard to imagine how it could get worse. Hackers and malware have long had nearly free reign over the Internet to hack and do maliciousness without fear of reprisal. A malicious hacker is almost more likely to be hit by lightning than to be arrested for a cybercrime. That might be a statistical exaggeration on my part, but you get the idea.

I remember back in 2019 as ransomware was taking down organizations including computer security companies as well as hospitals, police stations, and even multiple cities, thinking, "How could ransomware get worse?" And then it did. At the end of 2019, ransomware began to routinely exfiltrate data, exfiltrate authentication credentials (e.g., business, employee, and customer), threaten and extort employees and customers, spear phish trusting partners and customers, and publicly shame victims. I covered this in Chapter 1, "Introduction to Ransomware," as "quintuple extortion." In the years since, quintuple extortion has become the norm, representing more than 75 percent of all ransomware attacks, if not more. So, again I ask myself now, "How could ransomware get worse?" Based on three decades of experience and knowing that no widespread solution is going to be implemented anytime soon, I know it's likely to get worse before it gets better.

One day, like all popular cyber threats before it (e.g., macro viruses, email worms, boot sector viruses, etc.), ransomware will become a thing of the past or at least more of a minor annoyance for some unprepared defenders, but it won't be the major threat it is today. For now, it remains a major threat, if not *the* major threat, and it's likely to get worse in the near-term future. "How?" you might ask. The following sections cover my speculation.

Attacks Beyond Traditional Computers

Right now, ransomware almost exclusively attacks traditional computer devices. Ransomware targets mostly Microsoft Windows, although we are seeing ransomware variants that attack Apple and Linux computers. I believe we will see ransomware move beyond desktop computers to mobile devices, Industrial Control Systems (ICSs), Supervisory Control and Data Acquisition (SCADA), Programmable Logic Controllers (PLCs), and Internet of Things (IoT) devices.

So far, ransomware threats against these types of systems have mostly been demonstrations or very rare events. Here are three examples of ransomware demonstrations against those types of systems:

- ClearEnergy ransomware aim to destroy process automation logics in critical infrastructure, SCADA, and industrial control systems (https://securityaffairs.co/wordpress/57731/malware/clearenergy-ransomware-scada.html)

- Researchers Create PoC Ransomware That Targets ICS/SCADA Systems (https://www.bleepingcomputer.com/news/security/researchers-create-poc-ransomware-that-targets-ics-scada-systems/)
- Proof-of-concept ransomware locks up the PLCs that control power plants (https://boingboing.net/2017/02/14/proof-of-concept-ransomware-lo.html)

It is clear, however, that these types of systems are definitely on the radar of both regular cybercriminals and nation-state attackers. Attacks against those systems don't even have to directly impact them. Simply attacking the computers around them can create a heightened risk that requires that the nontraditional systems be shut down. This happened in the Colonial Pipeline instance, for example, where the billing system was impacted and not the control systems. After decades of worrying about attacks against these types of systems, the last few years have shown a dizzying increase of successful and almost successful attacks against critical infrastructure and manufacturing targets.

Companies that use ICSs, SCADAs, and PLCs are usually involved in critical production of some sort and are under much more stress to stay operational. The publicly known attacks against the large energy and food production companies resulted in rapid payment of very large ransoms, and those ransomware attacks didn't even directly attack the noncomputer systems. Imagine if they did!

I think you're going to see real-world ransomware attacks against more nontraditional systems because they are more directly involved in critical operations and production, are more likely to be vulnerable, and have less options available for defense. The PC world is starting to be flooded by ransomware defenses. In the non-PC world, these same defenses are unheard of. Criminals go to where the money is and, as traditional computers get more protected against ransomware, the ransomware gangs will likely target less-protected systems, especially if the ransoms can be bigger and paid sooner.

IoT Ransoms

There are already more Internet-connected devices than people on the planet, and that figure is only going to rise. The buzzword *Internet of Things* (IoT) has arisen to describe noncomputer devices that now essentially contain Internet-connected computers. This includes surveillance cameras, toasters, devices to find things, "smart home" devices, cars, refrigerators, televisions, etc.

Bruce Schneier, in his book *Click Here to Kill Everybody* (https://en.wikipedia.org/wiki/Click_Here_to_Kill_Everybody), states that in the near future, IoT devices will be so plentiful and cheap that it will be more wasteful for someone to bend down and pick up a dropped IoT device than to just use a new one (I'm paraphrasing). He's likely right. IoT devices will be everywhere or built into everything. And as they increase in popularity, they are more likely to be targeted by ransomware.

We already have ransomware encrypting smart televisions as covered by the article at https://www.pcworld.com/article/3154226/ransomware-on-smart-tvs-is-here-and-removing-it-can-be-a-pain.html, and the YouTube video at https://www.youtube.com/watch?v=0WZ4uLFTHEE. Figure 12.1 shows a screenshot of the actual smart TV ransomware event.

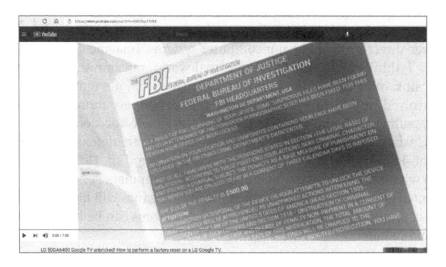

Figure 12.1   YouTube video showing television ransomware event

NOTE: A large version of this figure is available for download at www.wiley.com/go/ransomwareprotectionplaybook.

You can see that it appears to be similar to one of the fake FBI scareware attempts covered in Chapter 1, except that rebooting the television did not clear it off. The recovery involved resetting the TV to its original firmware state (i.e., a hard factory reset).

After a few of these were reported in 2016 and 2017, I expected to see a rash of televisions held for ransom. It didn't happen. I did read about a few more smart televisions being hit, mostly in Asian countries, but they all seemed to be the same television, one made by LG Electronics and running Google's Android television software (https://www.android.com/tv/). Since then, nothing.

My best guess is that the particular ransomware in question that hit those TVs was really directed at Android mobile phones and only this model of television was susceptible to the mobile trojans, because of the Android software and components they shared. Also, TVs rarely store things of great value (maybe a single credit card), so people are far less willing to pay a ransom. So, the big fear of millions of TVs being hit by ransomware did not come to fruition. That's a great thing! One for the good guys.

Still, hackers always hack what gets popular. They used to hack Apple computers back in the 1980s when they were the most popular personal computers. Then they moved on to DOS and Microsoft Windows computers when they became more popular. And now, they are back to hacking Apple's computers more often than Windows.

I expect that as IoT devices proliferate we will see more attacks against them. Like ICS, PLC, and SCADA systems discussed earlier, they are far more vulnerable and have far fewer available defenses. The offsetting fact is that most IoT devices don't have a lot of valuable data that the victim would not want to lose or be afraid of being leaked to the Internet, but that could change. There is already an extortion industry around private web camera videos and cell phone pictures, just not exploited by ransomware gangs. . .yet.

Mixed-Purpose Hacking Gangs

Mixed-purpose hacking gangs are already happening today and are a natural extension of the quintuple extortion tactics used by today's ransomware gangs. Ransomware criminals realize that they can do anything once inside a victim organization or device. Traditionally, ransomware gangs did ransomware. Bot net purveyors created and used bots. Crypto-miners stole computer resources, and so on.

Nearly a decade ago, cybersecurity reporter Brian Krebs published his summary (https://krebsonsecurity.com/2012/10/the-scrap-value-of-a-hacked-pc-revisited/) of the value of a hacked PC. It discussed all the ways a compromised PC and its data could be monetized. Today's professional criminal essentially has the same value proposition across the entire environment of a compromised victim. Here are some of the potential uses of a hacked victim organization:

- Sell exfiltrated data to highest bidder
- Use stolen resources for crypto-mining
- Use stolen resources for unauthorized storage, child sexual abuse material, etc.
- Take, use, or sell stolen passwords
- Create bot nets to attack other victims
- Launch distributed denial-of-service (DDoS) attacks
- Craft spear phishing attacks against trusted contacts
- Send spam
- Encrypt and extort a ransomware payment
- Establish command-and-control servers
- Other uses

These uses are already happening today, just usually by individual players with particular specialties. Smart ransomware gangs, especially the ones that survive and thrive as traditional ransomware gets mitigated, will move beyond just doing ransomware. They will look at every victim to see what's the best, highest utilization of a compromised client. How can they maximize profit on each compromised victim? It will only be the immature, dumb cybercriminal groups that don't attempt to maximize uses and profits of all compromised victims. Most criminal groups have gone professional. Maximizing profits is the goal of all professional groups.

So, how could it get worse than today? I expect ransomware groups will start attacking nontraditional computer devices and start to do far more things than just quintuple extortion. I'd love to be wrong.

Future of Ransomware Defense

This is not to say that defenders are going to take the growing threat of ransomware without responding. No, as the pain gets worse, the responders and defenders eventually fight back. Eventually, society will defeat ransomware.

As covered in Chapter 2, "Preventing Ransomware," it's going to take a combination of better individual security controls, focusing on and mitigating the root causes of successful ransomware attacks, fixing the entire Internet to make it significantly more secure, and other political solutions. The following sections are a continuation of how to prevent and defend against ransomware as I think it will evolve in the near-term future, split technically and strategically.

Future Technical Defenses

Future technical defenses can be broken down into two main classifications: local ransomware countermeasure applications and artificial intelligence (AI) defenses.

Ransomware Countermeasure Apps and Features

As ransomware continues to be more successful and do more damage, computer defense vendors, seeking more profit, will develop more ransomware-specific defenses. These defenses will be either entire products dedicated to defeating ransomware or additional features added to existing products.

Ransomware Heuristics

Certainly, the most obvious future defenses are applications or features that detect, alert, and block ransomware-like activity. Most of this involves monitoring the file system and doing anomaly analysis. If a defense system detects an abnormal level of read/writes, changes in file names or extensions, changes in file hashes, or excessive moves, it may detect the beginning of malicious encryption. Data-leak detection mechanisms can look for abnormal levels of data exfiltration.

Canary Files

Ransomware make a strong case for the use of deception technologies like "honey files" (aka canary files, red herring files, etc.). Essentially, the deception system places a few or more "fake" files around the file system or network. They serve no purpose other than to be monitored. If some unauthorized process touches them, it immediately sends out an alert for an incident response investigation.

Blackholing

When ransomware-like activity is detected, the process involved can be redirected to a fake file system, where its potentially malicious activities continue to happen. Blackholing has been around for decades and used successfully against malware. We just need to update it to look for ransomware-like behavior.

Encryption Key Capturing

There are some ransomware defenders who are promoting defenses that look for and capture ransomware encryption/decryption keys. The tools monitor processes and, when a ransomware-like process is detected, specifically look for and document the involved encryption/decryption keys. All encryption/decryption keys eventually have to be used or can be derived to a plaintext form to be used. Encryption key capturing software can capture ransomware encryption/decryption keys as they are used and allow easy recovery. Some researchers have already successfully showed a crude program, called Paybreak, that would have worked against Wanna-Cry ransomware: https://eugenekolo.com/static/paybreak.pdf.

AI Defense and Bots

AI and AI-enabled bots (and machine learning) are already being used to improve cybersecurity defenses. Certainly, AI and their bots will be used to identify and remediate ransomware programs. I expect the future of all cybersecurity to be a war of the good side's AI and bots against the bad side's AI and bots, and whoever has the best algorithms wins. There will always be human involvement in defenses and attacks, but over time you will certainly see increased automation on both sides.

But every tactical defense can be defeated by the attacker analyzing what allows ransomware behavior to be detected and then modifying that behavior, be it slowing down, doing the same things differently, or doing different things. As long as ransomware criminals can make money and get away with their crimes with a low chance of being punished, ransomware will continue to be a problem. That is why we will have no ultimate defeat of ransomware until we have strategic wins that work beyond the level of the individual device, system, and victim.

Strategic Defenses

Strategic defenses were covered in Chapter 2 but bear quick repeating here, in a chapter on the future of ransomware defense.

Focus on Mitigating Root Causes

If you want to defeat hackers and malware, you need to focus on the exploit methods that allow them to break in. Only by closing the holes (e.g., social engineering, unpatched software, weak passwords, eavesdropping, etc.) can we begin to stop hackers and malware from breaking in. Focus on determine what your biggest risks are. For most companies, it's social engineering, unpatched software, and password issues. But whatever it is, determine what your organization's biggest threats are, and then implement mitigations to reduce risk. Start with the biggest, most likely threats first, and work your way down the priority list.

Geopolitical Improvements

Hackers and their malware creations proliferate because we can't arrest them. We need a digital Geneva Conventions–like, global agreement on what is and isn't allowed across nation-state lines and what each nation agrees to do when given proof of unethical or illegal hacking. Until every nation agrees that ransomware is illegal and should be strongly disincentivized, it will continue from those cybercriminal safe havens. We need to strongly incentivize all nations that it's in their own best interest to help defeat ransomware.

Systematic Improvements

We also need national-level, systematic improvements that each nation and its allies agree to do. The IST's "Combating Ransomware: A Comprehensive Framework for Action: Key Recommendations from the Ransomware Task Force" (https://securityandtechnology.org/ransomwaretaskforce/report/) is an excellent summary of these sorts of needed systematic improvements. It lists 48 separate actions recommended for the US government to take to mitigate ransomware.

Many of its recommendations call for a centralized, coordinated, government/private-sponsored organization to directly fight ransomware. It recommends many actions, including the following:

- Establish an inter-intelligence agency working group and team to fight ransomware.
- Designate ransomware as a national security threat (this was done after the report was issued).
- Establish an international coalition to fight ransomware criminals.
- Create a global network of ransomware investigation hubs.

Use Cyber Insurance as a Tool

Many ransomware defenders cite the rise of cyber insurance covering ransomware attacks as a major factor in the increase in ransomware attacks. However, the incredible increase in ransomware attacks and their extortion demands has also created a huge challenge in the cyber insurance industry. Today, ransomware insurance coverage is more difficult to obtain. As covered in Chapter 3, "Cyber Insurance," today there are fewer insurance companies willing to offer ransomware coverage, and those that do offer smaller coverage, increased premiums, increased deductibles, and more exclusions.

The result is that the cyber insurance industry is no longer offering ransomware coverage to just any potential customer. Today, customers must prove they are cyber-resilient and following industry best practices. I think cyber insurance can be used to help push better local cybersecurity into more organizations. There is a sizable percentage of organizations that are first forced to address their lax cybersecurity practices when applying for cybersecurity insurance. If the cybersecurity insurance industry can be blamed for increasing the plague of ransomware, I think they also offer another way to mitigate it.

Improve Internet Security Overall

We must also modify the Internet so that it is a far safer place to compute than it is today. I covered this recommendation in Chapter 2. I provide a more detailed solution of how to do it at https:// www.linkedin.com/pulse/why-isnt-internet-more-secure-roger-grimes. Until we significantly improve the security of the Internet to allow us to better identify and block malicious actors, hackers and malware will continue to flourish.

Summary

Chapter 12 covered what I believe is the future of ransomware and ransomware defenses. The ransomware of the future is likely to routinely attack nontraditional platforms, such as ICSs, PLCs, SCADA, and IoT devices. We will also see ransomware gangs morph from today's quintuple extortion techniques to mixed-purpose hacking groups that look to maximize their rogue revenue gained from each victim.

This chapter also covered likely future ransomware defenses including technical defenses, better ransomware heuristics, canary files, blackholing, encryption key capturing software, and

AI defenses and bots. Strategic defenses may include geopolitical improvements, systematic improvements, using cyber insurance as a tool to improve local security, and improving the overall security of the Internet.

Parting Words

This concludes this book. I hope you have learned more than a few ideas about how to prevent and mitigate ransomware. The most important concepts to take away are how you must try harder to prevent ransomware from being successful in the first place. That means identifying, concentrating, and mitigating the most common root causes that allow ransomware to be successful. Usually, this means better fighting social engineering tactics, better software patching, using multifactor authentication (MFA), and using good password policies. Doing a significantly better effort of focusing on these recommendations will make it far harder for ransomware, as well as all hackers and malware, to be successful.

Lastly, don't wait for ransomware to successfully hit your environment to decide what you would do. Instead, be proactive. Think ahead. Develop a ransomware incident response plan as shown in Chapter 5. Think about what you would do, how, and in what order. Don't be a victim that has to think of all the appropriate things to do, how, and when, during a ransomware emergency. People and organizations who thoughtfully plan ahead for emergencies almost always do better than those who don't.

Feel free to email me at roger@banneretcs.com with any questions, comments, or suggestions. I will always answer your emails. You can also follow me on LinkedIn (https://www.linkedin.com/in/rogeragrimes/) and Twitter (@rogeragrimes).

With that, continue to fight the good fight!

Index